"We dedicate this book to our Mother and Dad, Catherine and Frank Bernatonis, who gave us a solid foundation of home, family, loyalty, strength, and courage that sustained us all thru childhood and that has left us a deep well of love that we continue to draw from".

Stone Age Divas
Their Mystery and Their Magic

by Gloria Bertonis, M. Ed. with Carol Miranda

authorHOUSE®

AuthorHouse™
1663 Liberty Drive
Bloomington, IN 47403
www.authorhouse.com
Phone: 1-800-839-8640

© 2011 Gloria Bertonis, M. Ed. with Carol Miranda. All rights reserved.

No part of this book may be reproduced, stored in a retrieval system, or transmitted by any means without the written permission of the author.

First published by AuthorHouse 11/17/2011

ISBN: 978-1-4490-6418-1 (sc)
ISBN: 978-1-4634-6516-2 (e)

Library of Congress Control Number: 2010909444

Cover Design by: DAYA CEGLIA www.dayaceglia.com

Goddess at the Parthenon, Getty Image, Photographer/Artist: Harald Sund

Printed in the United States of America

This book is printed on acid-free paper.

Because of the dynamic nature of the Internet, any Web addresses or links contained in this book may have changed since publication and may no longer be valid. The views expressed in this work are solely those of the author and do not necessarily reflect the views of the publisher, and the publisher hereby disclaims any responsibility for them.

Learn Why We Think and Act the Way We Do!
It's Rooted in our Ancient History!
Stone Age Divas
Will take you there
and:

- <u>Give you back your cultural and spiritual roots</u> as a woman with a fabulous history reaching as far back as the dawn of humanity;

- <u>Create a brand new self-concept</u> based on the insights you will uncover page after page;

- <u>Motivate you to be your personal best</u> by tapping into ancient role models of strength, power, and full-figured beauty as the Goddesses;

- <u>Increase your self-confidence</u> by remembering a time when women were sacred, magical beings who held all the arts of civilization in their hands;

- <u>Expand your grasp of prehistory</u> with a few simple word 'tools' that will help you trace your female roots in ancient history;

- <u>Increase your self-esteem</u> by including yourself in the vast pool of innovators called 'women';

- <u>Build your personal strength</u> based on an unshakeable foundation of your early ancestors' accomplishments and contributions to civilization.

Acknowledgement

I dedicate this book to my cherished sister, Carol Bernatonis Miranda. It was her insistent, gentle persuasion, over twenty-seven years of study and research, that convinced me to put my startling conclusions into a book form.

Carol's editing, typing and computer skills have brought this manuscript to its fulfillment. It was her love and devotion to this sister project, that this book has been written.

She persevered under a life-changing diagnosis of breast cancer on three separate occasions over the years and through the stresses of her many surgeries, chemotherapy, heart and lung complications, radiation therapies, and miraculous healing.

Her courage, her strength, and her unyielding determination are to be commended. Her husband and four beautiful daughters who came to her aid while in the selfless pursuit and dedication to the project, and countless hours of referencing, researching, and editing are deeply thanked!

For all of Carol's efforts and her many contributions to this book over the years, I owe my deepest gratitude.

Women have made an enormous impact on life on the planet. They are deified and remembered in song, story, legend, and statues since at least 30,000 BC.

We are, and have always been, brilliant inventors, innovators, and leaders for hundred and thousands of years. We are the survivors of everything that came our way and passed on our culture.

Women are the creators of life! A woman can create life inside her own body, give birth to another human being, and make milk from her own breasts to feed her newborn life.

The Goddesses are real mothers, actual women who lived, and created beautiful handiwork and incredible usable things from next to nothing; such as: spinning and weaving, making pots from dirt, farming, medicine, and writing.

What a history! What a Gift to Civilization! Women were, and continue to be, the true Mothers of Invention!

If every girl in the world reads about the Goddesses found in this book, she will have a firm foundation of self-esteem and inspiration to make wise choices in her life. Since time immemorial, women have bonded together in sisterhood to fight for noble causes in nonviolent ways. Women have always been, and continue to be, great benefactors of humanity.

'STONE AGE DIVAS', takes an astonishing look at human beginnings never before attempted. It challenges our basic assumptions about gender, religion, and our civilization.

Warning: This book may be dangerous to your beliefs.

Ivory Silk

An ordinary day at work
Cutting up yards upon yards
Of fabric
I came upon a length
Of ivory silk.
Grasping the end,
I toss it up.
It billows and ripples,
Unfurling a river of moonlight.
A river that carries me away
To other places,
Other times,
Mirrored in the shimmering
Surface of that river,
To a lifetime
Where I lived
Adjacent to a temple
And woven garments
For the Goddesses and Gods
And chief among them
Was She
Who stood between the horns
Of the crescent moon,
She who's dusky locks
Were anointed
With attar of roses.
She who had starfire in her eyes…
The scenes and images
Shift and shiver
Dissipating like mist,

Rising from the river,
The river of ivory silk,
On an ordinary day at work.

Then I ask myself,
Who was She?
Who was this Goddess?
And the answer comes:
She is a part of myself,
A part of me that has existed
Since the beginning of time,
A part of me
Still waiting to be born.
Yet I got a fleeting
Glimpse of her
In a shining length
Of ivory silk
In a single, magical moment
On an ordinary day at work!

Maryly Hossein
9/20/00

Preface

With this book, I hope to give women their proper place in history.

I have tried to reach the reader with a fresh look at the Middle Stone Age when the Cro-Magnons, 'modern' humans, much like ourselves, arrived in Europe and displaced the earlier Neanderthals. Cro-Magnon origins are uncertain. All we know is that they brought unsurpassed creativity, innovations, inventions, and a highly developed sense of beauty which is still evident, millennia later, in their cultural remains.

I have diligently studied the achievements of our Stone Age ancestors with new eyes, leading me to believe that civilization was founded on the backs of women, which were probably beautifully and artistically tattooed.

It is my hypothesis that females used bone needles to sew furs and animal pelts into form-fitting clothing, and created nets out of knotted vines to do extensive fishing and hunting of small game. They crafted clay domestic vessels from the earth itself. They sculpted and painted many female statuettes of bone, ivory, horns, and clay; made necklaces and other body ornaments, jewelry from findings in the environment and manufactured very fine tools of tiny flints and obsidian, some shaped like lovely laurel leaves. They developed a religion centered on mother-power what they observed in nature all around them, and a great Mother Goddess Creatress.

There is some evidence that this belief system included resurrection from the dead, as the dead were painted with red ocher before burial, possibly to simulate menstrual blood, which was thought to be a source of life when it was withheld in the female body. Because menstruation ceases at onset of pregnancy, many ancient peoples may have thought that this blood formed the embryo.

Their most impressive art has remained to this day, in the cave paintings, which are unsurpassed in beauty, grace, and in the realistic outline depictions of the animals in their environment, as well as nursing mothers and the magic of birth.

My dates are very tentative, as the different ages occurred at different intervals in different parts of the world. For instance, the Americas and Australia never had an Iron Age. Dates change, as new archaeological discoveries are made almost daily. I beg the reader's pardon for errors in the time frame I have chosen to use; and strongly encourage them to read all they can, as reading is a wonderful avenue to expanded tolerance, wisdom, and appreciation of the gifts of our ancient forebears, both male and female.

There is wisdom that resides deep within our cellular memory. Our bodies are sacred beings, as well. In the Roman Catholic tradition, the body was to be respected, even after death, as 'The Temple of the Holy Spirit'. This is a beautiful metaphor that I have found helpful all throughout my life.

When we visit our ancestresses, who still live in our cellular memories, we can access the abundant wisdom available to us through an expanded awareness. The entire universe is ours to draw upon, for energy, for acceptance, for inspiration, for our health, for self-esteem, and for self-empowerment.

As women, we have a long and proud history of accomplishments always leading our human families forward. From the dawn of time, WOMEN were not only the carriers of Divinity; but the carriers of Culture as well. Everything that our modern technology is based upon is rooted in the female cultures of the Paleolithic.

I invite everyone to acknowledge the contributions of women to the origins of civilizations for our powers are truly immersed with the STONE AGE DIVAS.

Chapter Contents

I.	Women and the Evolution of the Species	1
II.	The Domestication of Animals	39
III.	Bronze Age Patriarchal Shift	47
IV.	Writing - Women's Gift to Civilization	71
V.	Textiles - Women's Work	97
VI.	Women as the First Doctors	121
VII.	An Herbal Grimoire	157
VIII.	Goddesses as Sources of Women's History	177
IX.	The Mother Syllable or Mother Tongue	203
X.	In Conclusion	231

The return of the Goddess as an Archetype of Meaning: restoring women's history to ALL women and creating a worldwide society where women's intelligence is valued and women's values are <u>restored</u>.

Introduction

With this book, I am going to delve into a time frame of history that was never well documented. This book will take you on a span of history (I prefer to call 'herstory') of women from the first faltering steps of our hominid ancestresses about three and one-half million years ago, and forward to the feminist scholars of today. These brave women are causing entire fields of research in archaeology, anthropology, psychology, sociology, and theology to be re-examined in the light of our new awareness of the value of the female in the survival and evolution of our species.

In researching my work, I examined every scrap of information I could find. 'A thread from our foremother's tattered aprons' is what Dr. Clarissa Pinkola Estes called the tiny clues she found of women's lives in her own remarkable work, *'Women Who Run with the Wolves'*. As I taught a course based on her book to a Women's Spirituality Group, I became aware of the terrible loss to women who have not had female instinctual wisdom passed down to them through the ages. I became aware of the tremendous void in the lives of young girls and women of every age: the loss of their roots, their spiritual heritage, their knowledge of reproduction, their freedom of choice, and equality, their ancient roles as Goddesses, Priestesses, Doctors, Prophets, Queens, Creators, Warriors, Artists, Teachers, Manufacturers, and Carriers of Divinity and much more.

If every little schoolgirl were taught her remarkable history as a survivor of a long, unbroken heritage of female power and divinity, how much more self-esteem she would have!

She would have powerful role models on which to build her own life that would fire her imagination with the incredible images available to her in her own history as a woman who gave all knowledge to the world.

Because of the very fact of her menstruation, she was motivated to watch the heavens and especially the moon, where she learned to measure time and where she saw herself reflected in its cycles and phases.

She would know that from the dawn of human creation, she was seen as sacred, god-like, and worthy of great respect and admiration.

Timeline

The Stone Age encompassed a vast period of time, and so it has generally been divided into the Old, Middle, and the New Stone Age.

2,000,000 BC to 40,000 BC
Paleolithic or Old Stone Age

40,000 BC to 10,000 BC
Mesolithic or Middle Stone Age

10,000 BC to 4000 BC
Neolithic or New Stone Age/Upper Paleolithic

6500 BC to 3000 BC
Copper Age, part of Neolithic

3000 BC to 1500 BC
Bronze Age - The beginning of writing as we use it today, war, and historical period.

1500 BC to AD 500
Iron Age

These are very tentative dates, as farming (which began in the Neolithic Age), the use for copper, bronze, and iron began at different times in different areas of the world. For instance, Native Americans never had a Copper, Bronze, or Iron Age; but enjoyed a Stone Age lifestyle and culture until the Europeans arrived in large numbers in AD 1700's.

It is probable around 4000 BC that most humans gained some degree of knowledge that a male had to mate with a female to make her pregnant. Intelligent women may have figured it out much earlier, but they would have kept it 'secret'. The priestesses, prophetesses, shamankas, psychics, wise women/witches, curanderas, etc probably would have known this. There is always a payoff for keeping knowledge secret since people will pay you to know that secret.

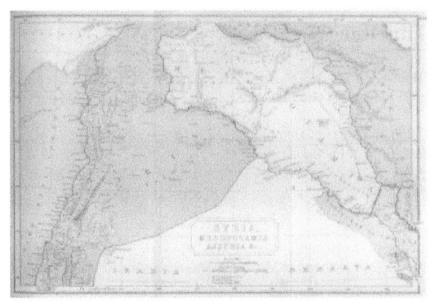

Map of Ancient Syria, Mesopotamia

CHAPTER I:
Women and the Evolution of the Species

At the very dawn of religion, God was a Woman. Do you remember? Do you perhaps have a fleeting memory of her when you walk through the woods or sit on a deserted beach? When you listen to the song of the brook, can you feel the stirrings of a yearning in the deepest recesses of your heart? When you hear the song of a bird and the whisper of the wind on a summer evening, do you hear her calling to you then? If so, you are connected at your deepest level to your primal ancestress, the Goddess. You are connected through your cellular memory to Maia, Isis, Astarte, Demeter, Hecate, Kali, and Gaia. She of a thousand names... You, to herself. She calls out to you, throughout the ages. Answer her! Recover her wisdom, her truth, and her power, her Divinity, in you.

LET HER LIVE AGAIN!

The earth lies wounded and bleeding. The earth's children are in pain. They call to their Mother, "Wrap your shawl around us, Mother; and teach us the ways of the wise women." And She answers, "There, there. There, there. Everything will be all right. I always knew you would come back to me. I've been waiting for you for a long, long time."

Will Durant once wrote that the story of civilization is the story of what happens on the banks of the river of activity we call "history". Sometimes the river is 'filled with blood' from armies waging war or defending themselves, killing, looting, expanding empires, doing the things historians usually record – while, on the banks unnoticed, people build homes, make love, raise children, sing songs, write poetry, create art. This then, is the story of what happened 'on the banks' of the pre-historic river at *The Dawn of Civilization* when women were still sacred, magical creatures and men were in awe of their mysteries.

'STONE AGE DIVAS' is the story of these women on the banks of the river, our ancient ancestresses, who led by their example, who tamed men by sharing the food they gathered with the men, who nurtured men, and gave them the first gift of civilization – the love bond: the family bond, the food bond, the mother-child bond, and the pair bond. For without the love bond, there is no civilization.

Without an enduring love relationship, the first mothers would not have nourished their offspring and none would have survived; as males had no idea the children were also theirs. The concept of fatherhood was unknown in most of the civilized world until just a few minutes ago, in evolutionary time. There are still extant Stone Age tribes, such as the Arunte of Australia, who do not understand the father's role in reproduction, and refuse to believe anthropologists who try to explain it to them.

Paternity then, was a completely unknown concept to early humans and the primate hominid, the human male ancestors of the human race would have had no reason to be interested in children or their welfare. In primate societies no fathering takes place even today. In almost the entire animal kingdom, the male does not perform any parenting functions at all. The male impregnates the females, and continues his carefree bachelor life, leaving the female to raise the young alone. This has the effect of placing an enormous burden on the new mother. For not only must she hunt and forage to sustain herself, in her already weakened postpartum condition, but she must also feed her babies lest they all perish. She can rarely sleep in her vigilance lest predators attack her young. Nature must certainly have thought highly of the female of the species, to place a burden of such magnitude on her!

This is the story then, of the females 'on the banks' of male history. They were white, brown, black, and various shadings in between. They were not Madonna's; neither were they whores. They were girls, (who in the Roman era were married at thirteen to older men), and they were women. We are their descendants.

Just as the Jewish and Roman matrons of AD 33 started the Christian religion 2000 years ago, so today also, women are awakening to their inner source of power collectively and calling it 'Womanspirit'. Suppressed by 4000 years of patriarchy, the worship of males, women's voices are proclaiming that we, too, are holy and there is ample historic precedent for this claim. We too are part of the Creative Force we call 'GOD', for want of a better name.

Starting as a faint whisper, the voice of Womanspirit has now become a roar; an insistence that every woman has a right to know her own gender's history and the right to participate fully in every area of life including her religious quest. Every woman has the right, and even the obligation to name her own life experiences as sacred, holy, and meaningful in the web of inter-relationships we call 'life'.

Women and Evolution

Human evolution has traditionally been taught in terms of 'Man the Hunter'. The tools and weapons he created were for the purpose of killing large animals for food. And later, using these same skills and more deadly weapons, to kill other 'animals' like himself: other tribes, clans, nations, in order to acquire their food, their territory, their possessions, their women, their wealth.

But what about the women? What were all the women doing down through the ages? The males were gone, often for long periods of time, performing so-called 'heroic' acts of daring and slaughter, which have been forever acclaimed in epics, sagas, inscriptions on stone, sacred scriptures, songs, dramas, books, monuments and historical texts.

Thus, 'history' has been a very appropriate word for the study of human civilization. It has indeed been 'his story' to the almost total exclusion of 'her story', which as we shall see, was just as exciting and dramatic in a totally different, non-violent way. For it was from the female of the species, and her contributions to survival as 'food gatherers', that everything that defines us as human, first originated. Yet to read the history books in the classrooms of today, one would hardly be aware that any females ever existed in the past; let alone, done anything worthwhile.

So, let us begin our journey back in time, approximately three and one half million years ago, when 'Lucy' took the first faltering steps that separated the hominids from their primate ancestors, the chimpanzees, the apes, and the gorillas of the African savannah.

This very significant first 'step' in our evolution was called 'bipedalism'. That simply means that we began walking on our own two feet instead of using our arms as an extra pair of legs, as the other primates do.

Bipedalism

Walking upright would have been more likely done by the females, who also had to hold their infants, while searching for food in trees and tall bushes and grasses.

It has been noted that because of the extremely hot climate in Africa, the most probable site of human evolution, the hominids had very little body hair (as we do today). The female mother had to hold her newborn infant upright, in order to nurse it from her breasts and forage in high places for food for herself and other small children in her family, at the same time.

In some species of animals, the female has a pouch in which to carry her young; or she has a lot of body hair to which the young can cling; and therefore she would not need to defy gravity by walking upright. Early female hominids, however, as they began to walk, lost the pouch in the fold of skin at their groin.

Bipedalism, or walking on two legs instead of four, was previously thought (by biased anthropologists) to have developed in males first, because of their need to see over the tops of high savannah grasses while hunting animals for food. However, in the last twenty years, with many women now allowed to enter the field of anthropology, (the study of human origins), things that were formerly taken for granted to be true about male superiority have now been challenged by feminist scholars.

It has come to light that hunting and gathering societies, formerly believed to be the very first human communities, were probably preceded by foraging societies. By 'foraging' is meant simply looking for, and gathering, whatever edible organic or animal substances could be found in the immediate environment. In foraging societies there is no hunting. Therefore, the human male would not have been required to develop weapons of destruction or stand upright to peer over high vegetation growth.

Foragers

Foragers eat whatever animal parts they find in their environment while searching for food. A larger predator animal may have previously killed a large animal and after the predators had eaten their fill of their feast, the human females and/or males would have eaten what was left over. Foragers also ate animals that died a natural death in their environment. Both females and males easily accomplished foraging, as it did not require exceptional bodily strength. The earliest hominids probably ate as they went along, without bringing the food back to their home or shelter (if they had one in those early years).

Anthropologists and archaeologists call this period of human development and evolution the 'Lower' Paleolithic. It simply means the time span approximately 300,000 years ago when Neanderthals, prototypes of humans, were roaming Africa and Europe. 'Lower' Paleolithic means earlier Stone Age; the time in prehistory when the earliest humans began to live in limestone caves and use tools made of stones.

Tool-Making by Foragers

Tool making was also considered one of the first capabilities that differentiated humans from animals. It was long believed that only humans used tools because of the unique way our hands developed when we stopped using them as extra feet, several million years ago. Our thumbs became more flexible and our fingers could more easily grasp small pieces of flint stone to be used as knives and scrapers. However, recent studies have indicated that chimpanzees also use rudimentary tools; and some birds like the thrush break open the shell of a snail by hitting in on a stone.

The female chimpanzee uses a pointed stick for 'termite fishing'; that is, poking into underground termite nests to catch the insects to feed herself and her young.

Female Use of Tools

Insects are a good source of protein, which are consumed by many indigenous peoples. This has led anthropologists and archaeologists to take another look at the tools found in earliest human settlements from the Lower Paleolithic. When man (until the last thirty years or so) dominated these sciences, male bias interpreted all stone tools (the only kind of evidence of human societies that survived for hundreds of thousands of years) as being invented by 'Man the Hunter'. Now, however, many scholars believe that the female played a crucial role in the invention of tools.

Because she was constantly foraging for food for herself and her young, she would have had more motivation to use sharp stones and sticks for digging out tubers and roots, slicing bark off trees, cutting leaves, stems fruits, berries, bulbs, fungi, grasses, grains, and seaweed. She would have had more reasons (her hungry children) to fashion sharpened flint into knives to kill and skin small animals such as rabbits, turtles, lizards and even shellfish. The female would have had more reasons and motivation for inventing tools because of her combined responsibilities of childcare and food gathering. One of the most early and most important tools would have had to be a container in which to carry her infant with her as she nursed it at her breast and searched for food at the same time. It was probably a sling made of an animal hide.

Mother and Child Family Unit

I am writing now of the earliest hominids, who lived in small groups; and who did not yet have any concept of fatherhood or the contribution of male sperm in the reproductive process.

The earliest human 'family' was therefore a mother with her children. The men very likely would have lived separately from the women and the children, as there would not have been any knowledge of paternity. In other words, the men would not have known that they were fathers; or that the children belonged also to them.

Without any science or the knowledge contained in books, we can see how it would be unlikely to associate the act of sexual intercourse with the birth of a baby almost a year later. We believe the knowledge of the reproductive process was recognized through animal husbandry approximately 4,000 BC during the Bronze Age. The mother and child image, without a father, was found frequently in the ancient art of Egypt. The Goddess Isis, the most beloved and longest lasting female deity, was often portrayed with her divine child, Horus. This theme was carried over into the classical Greek world of Goddess Demeter, which means "God-the-Mother", and often shown with her daughter, Persephone.

In the Roman era, when Christianity was spreading throughout the Roman Empire, the mother and child were again used to portray the family unit. The Madonna Mary with her divine Child, Jesus, was a favorite subject of all the old masters: Raphael, DA Vinci, Botticelli, and Michelangelo. It seems that today, we are reverting back to the Old Stone Age, with many of our family units consisting only of a mother and her children without the presence of a father. In some instances, a single-parent family consists of a father and child or children; but overwhelmingly, a woman is the head of a single-parent family.

Primate Sexuality

Even though today we know full well that the male's sperm contributed to the creation of a child, many men have chosen to deny or ignore their responsibility toward the children they have generated. This would make an interesting field of study for sociologists and psychologists: why are males, in increasingly greater numbers, abandoning their mates and their progeny? Why, in almost the twenty-first century of human progress and evolution are so many males reverting to patterns of behavior almost identical to the behavior of Neanderthals, our evolutionary ancestors?

Returning to the lower Paleolithic era, often called the 'Old Stone Age' circa 50,000 BC, the Cro-Magnon branch of the hominids (named after the locale in France where many of their skeletal remains were found) has replaced the Neanderthals (the prototypical humans). No one knows exactly when, or how, or why this happened. It is commonly believed that the Neanderthals (the ones with prominent brows, lots of body hair and lumbering gait that are often depicted as Stone Age people) were not able to adapt to the changing environment. They did not improve their tools over millennia and were not able to pass on knowledge to succeeding generations.

Development of Cro-Magnon Brain

When they came in contact with the other branch of the human family, the Cro-Magnons, they were either killed or died off, or simply absorbed into the Cro-Magnon tribes. We can reflect now on the cranial cavity of the presumed to be superior Cro-Magnons. Because they were already walking in a more erect position, (remember how the female hominids learned to walk upright while holding an infant to their breasts and reaching for fruits, etc. in tall trees) their brains would have evolved quite differently than their primate ancestors. The force of gravity would have elongated the head, making more space for brain cells to grow and more neuronal pathways would have been generated by the innovative upright posture.

In the former studies of anthropologists, credit for the increased brainpower was automatically awarded to the males, who had to stand tall to peer over the high Savannah grasses in search of large animals to kill for food. However, newer scholarship argues that hunting large game animals did not come until much later, probably circa 30,000 BC.

That, in fact, the females probably foraged for most of the tribe's food which would have consisted of tubers, roots, berries, rhizomes, leaves, barks, grasses, seeds, shellfish, nuts, fruits, and perhaps some small animals, already dead that she found while foraging. The female's bipedalism would have led to increased brain size to fill the elongated head cavity; and if she was a mother, her brain would have been flooded with estrogen and progesterone, known to increase intelligence. Her need to carry her young while reaching high in trees and bushes for food, would have been a more powerful motivation for bipedalism than the males' motivation to look for large animals; as they were not yet part of the human diet. Much of this information has been extrapolated from observation of present-day 'primitive' societies and also chimpanzee and gorilla behavior such as the studies done by Jane Goodall in Kombe, Tanzania and Diane Fossey in Rwanda.

Scientists observing chimpanzees in Africa have observed that the female is more likely to use a tool to reach food, is more successful more frequently than males at securing food, and is more adept at manipulation of the tool. The first tool inventors and tool users may very well have been females. The female must hold her offspring with one hand, while doing the entire food gathering with the other; and she must secure enough food for two or more, depending on how many offspring she has.

Woman - The Tool Maker

The study of primate societies is especially useful because the males and females have not been subject to hundreds of thousands of years of societal conditioning to behave in certain restricted ways, as humans have learned to do.

So far we have seen how the female's motherhood and bipedalism may have led to increased brain size and her ability to use tools: sharpened sticks for digging out tubers and roots from the earth, sharpened pieces of flint stone for cutting bark from trees and cutting back vines and underbrush. She would have used sharpened sticks for skinning small birds and animals, and she used rocks for cracking open nuts and knocking down fruit, or stunning small birds and game.

It is quite probable that the very first humans were vegetarians as most primates still are. It is also quite possible that our bodies evolved 200,000 years ago from a diet of plants, vegetation, fruits, grains, seeds and tubers; and that, in fact, our bodies would still function optimally on such a diet.

Some doctors today are saying that animals and their by-products (aged cheeses, smoked meats, sausages, nitrates in luncheon meats, etc.,) are a primary cause of cancer in humans; and that we were never meant to eat animals. Naturopathic doctors tell us that our bodies evolved on vegetation as our nutrition; so we should use herbal remedies to cure what ails us.

Women in the ancient world knew every curative aspect of everything found in nature; and used this knowledge for hundreds of thousands of years. They were known as shamankas, medicine women, curanderas, midwives, wise old women; and most often, wiccans (pronounced 'witches'). They knew how to heal, how to ease pain, how to control reproduction so that there wouldn't be more mouths to feed than the tribe could sustain. The medicine women carried their herbs, salves, ointments, and pills, (which they rolled themselves from natural ingredients) in pouches around their necks or hanging on their belts, so they would always be ready for any emergency. They knew how to ease the pain of childbirth and how to comfort the dying. They were present at the beginning of life, childbirth, as well as at the end of life, death, performing their healing arts as a community service; as there was little or no money circulated those days, from our very beginnings to circa AD 1300.

The medicinal knowledge of traditional women, passed on from mothers to daughters for millennia, was virtually eradicated during the witch-hunts of the Middle Ages. The Catholic hierarchy, which also controlled most European countries' political power, put to death millions of women over a span of three hundred years, under the pretense of 'heresy'. Church Officials even published a manual, "Malleus Malleficorum" in which it outlined the tortures approved by the church. The women's holocaust was given official sanction under the title, 'Inquisition'; when in fact, it was an organized, planned way of wresting the knowledge and practice of medicine from the local village healers; and putting it in the hands of the men who were graduating from Catholic Universities. The practice of medicine was becoming very profitable by the 14th century.

The old peasant women (and sometimes men, of the Germanic and Celtic tribes) practiced medicine for no monetary pay, or for barter. Peasant families had little if anything that they could use for barter, like eggs or a piece of homespun fabric, but were still seen as a threat to the emerging profitability in the field of medicine. The Catholic Church decreed that only university-trained doctors would thenceforth be allowed to practice medicine.

Witches' Holocaust

Since women were not allowed into the church-owned universities, this dictum was supposed to eliminate this healing power of women. However, women continued to service those who came to them for relief of suffering; and for this, they were called "witches" and tortured and killed; sometimes burned alive on a pole of dried rushes, for the whole town to see as an example. It is said that in some European villages, not one woman was left alive. Sometimes their animals, their husbands, and their children were killed with them in the mass hysteria that took place in central Europe. Their property was then absconded by the church of

Rome to cover the costs of their 'trials'. The Vatican's wealth may have grown considerably by the acquisition of accused women's land.

The hysteria even crossed the ocean with the Puritans. As late as AD 1670 in our own country, in Salem, Massachusetts, there were several witch burnings. In this way, through the combined power of Church and State (always a dangerous alliance) the knowledge of millennia - old healing herbs, barks, roots, twigs, seeds, nuts, berries, leaves, flowers, oils, poultices, teas, infusions, liniments, tonics, salves and potions (all found in the local environment) were lost to the Western world, as those women who had the knowledge were systematically murdered under the pretext that they were 'witches'.

Wise Women

'Witch' is a corruption of the word 'wiccan', meaning 'wise woman' or a woman who has much wisdom and knowledge of the curative powers within nature. Because the 'c' in Wicca is pronounced 'ch' in the Celtic language (also Gaelic), the root word for wisdom, 'wic', or 'wit' came to be pronounced 'wich'. As yet, there was no writing in *The Celtic World*, no alphabet (except two rudimentary twig alphabets called runic and ogham), and no standardized spelling. Words, when they were finally written down centuries later, bore little resemblance to their original spelling and meaning. Therefore, for the remainder of this text, I will use the proper, respectful name of 'wiccan' for those wise women, and also some men, who practiced 'the craft' (formerly known as 'witch-craft'), a household religion based on the wisdom found in nature, the agricultural cycles, the hearth and the home.

Year of the Woman, 6010 AA (after agriculture)

Because women were the quintessential food gatherers, food preparers, and food preservers, they may have discovered and originated agriculture approximately 7,000 BC. Feminist authors sometimes use a time frame of reference based on one of the most valuable gifts to civilization, farming. The year that I am writing now would be 6010 AA (after agriculture), for this is the time span through which we can trace women's gifts to civilization with more archeological evidence. However, we can go back in time, thirty thousand years, to the first limestone cave shelters used by the early Paleolithic (Stone Age) people and find a carving of a woman at the entrance to the cave.

It was carved into a large block fallen in a limestone rock shelter (abri de Laussel) on the territory of the Commune of Marquay, in the Dordogne Department of Southwestern France. It is now in the Musée d'Aquitaine, in Bordeaux, France. J. G. Lalanne, a physician, rediscovered the figure in 1911.

The 'Venus of Laussel' is one of the earliest representations of a human like us. There is a great deal that is significant about this rotund female holding a crescent-shaped object. The first thing that is significant is that the human being painstakingly carved into limestone rock about 28,000 years ago is a female. There can be no doubt about her gender as is often the case in stick-figure cave drawings of the Paleolithic (Stone Age) without identifiable sexual organs.

This 'Venus', so named by archaeologists because this is the Latin name of the Roman fertility and love Goddess, has large breasts, the distended belly of late pregnancy, and the female's pubic area. Does this mean the Stone Age people revered women, especially pregnant women?

It could mean they held women in awe; or at least thought women were 'worthy', meaning worthy of worship. The old English derivation of 'worship' is worthy to be shaped, or worthwhile, worth shaping ourselves after, as in role modeling, or worthy of adoration, as in worship.

Menstrual Entrainment

The next significant feature of this bas-relief limestone carving is an object she holds in her right hand. It is crescent-shaped and can be either a crescent moon or a ram or bison horn. It has thirteen notches carved on it, which are believed by many scholars to represent lunar months. In ancient Stone Age societies, where many women would have lived in a cave, in close proximity to each other, they would have experienced their menstrual periods very differently than women do today.

A phenomenon called 'entrainment' would probably have developed among the women of the clan, all-living together in one shelter. This 'entrainment' means that the women's hormonal systems would have begun to operate in coordination with each other. That is, every girl past menarche and every non-pregnant female in the extended family (clan) would have had the same menstrual period, starting and ending around the same day of the month.

This natural phenomena occurs today in all-girl boarding schools or in the military, where the women might share a dormitory for sleeping; and discover eventually, that they are all menstruating about the same time each month.

Women in the Stone Age

Presuming that this is what happened in the Stone Age, when women lived communally (and possibly, in separate areas from the men), the monthly bleeding would have been very noticeable. Stone Age people did not have clothing, as we do today. They removed the pelts from dead animals found in their environment before they learned how to hunt and kill the animals themselves and they wore the animals' fur skins to keep warm. The animals were their teachers just as the Native Americans used the 'four-leggeds' as role models.

Animals as the First 'Gods' and 'Goddesses'

Remember that Native Americans were Stone Age people living a

30,000 BC lifestyle in the 17th century AD when the English encountered them in Virginia and Massachusetts. Because Stone Age people lived so close to nature, in limestone caves and makeshift shelters, the animals in their environment constantly surrounded them. This was especially true before the discovery of fire, which was later used to keep animals at a distance, as the animals were frightened away by fire. (In another chapter I will deal with the discovery of fire and its great importance in shaping human development, and the female's traditional role as 'fire-keeper' or 'keeper of the hearth/home fire').

Animals were not only walking 'encyclopedias' for the first humans; animals were the first gods. At first, this may seem absurd; but upon reflection, remember that animals must have seemed incredibly self-sufficient, wise, strange, and immortal. In a way, this was all true. Stone Age people thought the animals had always been there; long before they themselves were born, which was true. We now know that many species of animals, like the dinosaurs, were in existence millions of years before humans appeared. Stone Age people probably thought the animals were their forebears; or at least, related to themselves in some way. We now know that gorillas and/or chimpanzees are indeed our relatives, perhaps our evolutionary ancestors. Stone Age people thought animals, therefore, had lived forever and never died; but grew a new body from their skeletal remains. Could this be where we get our religious ideas of reincarnation and resurrection?

Catholics were taught that the long-dead bodies of the 'faithful' would magically rise from their graves on the day of the 'Last Judgment'. Stone Age people thought animals were wiser than people were, and more self-sufficient. This is also true. Animals are born with all the knowledge they need to survive. We call this 'instinct' and many psychologists believe that humans have no basic instincts. That is why humans can try new ways of doing things. We are not stuck in repetitive behavior patterns that are programmed into our brains. This freedom of choosing our own destiny and how to behave in each situation is called 'free will'.

Stone Age (Paleolithic) people observed the animals in their environment very closely in order to learn how to survive in a harsh climate (too hot in Africa, too cold in Northern Europe, Asia, China) with absolutely no technology, no tools, no weapons, no fire, and no shelter. They may have had shelter in a limestone cave if they were fortunate enough to find one. This is why we call our earliest ancestors 'cave women' or 'cave men' because the first human shelters were limestone caves.

Native Americans

The word 'Paleolithic' that I shall use from now on to refer to our Stone Age ancestors of 30,000 BC simply means 'old' (paleo), 'stone' (lithic) age. We know very little about them except that they were 'us' without our technology. They probably had no language, as we know it today; but they communicated effectively by vocal sounds, hand gestures, facial expressions, touching, body language, and symbols (drawings). Animals were their creature-teachers.

Animals also served in this manner, as teachers or role models, to Native Americans who named themselves, their family clans, and their tribes after the animals and admirable skills of animals, such as 'Running-Deer', 'Turtle Clan', or 'Bear Tribe'.

Destruction of Native American Communities

We can extrapolate from the Native Americans to the Paleolithic people; and get a clearer idea of how the very first humans survived: the foods they ate, how they made shelters and clothing, their world-views, religions, deities, and value systems.

There were hundreds of tribes living within one or two days walk of each other all over North America, one hundred fifty years ago. This was the case until they were chased from their ancestral lands, marginalized onto unproductive outreaches in the country, far away from industry and towns, and forbidden to practice their religion and culture and to speak their own language.

Pregnancy, the Magical State

Let us go backward in time now, to twenty thousand BC, and take a closer look at the amazing work of art that was found at the entrance of a Paleolithic limestone cave. It was the figure of a very pregnant woman, carved in bas-relief, and holding in one hand a crescent-moon shaped object with thirteen notches carved into the crescent. This one, powerful representation of a human like ourselves, tells us a great deal about women's history. First, it tells us that women were very important. So important, that the likeness of a woman was painstakingly preserved at a very significant location: at the entrance to their dwelling place. It also tells us about the kind of women that were revered, respected, and admired: 'fat' or pregnant women. Pregnancy was believed to be a magical state.

The holiest member of society was not the priest, nor the saint, nor the prophet. It was the pregnant woman who was held in awe as the Creatress, which means: She who brings forth-another human being from inside her own body. What could be more magical, more sacred, and more important to the survival of the clan? Not only did she reproduce herself but she also reproduced someone not like herself, boy babies. Not only did she create this new life out of her own bones and blood, but she also produced food for it that flowed magically from her breasts at just the right time!

How wondrous a creature was woman! How worthy of awe, how incredible, how mysterious, how infinitely wise and far superior to any other human! It was said by Native Americans that a man who did not have a woman, would die, if left to his own devices before Europeans arrived. His mate cooked his meals, made his clothing, shoes, and shelter, prepared his medicine, and nursed him when he was sick or injured. She also gathered and/or grew his food. Many tribes held women in the highest regard as European settlers wrote in their letters and accounts of life in the New World.

She could bleed for five days or more, every month and not die. She was the only creature who could do that! If a Paleolithic man bled continuously for five days, he would surely die. So would an animal. But a woman seemed to be a truly magical, God-like being. She could bleed without dying, she could make people unlike herself, (males), and she could manufacture food, her breast milk.

These were surely great supernatural abilities in the prehistoric world and for these reasons (as well as others) females were regarded as deities - Goddesses! And the woman was to retain this state of divinity, as the Great Mother Goddess, well into the Bronze Age.

The mysterious way women were able to create new life was their secret for millennia and it gave them tremendous power.

The 'Eleusinian Mysteries' was the name given to the female knowledge in the Aegean. The women's mystery religions were kept so secret that very little is known about them today. It has been said that Pythagoras, a male philosopher, was initiated into the mysteries, which would have been an enormous honor because men were not permitted to be initiates until about 100 BC.

Moon as the Cause of Pregnancy

No one knew, thirty thousand years ago, how the infant got into the women's body. There was as yet no knowledge of male sperm or its contribution to fertilization of the female ovum.

After all, sperm cannot be seen without a microscope (which our earliest ancestors did not have). There were many theories in ancient times of how a woman became pregnant. Our earliest ancestors probably believed that the moon had something to do with it because the woman's bleeding ('menses' means 'of the moon') seemed to be in some way connected to or caused by cycles of the moon.

The moon, therefore, became highly identified with women as a divinity in and of itself; and, also, because of its association with menstrual bleeding, women were perceived as being carriers of divinity, or Goddesses, because of their ability to create new life.

Sun, Moon, and Stars as Deities

It may seem ludicrous today, that our ancient ancestors believed the moon, sun, and stars were deities. However, without the science of Astrology, Astronomy, Physics, or powerful telescopes, what else could they think? They lived their lives mostly under the open sky, before they learned how to build shelters (by observing the animals and birds, their first teachers). Native Americans, as well as all early people, 'lived the sky', learning to foretell weather, preparing for each seasonal cycle.

They saw these strange 'eyes' in the night sky watching and following their every move, then disappearing from sight for intervals of time. One of the strange 'beings' in the sky even provided them with light and warmth - very essential services 200,000 year ago before lights or heaters. Today we call it 'sun', but it was worshipped as a major Goddess and/or God well into the Roman era.

The ancients recognized the sun as the source of all life on earth, which we know to be true today. Minerva Sulis was the name of the Sun Goddess honored and prayed to in England during the Roman occupation of the British Isles. She was known by many names in almost all countries in the ancient world, including Saule (Lithuania), Sonja (Nordic countries), Sunne (Germanic), Sulis (Celtic), Sole (Roman). The Japanese called their ancestral Mother, 'Amaterasu', their Sun Goddess.

Originally, women were the carriers of divinity in Japan, as they still are in Okinawa. Later, however their emperors were believed to be the incarnations of Amaterasu. Note that the Latin word for mother, 'mater', is part of the Japanese Sun Goddess' name. 'A-mater-asu'.

The shape of the sun, a round disk, also became a symbol of holiness used by Catholic artists as a halo behind the heads of holy people. Called the 'solar disk', it was also used about 2000 BC in ancient Egypt, as a symbol of 'RA', the sun god. As in most agricultural societies dependent on the sun for the growth of crops, Egypt also deified the sun.

Egyptian Sun Goddess, Ra-ta-uit

Originally, in pre-pharaoh Egypt, the sun was a Goddess, Ra-ta-uit, and the lady of heaven, which meant 'she who ruled alone'. Egyptian names are pronounced as separate syllables because each syllable has a meaning. The earliest Pyramid texts explained that she 'caused the sun, her divine child, RA, to grow old during the span of each day, die at sunset, then be brought back to life magically each dawn by his mother, the sun Goddess, Ra-ta-uit.

However, about 4000 BC, when a gradual shift toward the worship of maleness began to occur all over the ancient Middle Eastern Goddess-mother societies, Egyptian priests, and pharaohs also changed the gender of their deities from female to male. The sun Goddess, mother of the sun, became simply 'RA', the sun god. The pharaohs claimed to be descended from him, as they had earlier claimed to be the divine son of Ra-ta-uit; and thus proclaimed themselves gods. This was the beginning of the principle of the divine right of kings to rule and sometimes misuse their power-their absolute 'God-given' power.

Japanese Sun Goddess, Amaterasu

This principle was especially evident in Japan, in my own lifetime, where Emperor Hirohito was worshipped as an incarnation of the sun Goddess, Amaterasu. After the defeat of the Japanese in World War II, the United States forced the emperor, to tell his people that he was not a reincarnate god. This was extremely distressful for the Japanese, as it has left a huge gap in their spiritual belief system.

Later, Japan saw a proliferation of cults as the people of Japan tried to re-connect to their primal ancestress, the sun Goddess, and their spiritual mother. Japan still uses her symbol, the blazing sun, on its flag.

In former times, Japan was referred to as 'Land of the Rising Sun'. Far back in antiquity, Japan was a theocracy ruled by priestesses who traced their lineage to the 'Mother Sun Goddess'. Remnants of this theocracy still exist in the highly ritualized acts of the Geishas.

Female Carriers of Divinity in Asia

In parts of Asia, women are believed to be the carriers of divinity throughout the centuries to the present-day. In the indigenous Ryukyu Island religion of Okinawa, Japan, females carry the 'kami' or ancestral spirit.

In Korea today, the indigenous household religion is presided over by extremely intelligent female shamans. Eighty percent of the Korean population consults female shamans (priestesses of the ancestral religion). The South Korean government officially recognizes Buddhism as the state religion; and has been trying for decades to stamp out 'Korean Shamanism' and 'Household Religion' with little success. The indigenous Shinto religion of Japan contains a major element of ancestor worship, which includes the female ancestresses.

'Geisha' girls are a remnant of the ancestral Shinto religion with their highly ritualized behavior. Geishas used rice powder to paint their round faces like the moon, to symbolize their connections to divinity. They once held power as priestesses; but Japan has long been under the domination of Patriarchy and women's status has generally declined. Today, the Buddhist Mother of Compassion, Kwan Yin, is widely venerated in the Far East.

Sun Goddess 'Al-Lat' of Arabia

Another society that worshipped the Sun Goddess was Arabia, where the Goddess of the Sun, 'Al-Lat' was worshipped for over a thousand years of recorded history before she was masculinized by Islam, and became 'Allah'. 'Al-lat', as Queen of Heaven, was also Goddess of the Moon. Her ancient symbols, the crescent moon and star, are still used today on Islamic flags, although Moslems would probably deny any female symbolism in their predominantly patriarchal religion, even though their very name 'Moslem' contains the original mother-syllable, 'MO'. The meaning of the mother syllable will be explained in a later chapter as I show how it usually points to female origins of tribes, countries, accomplishments, and women's gifts to civilization.

Sun Goddess Arinna of Anatolia

In 1500 BC, the Hittites of Anatolia (present-day, Turkey) worshipped the Sun Goddess 'Arinna', usually pictured with the solar disk halo around her head. She was known also as Queen of Heaven and Earth. The round sun, or solar disk, around the head in art found in ancient Egypt, in Hindu and Buddhist art in India, and much later by Roman Catholic artists, was used to symbolically portray holiness, divinity, and sainthood.

Other Sun Goddesses

Other Sun Goddesses were 'Lethua', the Great Mother Goddess who gave her name to the Baltic nation of Lithuania; 'Lucia', Sweden; 'Brigit', Celtic Ireland; 'Mithra', Persia; 'Phoebe', East Anglia; 'Vesta' and 'Sulis', Rome; 'Sonja', Scandinavia; 'Shekinah', Hebrew; 'Isis', Egypt; 'Suriya', India; 'Sunne', Germanic Tribes; and countless others in the indigenous cultures of Australia, Alaska, the Americas and other countries.

Romans copied the deities of Greece because it (Greece) was a much more advanced civilization by the time the Romans conquered it, probably around 200 BC. The Greeks borrowed much from the high civilization of ancient Egypt, especially in medicine, religious concepts, etc. which the first Christians (who were Roman Catholics) then copied from the Greeks.

The Catholic male hierarchy copied the Roman Empires political organization: Pontiff, Priest, Nuns (vestal virgins), Diocese, and Cardinal. Some deities do not have Egyptian counterparts because ancient Egypt had a different value system and did not have a War God, like Mars. Isis (AuSet, the Spirit/Creatress) encompassed most female inventions or attributes.

Lithuanian Roots

The Lithuanian 'Ausros Vartai' is a solar icon of the Virgin Mary, Mother of God in the Catholic tradition. The Ausros Vartai is an arched gateway in Vilnius, the capitol of Lithuania. In pre-Christian times, it was the symbolic gateway to heaven through the Sun Goddess Liethua's opening of the gate that faced to the East, the direction of the sunrise. A miniature archway, the pagan symbol of new beginnings, is carried in Lithuanian religious processions today and symbolizes a new dawn for the recently liberated Lithuania. (This tiny Baltic nation was the first to break away from the Soviet Republic in 1990.)

A major incentive that inspired my own research into women's position in the ancient world was the seminal contribution of the noted Lithuanian archaeologist, Dr. Marija Gimbutas. Because I am of mixed Lithuanian and Welsh heritage, I felt a special kinship when I read of her search for her maternal roots in the rich soil of ancient Lithuania. This land had steadfastly refused to become Christian well into the AD 1400's, when most of Europe had already been converted (often forcibly) to Catholicism.

Because of Lithuania's long pagan history, Marija as a young girl heard the older women singing songs about folk heroines as they worked the fields. These traditional 'call-and-response' songs are called 'dainos' and still retain their ancient spiritual and cultural significance. This piqued her curiosity about women's cultural and spiritual history in Lithuania. She began her lifelong search for her own cultural roots in the archeological digs of Old Europe, where she personally led forty major expeditions.

I have seen a video on which my elderly cousin and her daughter sang a daino on the Bernatonis family homestead in Siliniai, Lithuania. It was very moving and poignant, and sung with much feeling for the love of their foremothers who sang these work songs before them. People sang as others answered, as if calling to each other, as they worked the fields, wove on their looms, canned foods for winter, or did many other tedious jobs. The songs relieved their tiredness and the monotony of repetitive chores.

Decoding the Symbols on Neolithic Pottery

Dr. Gimbutas was the first to decode the mysterious symbols found on Neolithic (c. 7000 BC) women's pottery and statuettes. Previous generations of anthropologists, who saw them as merely fanciful artwork, fertility symbols, or geometric designs, had dismissed the enigmatic markings in the wet clay of the ancient potters. However, Dr. Gimbutas' relentless pursuit of the meaning behind these symbols of Old Europe led her to reach startling conclusions. The markings were not just decorative artwork, but in fact, told a story to pre-literate peoples of their Mother Goddess and her attributes.

The most commonly found symbols on ancient Neolithic pottery and Goddess figurines were: the dot, the lozenge (diamond shape), the triangle, circle, egg (ovoid-shape), parallel lines, wavy lines, spirals, snakes and caterpillars, ram's horns, butterfly wings, (also called double ax or helix), squared cross (sometimes called 'swastika'), chevrons (V's and inverted V's), broken lines, crescents, and triangles.

There are five core elements to the symbols making up thirty core signs.

1. A straight line (could have meant the rain, or many lines in succession, a basket-weave)
2. Two straight lines intersected at the center (to form a chevron or a cross)
3. Two lines joined at the end (the supernatural pubic triangle)
4. A dot (or dots, could translate to tears or seeds),
5. And a curved line, or wavy line (perhaps running water or animals).

Stone Age Divas

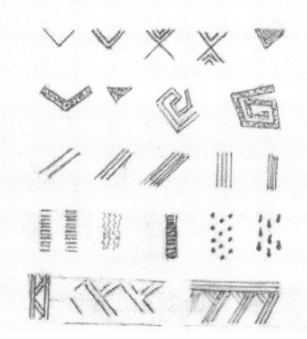

Sketch by Pres Miranda

These core symbols were markings from the Vinča culture (5200-4000 BC) About 70 of the 210 Vinča (Translyvania) signs were symbols universally used in Old Europe, and were incised on many of the goddess figurines. *

* Note:
  I still remind all that the font is in fact named 'Gimbutas', to the memory of Marija Gimbutas, American archaeologist at UCLA, of Lithuanian origin.
  Sorin Paliga, Dept of Slavic Languages and Literature, Bucharest, Romania

The old European sacred core script 8,000 years old, which is 2,000 years older than the Sumerian language, was discovered in Turdas (Tardas), as an early Vinča site in Transylvania was excavated in 1874.

Civilization of Old Europe

Dr. Gimbutas painstakingly analyzed thousands of potsherds, figurines, bowls, vases, lids, clay seals, jewelry, bone, ivory, and rock carvings, spindle whorls, pillars, altar pieces, and numerous other artifacts that she meticulously researched during her archeological digs in Old Europe, including the Aegean and Mediterranean areas. She based her work on the theory that southeastern Europe had evolved into a unique civilization, contemporary with the great civilizations evolving in Anatolia (present-day Turkey), Mesopotamia* (present-day Iraq), Syria, Palestine, and Egypt.

The growth and cultural development of the Middle East, Egypt, and southeastern Europe occurred during 6000 BC to 4000 BC, the period generally called 'Neolithic' or new Stone Age. This is the era that marked the beginning of the cultivation of crops; and the beginning of a more settled lifestyle that would eventually revolve around women's gardens, the first farms.

The reader is reminded that I have presented the most rudimentary explanation of the multiplicity of 'sophisticated symbols' that were used to communicate important concepts in the Paleolithic and Neolithic ages of prehistory.

The serious student of prehistoric symbology is directed to 'The *Goddesses and Gods of Old Europe*: Myths and Cult Images' by Dr.

---

* For years, scholars were not quite certain of this area. Parts of Mesopotamia undoubtedly were past the borders of present day Iran; but it is generally agreed upon now that it was actually Iraq. Southern Iraq was Babylonia and Northern Iraq was Assyria. These kingdoms were later, after Sumerian civilization was long gone and forgotten, the first high civilization of the Middle East, which was also in Iraq. Saddam Hussein was very well aware that he was sitting on 6000 years of incredible ancient history, so he felt secure that the Western governments would never invade or bomb his country because of its historical value. However, both United States Presidents, George Bush and George W. Bush, saw him as a serious threat to United States security, and waged war on Iraq. The world may have consequently lost valuable treasures of the ancient high civilization of Mesopotamia.

(added by author)

Marija Gimbutas, for an in-depth study of the mythical imagery of Old Europe before the Indo-European invasions which began c.4500 BC. It is also important to remember that all scholars and researchers do not yet share the conclusions reached by Dr. Gimbutas.

Sketch by: Pres Miranda

- Dots often stood for seeds.

- The lozenge was an early vulva symbol.

- Parallel lines generally stood for a plowed field.

- The triangle was a more obvious pubic symbol.

- The circle was the primordial female symbol of breast and womb.

- Wavy or meander lines often meant water, rivers, waves, and movement.

- The spiral commonly stood for a coiled snake, which was a dominant motif in ancient Goddess cultures. The serpent stood for regeneration, as it was able to shed its skin and continue living. The spiral also may have symbolized the development of the embryo from seed to infant, as the fetus turned around itself in the 'fetal position' in a woman's uterus.

- The serpent was a sacred symbol of the Minoans of ancient Crete and the Neolithic artists of Old Europe. This association of the female divinity and the serpent was even used in the Biblical Garden of Eden.

- The crescent could symbolize the crescent moon as a female lunar symbol; or it could also stand for the horn of a male animal like a bull or ram. The horn's mysterious ability to grow from the head of a male animal eventually came to signify male power and divinity.

- The butterfly is still widely used as a symbol of transformation from a caterpillar to a lovely winged creature.

- Double-ax or helix: this symbol derived from the original butterfly symbolism and came to mean an ending or death during the Bronze Age when violence entered the Mediterranean area via the invaders from the North.

- Wheeled cross or swastika: it represented the sun's movement across the sky or the movement of nature through its cycles and seasons. This symbol predates the invention of the round wheel most likely used by potters before it was adapted for use on vehicles like farm carts, and later, chariots.

- V's and inverted V's or chevrons symbolized status as it still does today in the military. It was copied from flight patterns of migratory birds. This is called the 'pubic triangle', because the **'V'** symbolized the sacred life source, the female pubis.

* The egg was the symbol of potential life. This oval shape could also represent a chrysalis on the verge of becoming something else.

* Broken lines were a rain symbol. To agricultural societies, this was a very important way to 'create' much-needed rain by 'sympathetic magic', evoking the spirit of the rain.

These were conventional signs used to stamp seals from the 7th and 6th millennia BC to mark objects, thrones, temples, pendants, plaques, and many other religious objects. Chevrons, Xs with Vs between the arms, zigzags, whirls, crosses, concentric circles and squares. These became many of the letters of our alphabet: V, X, T, C, I, M, Y, W, E, A, P, S.

This writing may have begun as a means to communicate with the

Mother Goddess and other Goddesses of a similar culture as it showed an eagerness to communicate with existing peace in the world they knew.

Agriculture: Women's Gift to Civilization

By 8000 BC, women had noticed that when they dropped seeds from the armfuls of vegetation they had gathered in their daily foraging for food, the seeds would often begin to sprout. Since these 'food-gatherers' had to keep a sharp eye on the ground for anything edible, they soon got the idea that perhaps they could deliberately put some kernels or seeds in the ground near their hearths, and see what happened. Of course, we all know the rest of the story. The seeds sprouted, the women carefully tended their gardens, and horticulture was born.

Horticulture, (sustenance farming), eventually, over the span of thousands of years, became agriculture. The ancients had no problem giving women credit for this magical gift to civilization - the gift of food - because were not women already known to be wondrous magical Goddesses who could create new life at will? Remember that there was as yet, no concept of fatherhood or paternity. This would come later, about 4000 BC, when women learned how to tame animals and raise them as they raised their own children.

Through animal husbandry, the mystery of the reproductive process and the male's contribution to it was finally understood. However, those societies in isolated areas that did not practice animal husbandry probably did not understand the principle of paternity until the nineteenth century AD. For instance, the Lenapes, Native Americans living in New Jersey in AD 1812, had only the most vague concept of paternity. Their mothers' brothers mentored the boys; and this mentoring (acting like a father) was the sacred, life long obligation of the uncles.

This was a matrilineal society, where only the mother's lineage was honored and understood.

There was only the all-giving mother! Ancient peoples believed that she created the baby out of her menstrual blood (which was retained during pregnancy); that she magically brought forth the baby when it had reached the right size, and that she nursed the infant with food she had magically produced out of her own body - mother's milk. It was not a difficult decision to reach then, that the Creative Principle in the universe, which we now call 'God', was female. Who else but the female could create new life? Everywhere in the natural world, all life came through the female. Because of this awesome power, the creator was conceptualized as a woman, the 'Great Cosmic Mother' from whom all life and all bounty flowed. This 'Great Mother God' was almost always envisioned as huge, almost monstrous, as the Goddess figures of Malta show us from 5000 BC.

All through the Paleolithic (Stone Age that encompassed a vast time period from c. 500,000 BC to 10,000 BC) the Great Mother Goddess was corpulent by our standards, a great, voluptuous being. She was very pregnant and full-figured with exaggerated breasts, hips, and buttocks. While she would be known by many names in all parts of the world and while she would be portrayed with many different attributes in diverse cultures, she was always <u>The One</u> unto Herself, the Mother Goddess.

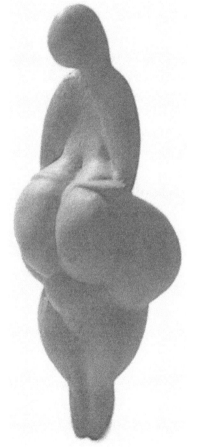

Great Mother Goddess

This was a monotheistic religion; for while she would continue to be represented in thousands of different images with thousands of different names, and for thousands of years, she was always One unto Herself; the giver and provider of all life on earth, in the oceans and in the sky. She could pass through the stages of life, like the stages of the moon, her sacred symbol.

Triple Goddess

She could be Maiden, Mother, Crone, the Triple Goddess, or 'Trinity' as the Christians would later call their male deity. But, she was always <u>The One</u>, the 'Great Cosmic Mother' who birthed us, who nourished us, who nursed our wounds, who helped us die, who eased our exit from this life as she had eased our entrance into life.

The rest of my book will be a journey through time and space, as together we visit our 'Great Cosmic Mother' Goddess. She was imaged by her human children from 20,000 BC and probably much earlier in that vast era of time we call the Stone Age or Paleolithic era, to 3000 BC, the Bronze Age. During the Bronze Age, she was given a male consort, husband, mate, or son to gradually diminish her autonomy and power.

Later through the Iron Age, c. 1000 BC, she was dethroned, debased, violated, denied, and demonized. Throughout the Christian era, AD 50, she emerged again as Mary, (the Mother of God, with only half of her power restored). From AD 50 to the present-day of Feminist Spirituality and the re-emergence of the Great Goddess, the Cosmic Mother holds for women a sense of self-worth. As a role model for women who want to make better choices in their lives, she will be unsurpassed.

Paleolithic Religion

But first, we must return to her roots in the Stone Age, 20,000 BC, where we first come face to face with her at the entrance to her limestone cave sanctuary. Many symbols of the Great Mother Goddess, used in Neolithic art, have their roots in the Stone Age; the snake, the crescent moon, the fish, the bird, and ram's horns are just a few. This union of the female and animal symbolism probably arose from the beliefs of our Stone Age, or Paleolithic, ancestors.

Paleolithic people, if we can extrapolate from our own indigenous Native Americans, believed that women gave birth to the first animals. To this day, some Native American societies believe animals are their ancestors. Their sacred animal ancestor is called their 'Totem' and 'Totem poles' are carved with their animal images. Tribal names include the qualities of animal role models; and clans (extended families) are named after the animal ancestor. For instance, in the Wolf Clan of the Massapequots of Connecticut, the typical Native American names are 'Running Deer', 'Sun Bear', 'Eagle Eye', 'Black Hawk', 'Corn Goddess', and 'Silver Fox'. In this way, the name would serve to evoke these qualities in the child.

Due to their isolation from the rest of the civilized world, Native Americans were caught in a time warp, still living a Paleolithic lifestyle in AD 1700. We can presume that the beliefs of our prehistoric ancestors coincided with what we know of Native American beliefs. This is called 'extrapolation'.

Anthropologists use this method to deduce prehistoric behavior and beliefs by observing indigenous tribal peoples in Africa, Australia, Philippine Islands, New Zealand, and New Guinea.

Paleolithic Cave Art

We know that we probably descended from at least one family of animals: mammals. It was formerly thought that we evolved from gorillas or chimpanzees; but the latest scholarship may trace our lineage to monkeys. At any rate, our earliest ancestors clearly felt that a strong link existed between animals and themselves. Earliest human art revolved around animals.

The cave art of Lascaux, France featured magnificent reproductions of animals on the walls and ceilings of a 30,000-year-old limestone cave inhabited by Paleolithic peoples. These magnificent animals, bounding and leaping across the high ceilings of the ancient caverns, rival anything that Picasso has produced. It is said that when one walks through the cave holding a torch, the animals appear to move and leap out at the visitor.

Some of the colors have faded; but it is believed the Stone Age artists used animal fat mixed with minerals they pulverized in order to create colored pigments. They then blew the paint mixture through reeds onto the outlines of the animals. This cave art is found throughout southern France, Spain, Portugal, and Italy. They are called the 'Stone Age Sistine Chapels'.

There are very few humans depicted with the engravings of bison, mammoths, antelopes, horses, ibex, and wild cattle. When humans are found, they are usually stick figures. But where it is possible to determine their sex, they are usually females.

A rock painting at the Cuevas de la Araña, at Bicorp, Spain, dated c. 7000-4000 BC shows a woman gathering wild honey. Since honey was the only sweetener available in the ancient world, the one who gathered it was highly valued as well as extremely courageous. She was not wearing a protective covering as beekeepers do today.

The Bee Goddess

The 'Bee' headed Goddess was one of the multitude of images combining human/animal or human/insect combinations. In order to understand ancient symbology we need to remember that the 'pagans' (non-Christians) of prehistory, long before Christ was born had a very holistic view of the world. Everything was connected, and everything was holy. They felt their entire landscape was peopled with unseen energies or 'spirits' (some benign, some harmful); and in this environment, everything had meaning and everything was connected.

Animals turned into people (as Darwin later hypothesized in his 'Evolution of the Species'); and people could learn from insects and animals and maybe even merge into them at some point. This theory is called 'the transmigration of souls' in Eastern religions. Therefore, a 'bee' headed Goddess would not seem unlikely to the agricultural societies of Neolithic Europe, the Middle East or Egypt.

The Egyptians, especially, were well known for their animal headed Goddesses and Gods. In a civilization without reading or writing (except for a privileged few scribes, clergy and royalty) imagery conveyed powerful messages of the continuity of life after death and the interrelationship of all forms of life. Aristotle is reported to have said that the Greeks were far superior to the Egyptians (who were already a very erudite, ancient race by 370 BC) because at least they - the "Greeks" - did not worship women and men with the heads of hyenas, lions, or hawks. We worship those like ourselves, the Goddesses and Gods of Mt. Olympus, and the heroines and heroes of classical Greek mythology, who were very human indeed.

Bee-Goddess and her Melissae

The priestess beekeepers of the Great Mother Goddess 'Demeter' of Greece were called 'Melissae'. (Note that 'de' means of; 'meter' means mother). Honey was considered food of the gods, reputed to prolong life. Honey was used to cure ills, as it still is today; and possibly mead, the mother's brew, is one of the earliest alcoholic beverages, made of fermented honey. Our craving for sweets is so strong that primitive people risked death to gather honey from beehives. This 'sweet tooth' is believed to come from our primate ancestors who lived on sweet fruits, berries and nuts high up in the tree branches of the primeval jungle.

Honey lasted forever in the days before refrigeration. It is the only food that never spoils. It has even been found in the tombs of Egyptian pyramids.

Souls were like bees and the Melissae (priestesses) drew the souls down from heaven to be born again.

Many gold rings found in Minoan ruins on Crete have had bee-headed Goddesses engraved on them. The bee-headed Goddess was found also in Rhodes where she was known as "Lady of the Wild Things", 700 BC.

At Ephesus (in present-day Turkey), the Goddess Artemis, 'Mistress of Animals', was associated with the bee as her sacred icon. Her sanctuary was organized like a beehive, with swarms of priestesses called 'Melissae', and numerous eunuch priests called 'Drones'. Eventually, just the image of a bee was enough to represent the Mother Goddess, a sort of 'Goddess shorthand' before writing.

For what it is worth, Napoleon Bonaparte chose the bee as his personal symbol, because he was always 'busy as a bee'. His Empress, Josephine, chose the rose for her symbol; so the rose with a bee hovering over it was the motif embroidered on their brocade draperies and velvet pillows at their palace in Fontainbleau, France.

Symbols were still being widely used to convey meaning in AD 1820 in France as they are today. Just think of the meanings encoded in our flag, if you have any doubt of the power of symbols. And so it was also in the ancient world.

The enormous creative activity and cooperation of swarms of buzzing bees in the production of their beehives and honey must have greatly impressed our foremothers and forefathers; and they used this imagery in a religious sense as a sacred symbol of regeneration and eternal renewal in the cycle of life.

Just as I had finished this chapter on the importance of the bee and its honey in the ancient world, my friend arrived to take me for an outing to one of our favorite places in Bucks County, Pennsylvania. New Hope is an artist's colony filled with charming outdoor cafes, sculptures in lovely gardens, and boutiques. After a delightful lunch at our favorite rendezvous, we strolled across the street to a beautiful shop that we always visit. As we browsed through the rooms, we spotted unusual linen clothing from Lithuania. I had never seen any clothing made in Lithuania (my heritage homeland). When I read the label, I was even more pleased. There, to my astonishment, was the "Bee Keeper" jacket, as it was written on the label, with a beehive symbol. What a stroke of pure serendipity! Now I am the owner of a beautiful olivine colored "Beekeeper" jacket made in the ancient land of the Great Mother Goddess, Lethua.

(added by author)

Beetle and Butterfly Symbolism

The Egyptian beetle or 'scarab' comes to mind as another powerful religious symbol that has come down through antiquity, symbolizing regeneration. The butterfly is another. Because the beetle steps out of its shell and the butterfly emerges from a cocoon, they both represent the Life-Death-Life cycle found in nature.

The chrysalis and butterfly are common Goddess symbols that were observed in nature and incorporated into religious symbolism eight thousand years ago. The chrysalis represented the transformation of an ugly caterpillar into a beautiful winged creature. Dr. Marija Gimbutas found the cocoon, chrysalis, and butterfly designs on Neolithic European clay pots, small Mother Goddess figurines, and frescos in Catal Huyuk, Anatolia (present-day Turkey).

Catal Huyuk was one of the oldest sites of human habitation in the world; showing that the butterfly was long recognized as a fertilizing force, a means of cross-pollination and symbol of resurrection and everlasting life.

The cocoon and butterfly symbols were also used to represent the qualities of the creatress Goddess in Vinča, former central Yugoslavia. The Balkans at that time were another ancient site of human settlements (c. 8000 BC and earlier).

From Butterfly to Battle-Ax

The butterfly eventually became highly stylized into a double ax; but it had nothing to do with the metal ax, which was not invented until several thousand years later. The ax and lightning bolt became symbols of the Thunder God of the northern tradition.

Starting around 2000 BC, invading hordes of nomads from beyond the Caucasus Mountains began to destroy the settled Mother Goddess agricultural communities. The butterfly evolved into the 'battle-ax', the symbol of the Goddess deity of the conquered. Near Eastern Mother Goddesses were made to endorse war by the Caucasian invaders. It is ironic that even today, to call a woman 'an old battle-ax' is to mean that she is 'an assertive woman who demands accountability', as Dr. Gimbutas reminded us.

From butterfly to double-ax is quite a journey, even in mythological time. From life-affirming, matrifocal and settled agricultural communities, to death-defying, male-focused warrior societies, was a long, bloody journey of the past 4000 years from which we are still trying to extricate ourselves.

The rest of my book will tell how and why this happened. It was a clash of opposing worldviews in a power struggle that met head-on, with monumental consequences that reverberated around the world; and, we are still reeling in its grip!

The Day the Horses Came

Dr. Riane Eisler, in her book, 'The Chalice and the Blade', dealt with the theme - the day the horses came. Highly skilled horsemen from north of the Caucasus Mts. came in horde after horde of devastating invasions that changed forever the 'Garden of Eden', the matrifocal, and agrarian, peaceful world of the Mother Goddess.

The combination of skilled horsemen with their new technology of iron weaponry would prove to be a deadly combination indeed! For it was this combination of high-spirited young males, with iron swords and swift horses, that was to mark the end of the Neolithic and Bronze Ages. It was they who ushered in the Iron Age with its increasing violence and forever change the way women and men would relate to each other and the world around them.

Who were these Iron Age nomads from the North who virtually destroyed the civilizations of the Goddess? Would it surprise you to know that they may have been our forefathers: Russians, Balts, Slavs, and many, many others that I will document.

About 4500 BC, they started coming to the peaceful, agricultural, matrifocal societies of Anatolia (present-day Turkey), Mesopotamia (present-day Iran, Iraq, parts of Syria), Greece, India, and Egypt. According to the sometimes-disputed theory of Dr. Maria Gimbutas, the aggressive invaders on horseback from beyond the Caucasus Mountains came in wave after wave of destruction. No one knows for sure who they were or where they originated. We know them as Aryans, Indo-Europeans, or Caucasians. You and I are probably their descendants. All we know is that they were very vigorous, aggressive, young males on swift, strong horses, carrying weapons of the brand new technology: iron. (The word 'Aryan' was used by the conquered peoples to describe their fearsome sword of 'iron'.) The name of one of the territories they conquered is known today as 'Iran', also derived from the word, 'iron'.

The combination of crazed young males, war horses and iron weapons would prove to be a deadly combination indeed. For they not only destroyed everything in their path: homes, temples, statues, literature, libraries, invaluable historic records of these ancient cultures; but they also brought with them their violent, militant gods of thunder, lightening, war, and destruction (Woden, Indra, Ahura Mazda, Zeus and Mars).

The entire mythic system changed gradually from a celebration of the female's fertility, to the celebration of the male's fertility and power. The marauding hordes brought their male (and some female) deities, their language (Indo-European), their system of government based on a hierarchy of power, competition, and war. Instead of accumulating wealth 'the hard way', by creating it themselves as the conquered societies had done, the invaders found an easier way to acquire riches: by the spoils of war.

About the same time, another group of restless nomads, the Semites, began to migrate from the deserts of Arabia, and North Africa. Instead of horses, they used camels and asses to migrate. The Semites included Hebrews, who were later to document their violent infiltration into the world of the Mother Goddess in explicit detail in the Old Testament of the Bible; as well as, Phoenicians, Chaldeans, and Armeneans. They brought with them, their jealous, fearsome, Yahweh or Jehovah, a father God.

The 'spoils of war' included women who were raped by their captives. Warriors always consider women to be fair game. Women were captured and carried back to the invaders' homelands, along with gold, silver, bronze artifacts, cattle and textiles, (which were mostly made by women). Textiles were very highly valued in the ancient world for use as clothing, blankets, and floor coverings.

This is how prostitution may have originated-by invaders capturing female war captives. The word prostitute derives from the Latin word 'prostrate', which means to hold down, to immobilize, which is what was done to women in order to have them raped by the soldiers. Prostitution was never a freely chosen profession, as we have been led to believe. It was a brutal way of life forced upon helpless girls and women who could not even speak the language of their kidnappers and were horribly victimized during all wars since the Bronze Age.

Starting perhaps as early as 4500 BC, the nomads from the harsh, semi-arid Eurasian steppes, Mongolia, Russia, Kazakhstan, and Siberia started to head south in wave after wave of great migrations. They had learned to domesticate the wild horses that roamed in great herds across central and northern Europe. It was through the domestication (taming) of wild animals, that humans finally, after hundreds of thousands of years of existence on earth, learned the secret of reproduction and the role of the male in conception and pregnancy. This knowledge was to upset the balance of power in almost every country in the world.

The male gods won, as we all know very well. The Great Goddess was dethroned - but not without one hell of a fight.

By 1600 BC to 600 BC, the invaders from the North had shaken up almost all the civilized world. Only the remote civilizations like those in South and Middle America (Olmecs and Chavins), and Native Americans in North America were unaffected.

CHAPTER II:
The Domestication of Animals

The Taming of Animals

After the controlled use of fire long before 500,000 BC, the discovery of agriculture about 8000 BC, the wheel, writing, weaving of textiles, and use of metals, the greatest advance for civilization was the domestication of animals, called animal 'husbandry'.

It is believed by some historians, that women had learned to tame individual animals about 20,000 BC. In her extraordinary well-researched tale of prehistoric peoples, Jean M. Auel, in The *Clan of the Cave Bear*, suggested that prehistoric women first learned to tame wild dogs by having them eat scraps of food out of their hands. Because animals were often seen as deities in antiquity, humans would have had a motivating desire to communicate with them. It would have had to be a non-verbal language; and it would have had to create a bond of trust between the human (predator) and the smaller-sized animal (wolf dog).

In the taming of a much larger animal, such as the horse, the newborn animal would have had to live with the woman who found it (usually orphaned soon after birth by the death of the mare who, in her weakened postpartum state, would have been easy prey). The very young horse would have then bonded to the human woman (who fed it) as its' mother, and learned to obey her.

The Beginnings of Civilization

Sharing food is a well-known bonding technique among humans. It is conceivable that women 'tamed' men in the Cro-Magnon era (c. 20,000 BC) by inviting the lonely male, sitting on his haunches on the boundary of the hearth the female mother shared with HER children, to join them and partake of their food. Remember the concept of fatherhood was still many millennia away. The beginning of civilization began around the mother/child relationship: bonding, loving, feeding, nurturing sharing, and communing.

Because she was possibly the chief food provider, by gathering plant foods and preserving them to last through the winter, she would have probably enjoyed the higher social status. Paleolithic and Mesolithic (Middle Stone Age) women observed the animals in their environment hiding food in the ground; and they imitated the animal's behavior. They hid roots and tubers in holes dug in the soft ground and covered them with a light layer of dirt.

By digging deeply under their limestone caves, they were able to reach the permafrost level of the earth where food could have been preserved by freezing. (And we thought we invented frozen foods!) This was where the winter food-supply of tubers, wild carrots, onions, seeds, nuts, herbs, fruits, vegetables, grains, and meats could be stored over the winter, relatively safe from animal predators.

I personally observed this behavior in the small mountain village where I grew up in the 1930's. Lithuanian immigrants, newly arrived, dug 'root cellars' under their homes where many foods were kept in the cool, damp earth over the winter. We had a 'root cellar' in our Pennsylvania home.

No doubt women would have learned the secret of crop growing as they noticed that some of the buried seeds had sprouted in the damp earth. People of the Paleolithic era ate the seeds themselves, before they developed horticulture; so the women would have laid away a large supply of seeds as winter food.

The males were probably living separately in male groups during the Stone Age because they were away for long periods of time stalking animals. The women were living together with their young. When the first woman took pity on the isolated male and invited him to share her food, the first nuclear family unit was begun. Remember women were the main food providers for the group through their foraging activity, before more effective weapons needed for hunting were invented.

The male eventually shared her sleeping mat as well as her hearth and her food. This bonding through food sharing, and eating together, which still works very well in the mating game, had a 'civilizing' effect on the males. Anti-social behaviors of the young males probably lessened; for the Cro-Magnon females would be more likely to invite to their hearths and sleeping mats, the most cooperative, congenial males. In other words, she bonded with the male who evinced the most gentle, loving behavior toward her and her young. The male who would be most protective and steadfast was the one she bonded to. This bonding through love, sex, devotion, emotion, and fidelity, would eventually enable humans to live together cooperatively and form larger and larger communities that would over time lead to magnificent cities in the Middle East.

Even today, people equate food with love: love is food. This is a major setback in combating obesity, for this 'food-love' association has been imprinted in us from birth.

Female to Animal Bonding

The 'bonding' behavior may have worked so well with males, that women probably tried it on the small animals that approached their cave homes and hearths for scraps of leftover food. By this time, several centuries later, men and women both hunted because men did not always provide food for women and children. Like the mother bear, who was highly revered in northern climates for her maternal devotion, the prehistoric mothers hunted for themselves and their children.

But later, the men would eventually hunt in organized groups; and leave the women and children alone for long periods of time while away on a prolonged hunt. Women would have been motivated to seek added protection from animals that they would have previously taught to bond with them. The latest research points to the domestication of wolves in Siberia as early as 70,000 BC. They would most likely be Siberian Huskies.

The women may have fed and cared for the feral dog-wolves just as they cared for their own children. They allowed orphaned pups to nurse from their own breasts. They gave the tamed animals shelter in their limestone caves. There are many stories in ancient myths describing how women bonded with animals.

Some Native American tribes even believed women gave birth to the first animals; and therefore, the animals in their environment were their relatives. So it is not too far-fetched to see Paleolithic women as the first to befriend animals, tame certain small animals in their environment; and form bonds of trust and love with those animals who were most amenable to forming such animal-to-human bonds. The dog, cat, goat, or pig would thus have become a member of the woman's household. The animal was available to provide a certain amount of protection during menstruation or after childbirth (when Stone Age women would have been more vulnerable to predators because of scents), and to safeguard the family hearth while the men were away on a raiding foray or hunt. An animal provided extra warmth through its body heat in frigid European winters; and, in case of starvation, a ready source of food.

In many cultures throughout the ages, animals such as goats, cattle, sheep, horses, and camels were a form of wealth. The family's wealth and status would be measured according to how many animals it owned. In some ancient tribes (and even today in many parts of the world) the women are the ones to care for this animal 'currency'. The goats (or other prized animals) slept in the women's tents; and the women were entrusted with the responsibility of keeping them healthy and safe. In Palestine even today, the family's animals are kept on the roof of the house for safekeeping.

This is not the only example of women being entrusted with the safeguarding of a family's wealth. In other world cultures where precious metals are the measure of the family's wealth, the wife will be expected to wear the family wealth in the form of enormous pieces of jewelry. She cannot remove them from her person: gold neck rings, silver, gold, bronze ankle bracelets, rings, earrings, and even coins were sewn onto her clothing. Certain Africans and Arabs still use this method of safeguarding the family's wealth by attaching it to the woman's body.

An African Woman wearing an enormous amount of gold rings around her neck was on the cover of National Geographic Magazine, Vol.169, No. 2 in February of 1986.

Other scholars believe that wild goats were probably the first animals to be domesticated, as they would have lived in the environments where the first Neolithic (new Stone Age or agricultural) cultures thrived: around the Mediterranean and south central Europe. The female goat had teats, which could have been used to suckle infants whose mothers had died in childbirth.

Actually a goat's teat was the first baby bottle thousands of years ago. (And we thought baby bottles were a 'modern' invention!). Of course, the goat was no longer attached to the teat. The nanny goat's bag of milk with her nipple attached was removed from butchered goats, cured and preserved for use as a milk bag/bottle for suckling human babies. Ingenious, those Stone Age ancestors! So, we can see that women would have had powerful motivations to domesticate, befriend, and tame wild animals.

Infanticide by Exposure

The folklore legends of many cultures are stories of human babies who were nurtured by animal mothers. The origin myth of the Roman Empire comes to mind. In ancient times, and even up to the present time (in some parts of the world), 'exposure' was an accepted way of getting rid of unwanted infants. There have always been unintended pregnancies; and one of the ways the ancients dealt with this tragic societal problem was to abandon the newborn to nature. To us, it may seem cruel and heartless; but in many parts of the world there were very few choices available to deal with the problem of too many babies and too few resources.

The great Hebrew patriarch, Moses, was himself such 'an exposed infant'. He was placed on a raft of bulrushes and left to float on the water in Egypt. This was done in many countries where water was nearby. Water was believed to take the baby back to the deity; but anyone who desired a baby could rescue it and raise it. In areas where no body of water was available, newborns were left on hillsides. The townspeople could hear the cries of the abandoned infant; but it was ignored and just accepted as part of normal life. This was a common practice in areas around the Mediterranean, circa 450 BC and earlier, according to historian Herodotus. The infants were frequently retrieved by slave-masters who raised the children and then sold them, and also by the procurers who trained them to be prostitutes. The origin myth of the Roman Empire revolved around twins, Romulus and Remus, who were exposed and abandoned on the sacred hill outside of Rome, suckled by a wolf-mother, and grew up to be kings. King Romulus was the legendary founder of the Roman Empire, 751 BC.

Female Domestication of Animals

Women about 7000 BC surely noticed that female animals produced milk for their newborns, just as they themselves produced their own breast milk. They would surely have noticed that the milk looked the same, tasted almost the same, and had the same consistency as their own breast milk and that it could be used as a food for humans. This would have been a major step forward in human progress. They could use the milk-producing animals by taming them and keeping them with the family as a steady source of liquid (milk), cheese, butter, cream, yogurt, buttermilk and curds and whey (which my Lithuanian father loved to eat over hot boiled potatoes).

The domesticated animals would also be ready-made food. Tribes could settle permanently in one place and not have to follow wild animals, their usual prey. They could now grow food beside a source of water, lake, or river, and also have a source of meat to sustain them through the long winter without crops.

Eventually, the Neolithic people would enlist the aid of dogs in hunting, and would use the muscles of their cattle to plow their fields. They would establish great herds of animals that would make them wealthy; and would harness the energy, strength, and speed of the horse to turn it into an indomitable war machine of the Bronze Age invasions.

But first, the Neolithic agriculturists had to learn the secret of animal husbandry: the secret of life, the secret of sex, and the male's role in procreation.

Cattle-Breeding and the Secret of Sperm

Because animals were now tamed, and living in close proximity with humans (usually in the same room, tent, cave or shelter) herders were able to observe their mating practices at very close range. The role of the male in conception was finally understood. Up until this time, many ancient peoples believed that the light of the moon impregnated women. Some believed the spirits of their dead ancestors caused females to get pregnant. Others believed seeds or invisible agents carried on the wind, caused pregnancy. Some may have believed that women withheld their menstrual blood at will, and the retained blood created the fetus. After the discovery of agriculture and the potential life contained in plant seeds, people may have reasoned that a woman could get pregnant by eating certain kinds of seeds. Cattle's breeding was the catalyst that finally solved the eternal mystery of the human race:

How did the baby get inside the mother?

The discovery of the fertilizing aspect of the male's sperm was to have far-reaching effects in the 'Garden of Eden', which some historians have located along the Syrian coast. The peaceful, settled, agrarian societies of the Mother Goddess would be only a far distant memory by the time Hebrew scribes memorialized the 'Land of Milk and Honey' and the 'Garden of Eden' in the old testament, about 1000 BC, during the Iron Age.

With the new recognition of the importance of the male in the creation of new life, the world would forever be changed; and, the female would, eventually, over the next four thousand years, be relegated to a position of greatly lessened power.

Because hunting was no longer needed as the major occupation of males, they were able to take over the breeding of livestock. Men were able to oversee large herds of cattle; and animals would also lose much of the mystery and divinity they had enjoyed as manifestations of the Great Mother. Now they became the means of power and wealth.

The word 'capitalism' derives from the Latin 'caput', which originally meant 'a head of cattle'. Animals were also a form of wealth in my hometown in Pennsylvania. In the 1800's, citizens were taxed according to how many horses they owned, as well as their real estate properties.

CHAPTER III:
Bronze Age Patriarchal Shift

Patriarchy was born when cattle breeders discovered the male role in conception; and that their own sperm had the power to begin a new life in the woman. With this awesome new knowledge, they could create more wealth in the form of children who could be used as workers; or, in the case of girls, be bartered for a 'bride price' or her labor used to create a new form of wealth, babies, and textiles.

The female body, long viewed as the 'holiest of the holiest', the vessel of the miracle and the mystery of new life, now became a 'machine' for producing wealth through unlimited pregnancies and never-ending domestic and farm chores.

The restless nomads of the North, who had domesticated the horse and turned it into an efficient war-machine by attaching a chariot, were poised to conquer the settled cities in the Near East. They had a mytho-religious philosophy of male supremacy, which they would superimpose on the Mother Goddess religion. This patriarchal shift to the worship of maleness took thousands of years; and many thousands of lives would be lost in this terrible clash of ideologies.

The female and everything she stood for - the oneness of nature, animals, humans, cycles of life and death, and life reborn - would be denied, disrespected, and eventually, demonized.

Genus Equus: The Horse

Eight thousand years ago, horses were found only in north Europe. We know the Paleolithics hunted them, or at least admired them, because of the magnificent charcoal drawings evidenced in their cave paintings. Horses were probably first domesticated by Central Asian nomads before 4500 BC.

There are also records of horses being used in Mesopotamia

(present-day Iraq and Iran), and China about 2000 BC, in Greece about 1700 BC, in Egypt c.1600 BC, India 1500 BC, and Western Europe about 1000 BC. (The ass was domesticated much earlier).

We call this period the Bronze Age.

The Warrior Horsemen

The Indo-European Aryans who first domesticated the horses were tall, light-skinned, and big-boned. They entered the stage of history with a superior war technology: the horse drawn chariot. Donkey drawn carts and wagons had long been in use in Europe and the Middle East before this.

However, the horse was a vast improvement over the donkey. The speed, agility, power, endurance, strength, and intelligence of the horse were exploited mercilessly by the restless northern nomads, who now controlled the secret of reproduction and used it to create new (animal) wealth.

The horse was an extraordinary animal: vibrant, strong, sleek, wild, knowing, and confident. Its flanks were incredibly responsive and sensitive to the slightest pressure from a human rider's thighs. In art and mythology it's majestic image would come to represent Freedom, Joy, Integrity, Maleness, Power, Speed, and Conquest. Early riders rode bareback. It was said by early historians that these skilled horsemen could do EVERYTHING on horseback.

It was said of the Scythians (those from present-day southern Russia) that they were able to control and stop their horses in mid-charge; and thus were able to fight from horseback. They didn't have to carry heavy shields; and could defeat any warrior on foot.

They were noted for fierceness in battle and often fought naked, with only indigo-blue designs painted all over their bodies, as their 'magical' protection. The Celts of the later Iron Age were also known to go into battle naked and tattooed in blue. Saddle and stirrups were believed to have been invented 1500 years later by Genghis Khan; and their use spread by Asian horsemen who settled in Hungary, the Huns. Nakedness would eventually come to symbolize male bravery in the sculptures of classical Greece, c. 500 BC and earlier.

Horses played an important role in the conquest of central Asia, south central Europe, and the Middle East. In successive Bronze Age invasions, over a period of three thousand years, beginning about 4500 BC, the warrior tribes of horsemen from the Russian steppes infiltrated the Neolithic world of the Great Mother Goddess Civilizations.

Kurqans

They were the Kurqans, Indo-Europeans who swept across Europe bringing war, barbarism, conquest, and violence. No one knows exactly what their tribal names were or exactly where they originated. All that is certain is that they originated somewhere beyond the Caucasus Mts. (thus the name 'Caucasians'); and that they had trained their horses on the harsh, semi-arid Eurasian steppes. They were called 'Kurqans' because of the method of burial they used for their dead. It was not a tribal name.

Various theorists place the homelands of the Indo-European speaking horsemen on the Baltic coast between east Prussia and Estonia; the steppes from the Carpathian Mountains to the Caspian Sea. South Russia and Eastern Europe was the horse-breeding zone with the ideal climate for raising and grazing horses, as well as riding them.

Timber graves of warriors buried with their horses were found from the Black Sea to the Caspian Sea. Armenia was technologically advanced for its time in 7000 BC. Slovakia to the Ural Mountains was a very advanced culture with domesticated horses, archery, wheels, chariots, and wagons.

Some scholars believe they were Mongolians, Russians, Turkistans, Kazakhstans, and Siberians. Starting about 3000 BC, they started arriving in Anatolia (present-day Turkey) and Mesopotamia (present-day Iran and Iraq) in great migrations. Other tribes who were probably on the move were the Germanics, Balts (Lithuanians, Latvians, and Old Prussians), Slavs (Russians, Poles, Czechs), and the Celts (a political alliance of many Germanic tribes).

The Slavs certainly had good reasons to attack the tribes around the Mediterranean. For centuries, the Slavs had been subject to raiding parties from the south (ancient Egypt and Assyria) who used the larger, stronger Slav captives as slaves to build their empires. The word 'slave', used by the later Greeks and Romans, is derived from 'Slav'.

The Bronze Age warrior horsemen not only infiltrated the Middle East, but also India c. 2200-1700 BC. They crossed the Bactrian plain of

Northern Afghanistan, scaled the Hindu Kush Mountains, and crossed the Khyber Pass into northern India; where they established themselves as the Brahman caste of light skinned dominators and perpetuated the terrible racism of the caste system for millennia.

The Superior Technology of the Chariot

The marauding Asian tribes who used it as an instrument of war and aggression introduced the chariot. It took enormous training and skill to wage warfare from a fast-moving chariot; but the invaders had mastered the skill very well. By 1150 BC the Eurasians from southern Russia had invaded India and by 1700 BC they were in Iran (Mesopotamia). They were called Aryans (because of their iron weapons) in Iran.

The Hittites were the invaders that conquered Anatolia (present-day Turkey), with their swift horses, chariots, and weapons of iron c. 1600 BC. The Hittites launched attack after attack on the Egyptian Empire, well known in the ancient world for its priceless knowledge and treasures. The Egyptians and Hittites used thousands of chariots against each other; and bankrupted their resources because of the enormous cost. Chariots and armies were very expensive in the ancient world, just as our military technology is very expensive in our modern world.

The Persians were also a group of Indo-European speaking tribes who settled in Elam; and became vassals under the Medes.

Semitic Invaders

From the other direction, by 3000 BC, the Semites (Hebrews, Phoenicians, Chaldeans, and Arameans) had come out of the deserts of Arabia and North Africa. They used asses and camels to migrate into Egypt and the Middle East and cause a threat to the relative stability there.

Invasions of the Sea People

By 1185 BC, the Sea Peoples were on the move. These were tribes who in migration came by galley ships to the Mediterranean Goddess civilizations. The galley ship became the new instrument of aggression. Northern tribes who attacked the coastal settlements with swords and pikes used sleek vessels with bird-headed prows and sterns. The Philistines were one group of 'Sea-peoples' who settled in Palestine and ended

Egyptian rule there. The name of 'Palestine' derives from 'Philistine'. This began an epic struggle with the Israelites and the Judeans.

By 1000 BC piracy was a major problem in trade routes that had been well-established routes for the exchange of goods and ideas for centuries. No one knows exactly why all these 'barbarian' tribes converged on the settled agrarian civilizations. It could be that, according to their nomad value system, people that stayed in one place were sitting ducks just waiting to be plundered. Nomads were on the move constantly; and thought that anyone who put down roots in any kind of permanent structure was a fool. Settled people had to pay taxes (even in ancient times) and could easily be targeted by their enemies. Nomads, on the other hands, were free, unfettered with possessions, unable to be caught by other human predators.

Of course, most of the nomadic tribes eventually became 'civilized' by the superior cultures they had captured and dominated.

When I use the term 'barbarian' I am using it in the sense that it was used in the ancient world. Everyone who could not speak Greek or Roman was called a 'barbarian'. It was a catchall generic word that referred to strangers, the unknown 'other'.

The barbarians brought their male deities, their Indo-European languages, their system of government based on power, might, and domination of women and people of darker color, competition, aggression, violence, and war. They planted the seeds of racism and sexism.

The enormous power struggle between the ancient 'Goddess the Mother' religions began and the new 'God the Father' religions would continue for several millennia. It would be more than a struggle over the sexual gender of the deity. It would be an epic struggle for reproductive rights: for the control of the female's sexuality and pregnancy and children and the potential for wealth that they represented in the form of labor.

For, while agriculture had been such a positive step forward by the Neolithic women, it was by this time (the Bronze Age) an enormous increase in the women's workload. It brought with it, as an unfortunate consequence, increased demands for child rearing, as more farm hands were needed.

The domestication of animals incurred many more daily chores: tending to the family's animals, milking them, and processing the milk into butter, cheese, and yogurt. The sheep were the source of the family's income. They had to be sheared, the yarn spun and then woven into textiles for clothing, blankets, coats, and rugs. The men would have done large-scale herding. Hostility among neighboring tribes increased about this time; and some historians have seen it as the origin of warfare.

This would have been the first time in human history that some tribes would have been able to accumulate anything that would have incited need or greed in another tribe. Textiles now took on increasing value; and would eventually become the basis of wealth of an entire nation as linen was in ancient Egypt.

Eventually, men improved upon the inventions of women. For instance, plowing the earth instead of hand-tilling the fields, making huge textiles in a factory instead of making woven fabrics on the women's smaller, home-based looms, and using domesticated horses and dogs to help control the huge herds of animals.

Women's status gradually began to decline. The rate of decline varied, however, throughout rural and urban societies in Europe, the Near East, Middle East, Asia, India, and Egypt. The rate of decline depended a great deal upon women's civil rights in each society. In some, the women were allowed to keep the 'milk money'. That is, the money they earned by milking the cows or goats that they tended. In other societies, women did the trading and bartering for the family's goods and services.

By creating networks of customers or clients outside the home, women could create the base of power or some wealth. Remember, in 2000 BC, 'wealth' was perceived as animals, textiles, food, jewelry, precious metals, etc. before coinage. If the woman were seen as owning the goods she herself produced, often objects and textiles of much beauty, ingenuity, creativity, and value, then she would have a higher status in her society.

If however, all of her work was done within the home to sustain only her family, her work would be mostly 'invisible' and thus devalued. This would have been quite exhausting, even if she had a small family, which would have been unlikely during the historic period, when fertility was highly prized as a source of cheap labor.

Women's status further declined with the accumulation by monarchs of metal wealth - gold, silver, bronze, copper, electrum, tin, and iron. With the proliferation of warfare to amass great quantities of metals to be used to wage more warfare, large scale farming, herding and textile manufacture assumed gigantic importance. Due to this, the position of women as chief provider of the family's, the clan's, the tribe's, the community's most vital resources gradually lessened.

From Goddesses of the Neolithic age who had discovered the secrets of crop growing - to second-class citizens with no civil rights - (by 500 BC in many world cultures) was a long, perilous, slippery slide. It involved the destruction of deeply rooted mythologies, religions, values, customs, as well as reproductive and civil rights. It is still in process. We call it 'Patriarchy'.

The Patriarchal Shift

The Bronze Age, about 3000 BC to 1500 BC, is so called because bronze, an alloy of copper and tin, was the primary metal used for making tools, weapons, pots, vessels, jewelry, coins, objects of art and religious statues. There was now another way to accumulate individual wealth and to display it. This had a significant effect on the lives of women.

In some societies women were used to display the wealth of males. Women wore ornaments and jewelry and the women themselves were used as a medium of exchange in dealings between men. This created a mixed message. The woman was the one who was trusted to safeguard all of the family's worth by wearing it on her person as is still done today in parts of Africa; while on the other hand, she was dismissed as inferior intellectually, religiously, and politically.

The Great Mother Goddess was still worshipped in the Bronze Age; but instead of priestesses serving her as healers, midwives, herbalists, and oracles, a mostly all-male priesthood developed. The gap between the sacred sphere and the sphere of daily life was widening. The first female religions had been holistic - seeing everything and everyone as infused with holiness. After all, the Great Mother was present in her creation: in the animals, the plants, the people, the mountains, the trees, the rivers, and the wells. The country of Wales was even named for Her sacred wells.

Her power would be wrested from Her as powerful male rulers established kingdoms in what had formerly been peaceful Neolithic farming communities and settlements. With the new, stronger bronze weapons and their heady new knowledge of paternity, the invaders from the north imposed their will through violence and destruction of societies.

It is during this period (2000 BC) that 'gender roles' almost exactly like those in our Western world today, became established. These were still prehistoric cultures, as we have no written records of these peoples' lives or attitudes. In Egypt, writing in the form of pictures (hieroglyphics) was already in use since 3000 BC. The Pyramid Texts (writing on the walls of the pyramids) was mostly concerned with religious concepts portraying the Pharaoh as a composite god with the other deities (both female and male) in the Egyptians divine pantheon. As we came to the end of the Bronze Age invasions, writing was developed in many parts of the world, and what do you suppose the scribes wrote? They glorified the violence, deified the male as conqueror of life and death, and devalued women in very disrespectful texts, c. 600 BC, in the Old Testament especially.

Because writing began (in the sense of a linear script) when violence, war, male ascendance, and devaluing women were being put into the permanent literary historic record, many people today believe we have always been violent. Many people believe that men have always waged war, that God ordained patriarchy, and that women are inherently inferior.

<u>This is definitely not the case!</u>

Misinformed people do not realize that for the first 300,000 years of human life on this planet, people lived in relatively peaceful cooperation, and that men and women had a great deal of equality, and that their GOD WAS A WOMAN.

Actually, a woman, Enheduanna, Priestess at the temple of Goddess Inanna in Summeria, about 2300 BC, is history's earliest known author. "My Queen you are all-devouring", she wrote in a hymn. By 'author', I mean, one who wrote what was in her own heart and mind; not just a record of temple accounts or propaganda of a Pharaoh.

> "Lady of all essences, full of light,
> Good Woman clothed in radiance,
> Whom heaven and earth love...

You are a flood descending from a mountain,
O Primary One,
Moon Goddess Inanna of heaven and earth"
   Poem by Priestess Enheduanna, c. 2300 BC

Goddess of the Earth and Fertility

Sperm Became God the Father

Because women value the quality of life experienced by their children, women throughout history have done what they could to keep populations in balance with the environments. Herbal teas, artificial blockages, such as a stone or a sponge were used in prehistory as contraceptives.

Abortion was always a last resort, after much agonized soul

searching, and always with great sadness and a sense of loss. Tribal women averaged four children in their lifetime; each child receiving maximum intense maternal devotion during the critical formative years. No method of birth control is foolproof, and some are very dangerous. But when conception and abortion are not practiced, the results are even more horrific: infanticide, malnutrition, infant starvation deaths, and abandonment of newborn babies on doorsteps.

In ancient times, newborns were abandoned on the hillsides at the edge of the town as a means of population control. Because male sperm was not yet clearly understood, getting rid of female infants was the solution to over-population.

Because water was worshipped as a deity in many ancient cultures, putting the newborn out to sea was a symbolic way of returning the infant back to the divine source of all life. Even today, many Roman Catholics believe the Mother of God manifests her presence by making her holy, healing waters flow, as at Lourdes. A river, canal, or stream was used to set the newborn adrift, as well.

No woman, allowed to make her own choices, would deliberately bear children with the tortuous discomfort and excruciating pain of childbirth, bond with her infant even before birth, then watch it starve to death because the clan's resources were too meager to feed everyone. Among people practicing abortion, even infanticide, the spirit of the dead child was returned to the earth-womb to await new birth, partaking still in the substance of the Great Mother. It was not lost; and the well being of the living group was maintained.

Patriarchy arose among cattle breeders who discovered the male role in conception. They believed that the entire life force was contained in the male semen and that the female was only the 'vessel' to receive the male seed, which was elevated into the 'Father God.' Thus, semen, because of its 'magical' ability to fertilize and to create new life, became deified as 'God the Father'; which eventually encompassed all that was male, to the exclusion of everything female.

The Caucasians bred horses on the Russian steppes and invaded Asia Minor (Turkey) and Mesopotamia (Iran and Iraq) starting 4000 BC or earlier. They were the first patriarchs; and they brought their violent male deities with them. These 'northern tradition' deities rewarded (mythologically and religiously) violence, warfare, plunder, rape, and the 'macho' (masochistic) death of warriors engaged in killing others in their endless battles. Their names have come down to us through literary sources as Wodin, Frey, Mars, Zeus, Indra, and Seth. From the other direction, the Semitic followers of the vengeful, violence-loving Yahweh were attacking settlements in the Middle East. Yahweh's followers documented their violence in the Old Testament of the Bible.

The Bronze Age Invaders

Patriarchy arose with the Bronze-Age Indo-European speaking Caucasian invaders who had discovered the secret contained in male sperm. The woman was no longer the magical Goddess who created life in her own womb, as she alone willed. The woman had value only as the proof of male potency - the one that birthed his offspring. The Near East was delighted to receive this new knowledge of how life was created; and Father God religions began to replace the ancient Mother Goddess religions wherever the Indo-European nomads put down roots: the Near East, the Middle East, Southern Europe, North Africa, Egypt, and India.

Today, the Roman Catholic Church maintains that humans receive life entirely from God the Father. The nearly ten months of biologic labor put into this child by its 'female life-giver', the mother, means nothing.

Pope Paul VI announced in 1972 that no woman has the right to abortion even if her life depends on it, even if she has other children who need her, even is she is a full grown conscious human being who might desire to live. This is Patriarchy carried to its extreme: contempt for women and almost total negation of the female role in the creation of a new life.

By giving a supernatural male deity entire credit for the development of the fetus, the mother's super-human self-sacrifice is cavalierly dismissed. The mother's contribution of calcium for the child's skeletal system drawn from her own bones and teeth, as well as the formation of all the child's vital organs at the expense of the mother's own vitality, cannot be overlooked.

Thus the fundamental creation cycle in all of nature was turned upside down: new life did not come through the female, but through the male, according to male scriptures. Patriarchal Middle Eastern animal herders who wrote the Old Testament used this 'men give birth' myth in the story of the creation of Eve from Adam's rib.

The use of subtle imagery, as well as the actual smashing of her statues in her ancient temples toppled the Mother Goddess.

The Pharaohs of ancient Egypt were particularly skilled at manipulating their diverse populations through the use of symbols (glyphs) that had meaning through the visual impact of the symbol/word/hieroglyph itself. For example, the sun god, RA, (who replaced the ancestral Egyptian Mother Goddess, Ma'at) was said to be able to see all that went on in each individual's life, just as the sun itself 'saw' all that it shone upon. Before Patriarchy in Egypt, the compassionate, protective Goddesses Isis and Ma'at had kept watch over their people with their eyes.

By repeating the 'eye' symbol pictorially over and over, with accompanying texts, for centuries, just the eye, all by itself, became a symbol powerful enough to frighten and control the population. The stylized, large eye, emphasized with black kohl eyeliner, is still, even today, one of the most identifiable symbols of Egypt all over the world. From the watchful eye of the Mother Goddess protecting her children, the patriarchal shift diabolized the Mother's eye and turned it into the 'eye of God', a sort of political heavenly spy of the Pharaoh, and the god, Seth. Eventually, Isis' beautiful cosmic eye became the 'Evil Eye', which could do harm to the one it looked upon.

Stone Age Divas

Sketch by: Pres Miranda

The 'Eye of Isis', also called the 'Wedjet Eye' and
The 'Eye of Horus' and the 'evil eye'

Egyptian texts from circa 1500 BC are full of magical protection charms on papyrus; and archeological digs have found thousands of amulets worn to protect against the 'evil eye'. This widespread fear created enough anxiety to support a wealthy priesthood. They performed magical spells to ward off the 'evil eye', which became a metaphor for unexpected misfortunes ranging from infant death to scorpion bites.

Women in ancient Egypt used these protective amulets in increasing numbers as the patriarchal shift in Egypt continued to threaten their societal and economic status. The women of Egypt, whose skill in turning the flax they grew into the highly-coveted (even today) textile fabric that we call 'linen', found their home looms being increasingly devalued in place of a large state run linen industry dominated by men.

For centuries, much of Egypt's wealth had come from its female-based linen trade. But this 'cottage industry' of Egyptian women and their children was being phased out, in favor of mass production to meet worldwide demand for this most extraordinary fabric, which came only from Egypt. It is hard for us to appreciate the importance of a piece of cloth in the ancient world. It was almost worth its weight in gold. Fabrics had to be woven on looms; a difficult, complex, time-consuming skill that women had developed. Most societies had no clothing at all. A scrap of hide was all that protected the average person from the elements, before cotton and before silk or wool.

Women in pharaoh-Egypt began to feel especially stressed, perhaps because of the patriarchal shift in societal attitudes, which began to devalue everything female. This conclusion was reached by some historians and archaeologists who noted the increase in the number of women's protective amulets and prayers found in the archeological record of this era, circa 1500 BC. Dr. Geraldine Pinch in *'Magic in Ancient Egypt'*, UK, British Museum Press, 1994, wrote about the quality of life of the women and children in ancient Egypt.

The previous paragraphs gave examples of how symbols were used to manipulate the behavior of populations in pre-literate societies. The huge statue of the Goddess Isis and later, the God RA, was simplified to just one eye in a hieroglyph. The all-seeing 'Eye of God' became the 'evil eye' of Egypt, Greece, Italy, and Africa. The power of the symbol cannot be understated in societies where no one, except a few scribes and learned priestesses or priests could read or write.

Another way that was used to subtly dethrone the powerful Mother Goddesses was to give them a mate. The ancestral Egyptian Mother Goddess Ma'at was first given a consort or co-ruler, in order to lessen her authority mytho-religiously. She was also known as Au'Set, which became 'Isis' in the language of the Greeks who conquered Egypt under Alexander the Great; and ruled Egypt under the Ptolemies and Cleopatra (Egypt's last Pharaoh before the Roman invasion). The Egyptian Mother Goddess was first given a male consort, Ra, which diminished her position slightly, as she now had to share her divine powers. However, she was still the Supreme Deity, 3000 BC.

Goddess Isis or Au'Set

Bronze Age Patriarchs

By mid second millennia BC, Isis (Greek) or Au'Set (Egyptian), a very powerful ancient Egyptian Goddess was given a son with whom she shared power.

Isis and Horus were the first Divine Mother and Child, millennia before Mary and Jesus of Christian symbolism.

The Goddesses of Egypt were gradually deprived of their protective, leadership functions in the societal religio-mythic system; and the male gods assumed total power. This happened in Greece, Rome, and all through the Near East, Middle East, Mediterranean and southern Europe. The one exception to this pattern was Isis, who was universally loved and worshipped until well into the Roman era, c. AD 300 even with diminished status. Eventually, Mary took over Isis' position in the hearts of those who embraced Christianity, a Middle Eastern Savior religion which spread throughout the Roman Empire, including the Near East, Greece, Europe and Britain by Roman soldiers, their wives, their slaves, and their captives.

Even though the Paleolithic, Neolithic and Bronze Age Goddesses were often depicted with exaggerated breasts, buttocks, bellies, and thighs, there was nothing pornographic about them. This would come much later in the patriarchal era when women were increasingly debased in patriarchal myths, religions, and customs. Even though some Goddesses were usually depicted unclothed, these Goddesses had a regal poise. There was precious little clothing available in the Paleolithic,

Neolithic, and Bronze Age and even into the Classical period of 500 BC. Goddesses had a naked courage and sense of power that inspired respect. They were proud of their bodies, from which all new life entered the world.

One of the oldest human images in existence is a female figurine called 'Venus of Willendorf'. Her lack of facial features may represent an ego-less, trance like, meditative state. She is only a few inches tall, but overpowering in her abundant presence.

Though Paleolithic images of copulation between women and men occur, icons and myths of the Great Mother do not show her actually mated with a human lover/mate/husband until after 5500 BC. At this time in the Near East, there seemed to have been a phallic obsession, as this time frame coincided with the discovery of animal husbandry, and the male penis took on a new, more cosmic significance.

Representations of the penis, in the form of standing, phallic-shaped stones called 'menhirs', were revered in Britain and parts of Europe. Unusually shaped stones were considered sacred in every part of the ancient world. 'Menhirs' represented places the Goddess could take up residence in the deserts of Mesopotamia in antiquity. They are still there, between Egypt and Israel, and they represent the ancient Hebrew Goddess, Asherah/Astarte/Esther. As maleness became more highly valued, statuettes were carved with exaggerated erections. In Benares, India, today there are temples filled with hundreds of large phalluses (penises), the symbol of the male warrior god Indra. These were brought there thousands of years ago by the Indo-European invaders. Indra's phallus symbols are objects of worship by devout Hindus who flock to his temple on the banks of the Ganges River.

Venus of Willendorf, Austria c. 25,000 BC

There were many Goddess-Phallus stones with the figure of the Goddess carved on phallic-shaped bones or rocks. This tells us that prehistoric peoples struggled with ideas about sexuality and reproduction. They were trying to image human genitalia in rock carvings to try to make some sense of them. These poignant, powerful images found in Mesopotamia (Iraq) suggest the potential unity of the sexes, in mutual love and service before their disastrous splitting apart by patriarchal misogynists and repressive sexual codes of behavior for women, according to Sjöö and Mor in *The Great Cosmic Mother*.

By 500 BC, in Athens, Greece, women were virtually prisoners in their homes, allowed in the street only for religious festivals. Roman women were expected to have as many children as possible, probably because of high infant death rates. By the time of the Roman Empire c. 300 BC, the father of the family, 'Paterfamilias', had supreme power of life and death over his wife, his children, and his slaves.

Patriarchy had reached its pinnacle. Or had it?

The Serpent: Female Connotations

Patriarchal texts started appearing in Egypt about 1700 BC, in which the serpent symbol came to be associated with evil and sexuality. The serpent had long been a symbol of transformation, rejuvenation, and immortality in the ancient world of the Goddess.

Female oracles in temples of Crete and Greece often prophesied holding snakes; as serpents also stood for wisdom and sometimes an altered consciousness induced by certain venom. As late as the Gnostic Gospels (c. AD 100), the serpent symbolized the principle of Divine Wisdom. The Caduceus, symbol of doctors, which shows entwined serpents, points to the female roots of medicine; and clearly demonstrates how highly the snake was respected in the integrated world of the Goddess.

Photo by: Patrice Wynne

Minoan Snake Goddess, from Knossos, Crete c. 1600 BC, height 13 1/2 inches (34.3 cm) (Archeological Museum, Herakleion)

The serpent was demonized by the patriarchal Hebrew scribes in the Garden of Eden myth. This cleverly disguised myth probably has done more harm to more women's lives than anything previously recorded. In this allegory, the ancient symbol of the Goddess' religion, the serpent that sheds its skin but does not die was turned into a symbol of evil; and all women and their knowledge would be demonized from then on.

Instead of celebrating Eve for her desire to attain knowledge (of life and death); or the secret of reproduction, she was forever labeled as the evil woman who is responsible for bringing sin into the world, along with suffering, pain, and death.

Could there be a worse 'rap' for women to bear for the next 2000 years? I hardly think so.

Imagine if young girls in the Western world were raised with a different myth: a myth about the power and the beauty of the female body, and female intelligence, and female ability, and the female's gifts to civilization!

AS A WOMAN YOU ARE THAT GIFT!

Eve's Song of Temptation – The Serpent

The diabolization of the serpent by biblical scribes was a metaphor for the diabolization of everything female - her body as well as her ancient female centered religion - which was effectively accomplished by a very political as well as a very fascinating and poetic book, we call the Bible.

Eve listened to the serpent and picked the forbidden apple, which gave her the seeds, knowledge, and understanding of human reproduction and sexuality. This knowledge made women 'god-like' for millennia.

Patriarchal Shift in Values

The Bronze Age saw the elimination of cooperative farming communities by the powerful Caucasians with their weaponry. Kings, priests, warriors and accompanying specialists associated with a warrior society such as charioteers, scribes and priests, seized the agriculture-based wealth of the Goddess cultures.

The invaders also stole their spiritual wealth: their holistic life views as shown in their arts, their symbols, and their textiles.

The Neolithic peoples, as well as the Paleolithic for millennia before them, saw their world as interwoven with holiness and meaning. Goddess as nurturing mother, reverence for the earth, animals, mountains, springs, rivers, lakes, male and female working together to sustain the clan, the tribe, the community, a respect for life in all its myriad forms and its many cycles and seasons. These values shaped the consciousness of prehistoric peoples.

The pomegranate is another fruit used in the Middle East to symbolize the seeds of knowledge of reproduction. Women were thought to be impregnated by ingesting seeds, just as the earth grew new life from seeding. Women most probably discovered horticulture c. 8000 BC.

Bronze Age Warrior Societies

In the Bronze Age Warrior societies, a new hierarchical class system emerged. The King, Pharaoh, Priest, or Chief was at the top. Sometimes they were interchangeable: the Priest/Kings or God/Kings of ancient Pharaohs of Egypt often combined religion and politics as Henry VIII would do much later in Britain, when he named himself head of the Church of England.

Guarded in their palaces by a new specialized class of trained warriors, charioteers and horsemen, they began to systematically rape and plunder the ancient cultures that had previously existed for millennia without warfare. They 'raped' the female brain as well; taking the ancient discoveries of women, animal husbandry, weaving of textiles, twisting strings of hemp into rope, grinding of seeds and grain into breads (that would later be used to feed armies for extended periods), making pottery vessels to hold water, oil, wine, inventing mathematical signs (as they tracked their monthly menstrual cycles) – all of these would be co-opted by the Bronze Age patriarchies who would later take credit for them.

I am well aware that many scholars do not agree that a matriarchal social structure ever existed in the far distant past because they have not seen any recent societies where women hold most of the positions of power.

Was Matriarchy ever a social system in which women were held in great respect? The answer lies in the far undocumented mists of time. While the brutal despoilers burned the evidence of matriarchies, they could not destroy the languages in which much female history still survives – in the roots of the words themselves, and in the women's oral histories, myths, songs and Goddesses, and tales from their hearts, which were passed on through the generations. Writing eventually corroborated the violent conquests of the Bronze Age warriors and omitted female contributions to civilizations.

It is quite possible that a more equitable distribution of power existed in prehistory, although men may have held the leadership roles and political power. We do know, however, that matriarchal societies exist in the mammal world: elephants, gorillas, lions, foxes, bears, and horses among others. After all, women were constantly preoccupied with child care and producing the next generation, and men would have been already freed from the pressures of the hunt after agriculture was well established, c. 8000 BC by the women.

The political organization of the Neolithic era with men in leadership roles, but without the need to oppress women, I will call a Matrifocal social system, one in which the women were highly valued or at least valued equally.

Neolithic Burials

There has been some archeological evidence to support the idea that Neolithic communities were peaceful agrarian settlements. There were no heavily fortified towns, no walled settlements, few weapons, no mass graves, and no 'chieftain burials'. Most archeological evidence of this era, c. 9000-2000 BC, comes from gravesites. The method of burial tells researchers a great deal about the person who died; and what type of society the deceased inhabited.

A 'chieftain burial' is one in which a wealthy ruler is entombed with heaps of grave goods (usually of the finest metals and workmanship); and also, those he would have chosen to die with him, either willingly or unwillingly. These burials were not found for this period, the Neolithic. From the many burials found dating from this period, equal numbers of women and men had grave goods, such as jewelry, utensils, Goddess figurines, personal grooming items, or anything used by the deceased which would have been deemed too personal for anyone else to use.

This indicated equality of the sexes. In this period also, deceased men appear to have had their bodies painted with red ochre, which was often a symbol of menstrual blood and the magical propensities it was believed to have in the creation of new life.

Sometimes this (painting the body with red ochre) is interpreted as a plea to the Mother Goddess to grow a new body over their own dead bones, the skeletal frame of the deceased. Animals were commonly believed to be able to do this. This may be one of the reasons animals were held in great awe and reverence, and even deified as evidenced especially in the tomb paintings of Egypt.

Even in our own country, certain Native American tribes believed that when they threw the bones of the salmon they had eaten back into the river, it flowed downstream and grew a new body. Catholics are promised that their bodies will rise from their graves and be taken into heaven at the Last Judgment Day, presumably after a new body has reformed on the skeleton. It is not so far fetched then, to think that the Neolithic people also had a similar idea of reincarnation. After all, if woman could create a body once (during pregnancy), could she not also create a new body when the original one was used up?

Men of the Neolithic era were also buried with antlers (always conveying enormous spiritual significance of the animal kingdom); and men and women were both buried with stone artifacts such as flint blades, figurines or just unusually shaped rocks. In the world of the Goddess, everything had meaning and significance. Rocks were no exception.

A total lack of material wealth and meager possessions would have precluded a motive for warfare in Matrifocal societies. The debate continues in anthropology today: whether or not there ever were any matriarchies in the distant past. The answers lay deep in prehistory and future archeological finds; though many feminist scholars believe that there <u>was</u> such a time of cooperation between the sexes. It was before the domination of one gender over the other; a time when women were actually valued for the vital role they played in the life of the community.

Under the patriarchy of the four major religions, Judaism, Christianity, Islam, and Hinduism, the compulsion to label women negatively in order to control them has become firmly entrenched. This has been completed through brain washing, mind control, sexist language, sexist religious myths and imagery that pervades the entire culture and spews out of the media every minute of every day creating a toxic psychological environment for every female and male within such a woman-bashing culture.

"Patriarchy includes a literal belief that all of life is created for men to use. And what they find usable, they usually show contempt for." Such as, the women whose bodies bring forth their offspring; and who are then criticized when they lose their wasp waists, their tautness and 'helpless little girl' look that is so highly prized in our culture today. The gaunt, anorexic models of female beauty do not reflect the ample proportions of the great Goddesses of the past. But, there is hope. A new line of 'Goddess clothing' was recently unveiled for women's naturally rounded contours.

European Witch Hunts

The patriarchal shift that occurred in Europe during the Dark Ages and Medieval Ages created "a chronicle of horrors almost without parallel" in human history.

It is estimated that 4 million women, and often their children and husbands, were drowned, burned alive, and tortured in the 'Witch-Hunts' of Europe from 1200 AD to 1500 AD. The saddest part is that the conversion of Europe to Christianity played a major role in the hysterical rage against women, which spread like wildfire through towns and villages.

It was an attempt by the male clergy to stamp out the last vestigial traces of the ancient (since 300,000 BC and maybe earlier) mother religion, which empowered women to be wise and skilled in the healing arts.

Old women, widows, the handicapped and gifted, educated, and the hardiest women often earned a living by acting as midwives to ease the pain of childbirth, with their generations-old knowledge of herbal remedies. The Church took exception to this, branded the old, wise healers 'witches' (derived from Wiccans, 'wise ones') and decreed in 'Malleus Malefactorum' that the women were heretics, followers of Satan; and should be tortured until they admitted to it.

"Priests and nobility were the only people allowed an education. The great masses of people, denied access to their ancient Neolithic knowledge, and were kept in profound ignorance. The intellectual and cultural squalor of Europeans under the Christian Church was truly appalling. Periodic injections of Arabic brilliance saved it", according to Monica Sjöö and Barbara Mor, feminist researchers who wrote "*The Great Cosmic Mother*".

Origin of Caduceus, the Symbol of Medical Profession

We can see the origins of the caduceus symbol from this relief of Goddess Demeter holding vegetation and serpents. The entwined serpents around the staff testify to the female roots of medicine in the ancient agricultural Goddess civilizations.

Demeter Holding Sheaves of Grain
Goddess Demeter, bas-relief terra cotta, c. 2000 BC, Roman.

Medicine Women: Wiccans

Since the beginning of time women had been the healers, the nurturers, nurses, curers, curanderas, medicine women, herbalists, naturopaths, shamankas, and practitioners of all the healing arts.

Female origins of medicine are acknowledged in the symbol of the medical profession, the Caduceus: a healing wand entwined with serpents, the primeval symbols of the immortal Goddess. Pre-historic women had become physicians as naturally as they became mothers - by caring for their own infants and children and other clan members of the extended family.

In their daily foraging for plant food, prehistoric women familiarized themselves with everything in their environments; and learned, through trial and error, the properties of every seed and grain, twig, bark, leaf and fruit, root and nut; and whether they nourished or poisoned. The female brain was the first pharmacopoeia.

Women changed the chemical composition of organic materials they found in nature - by heating or crushing or mixing and blending. The first prescriptions were women's recipes, the Latin "Rx", means, "recipe". Women's gardens were the first pharmacies; their kitchens, the first laboratories; their recipes, the first prescriptions.

Before writing, women passed on their knowledge orally. Women historically administered their healing potions or (medicines) without regard to whether the sufferer could pay. They did it as a community service. If the sick person could 'barter' something in payment such as a chicken, a piece of woven cloth, or some flints, so much the better.

Medicine, as a profitable specialization, did not come till much later, when the Church proclaimed that only their university-trained men would practice medicine. The wise women, who had eked out a meager existence for millennia, by their hard won knowledge of the healing properties of plants, were forbidden to heal or to offer their services to those in need, especially women in childbirth.

The battle for reproductive rights began about AD 1200 when the Church declared war on the Wiccans - the witches who possessed the 'forbidden' - the knowledge of family planning, contraception, abortion, midwifery, the alleviation of labor pain, and all the monthly distress women were prone to during menstruation. Throughout the European countryside, the wise women were called in at childbirth. They were highly skilled: it is on record that some could perform caesarean sections with complete success for mother and child.

But during the late Middle Ages, which were dominated by the Inquisition, child delivery was no longer considered a suitable occupation for women. The women who attended the poor at childbirth became social outcasts or worse. They were charged with witchcraft; tortured, and burned alive at the stake. One 'witch' was burned alive in Scotland for the sole crime of bathing some neighborhood children, for hygienic reasons, during an epidemic.

Health care and healing were publicly discouraged by the Church, which officially believed that life was supposed to be diseased, wretched, and painful.

This was God the Father's punishment for being born...in Original Sin, from a woman's vagina.

CHAPTER IV:
Writing - Women's Gift to Civilization

She-Who-Speaks-With-Reeds

The relatively new technology of writing, c. 3000 BC would prove to be invaluable in spreading the doctrines of the dominators' religion of God the Father. Their 'holy' scriptures would ultimately disrespect, slander, and demonize everything female, by using the very technology that the women themselves had invented: Writing.

The first alphabet is generally believed to have begun with the ancient Phoenicians, c. 950 BC. (1) They were accomplished seafarers and traders who needed a method of keeping track of the goods they transported from country to country in the prehistoric world. The act of recording information by using incised symbols is actually much older.

With the invention of clay blocks, c. 4000 BC, the recording, and storing of information at the temple complexes of Egypt and Sumer became possible. Making marks with a sharp instrument in the wet surface of the mud brick tablets was the system of accounting used to keep records of temple donations, dues, taxes, gifts, offerings of livestock for sacrifices, and other obligations. This 'temple economy' of ancient Egypt, Sumer, and Crete (frequently at the temple of an ancestral Mother Goddess) was the lifeblood of the cities of the ancient world. The temple complex often included food storage areas, workshops, hospitals, birthing centers, priestesses' and priests' living quarters, an underground room for an oracle/advisor (almost always a woman), a scribes' room, library, money-changing and money-lending area, marketplace, ceremonial altars, statues, and a lake.

Archaeologists, within the last one hundred fifty years, have unearthed written records of the Sumerians, a non-Semitic people who infiltrated or invaded Mesopotamia (the area between the Tigris and Euphrates Rivers, present-day Iraq) c. 3500 BC. (2) The Sumerians developed a very advanced culture and founded a number of city-states that came to be known collectively as Sumer.

It is believed that the ancient Egyptians derived some of their prodigious knowledge from the even earlier Sumerians who were 'lost' completely for two thousand years. Only the discovery of an Assyrian inscription in 1850 hinted at the existence of this ancient Sumerian civilization, which was then proven by archaeology.

Although Paleolithic women had been 'writing' on their clay pots, spindle whorls, and clay, bone, stone, and ivory Goddess figurines for 20,000 years, there arose for the first time in human history an alphabet that an advanced civilization could use to record its activity and thought.

Uruk was one of their major cities; only the ruined stump of a ziggurat remains. A ziggurat is an artificial (built by humans) mountain sanctuary for a Goddess or God. Ziggurats were triangular, with a flat top: the precursors of the Egyptian pyramids. Small clay tablets inscribed with crude pictographic signs dating from 3100 BC were found along with the ruins of the ziggurats.

That is how writing began: using simple pictures (symbols) to represent objects that were later associated with whole ideas. Later, the pictures were simplified into cuneiform, one of the earliest alphabets, in which symbols could more rapidly be impressed in wet clay with a wedge-shaped stylus (pen).

'Cuneiform' derives from Sumerian 'kunte', meaning female genitalia. It survives in the patriarchal slur, 'cunt', the pornographic term for 'woman'. Cuneiform consists of arrangements of pubic triangles or "V",s which is the ancient Paleolithic symbol for woman.

Tablets such as these, from many ancient societies, survived for the precise reason that the invading hordes set <u>fire</u> to the temple complexes where the scribes stored their 'libraries' of clay tablets. The terrible heat of the fires, instead of consuming the clay tablets, hardened and preserved them for future generations, just as firing in a kiln hardens and gives a permanent finish to ceramics. This is one of the great ironies of history. The violence meant to destroy the evidence; in fact, preserved it.

The oldest literature of Sumer, dated c. 3100 BC (using carbon dating technology), had been used exclusively for administrative records. But by 2500 BC, it had developed into a more sophisticated literary style, capable of expressing a complex mythology and historic ideas.

From these later tablets (2500 BC) we learned about the Goddesses and Gods of ancient Sumer.

Sumerians had a highly developed theology and were profoundly devout. Innumerable figurines have been excavated showing people in poses of reverence, hands clasped, eyes wide with awe, deposited as votives (offerings), and dutifully recorded by the temple scribes.

Menstruation: Marking Their Moon-Time

However, an earlier script of pictographic 'writing' was used by women 6000 BC and earlier in Old Europe. (3) Because prehistoric women lived together, they 'cycled' together, that is, their hormonal systems would have been entrained. Entrainment means that each woman in the cave would have begun and ended her menstrual cycle on the same days of the month as the other clan women.

Tracking their 'moon-time' (as the menstrual cycle is known in indigenous societies where the moon's cycles are more easily witnessed) would have been precisely the stimulus needed for the invention of counting, the precursor of mathematics. Keeping a record of their 'moon-days' by means of pictures or count marks would have been a powerful stimulus for creating picture-symbols, which are the precursors of writing.

Watching the moon as it went through its monthly cycles just as they themselves did, the prehistoric women began marking the passage of time calendrically; thus creating the first lunar calendars which were used by agriculturists for millennia, even up to the present. We call this lunar calendar the Farmer's Almanac.

The prehistoric women's calendars were bones or pieces of ivory or antler marked with symbols that would help them remember. The women needed a record of the cycles of their bodies; as they needed to know where they (the tribe or clan) would be when the baby was born. They were not settled societies; they were nomadic, meaning that they followed the seasonal food supply of fish, vegetation, and small birds and animals, as foragers do.

It is impossible to overestimate the importance of menstruation in the development of writing, counting, accounting, and time keeping: marking the passages of time by the moons (months).

Although prehistoric women did not yet know that the cessation of menses meant that sperm had fertilized an ovum, they did know that the withholding of the menstrual blood meant that a child was growing inside their own bodies. Some ancient people believed the menstrual blood itself created the baby; which would be a logical conclusion since menstrual blood did not flow during pregnancy.

Keeping track of monthly menstrual periods was therefore incredibly important to our Paleolithic ancestresses, just as it is to women today.

The birth of a baby is always a life-altering event, especially for the mother. Menstruation would have been just the stimulus needed to invent a way to mark one's 'moon-times' and to record this information for retrieval at a later time. Men would not have been motivated to take an interest in women's mysterious body cycles, because they were not involved in the process (or so they thought).

Before the discovery of clay (earth) as a useful medium on which to record information, Paleolithic women in Europe carved their picture symbols and count marks on pieces of bone and ivory from the tusks of woolly mammoth elephants. These first 'calendar sticks' were probably early women's records of their menses, as they perceived their periods connected to, or influenced by, the waning of the moon.

Stone Age women lived mostly out of doors, in caves, and in rock shelters. In this way, by making calendar sticks, women sought and learned to understand the abstract concept of the passage of time. "By carving tiny moon shapes onto bone, by placing counting sticks in a basket, by tying knots in string, by stringing beads in a particular manner, by making dots in half moons and circles", (4) women created counting and accounting.

The shell bead, a symbol of a women's genitals (the cowry shell), was valued so highly that they were used as money in trade as well as for aesthetics, statues, jewelry, and counting. Beads are still used for counting and remembering in the abacus and the rosary.

Bones, ivory, antlers, and stones, as well as the walls of their limestone caves were the first surfaces utilized for writing. People of the Paleolithic era (30,000 BC and earlier) left us their magnificent, graceful cave art, rock paintings, and bas-reliefs of their Mother Goddess. They also left representations of animals, male and female hunters and dancers, women giving birth, dancing, hunting, planting, gathering honey, wearing animal masks in shamanic rituals, breast feeding, and playing with their children.

Pictures were the earliest forms of writing. They were a means of recording and a passing on of information.

Stone Age Divas

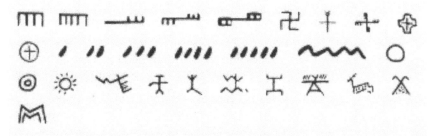

Symbols dating from the oldest period of Vinča culture
(6th-5th millennia BC)

As the pictures became miniaturized to fit on very small objects used by women in their daily lives, they became pictograms or picture writing. Pictograms were found on thousands of painted clay pots found in Europe, the Near East, Middle East, and Egypt.

Another form of early writing was carving. Our ancestors used a sharpened flake of flint stone to carve* their 'moon days' on various hard surfaces found in the immediate environment. Later, these markings (carvings) would come to have a shared meaning for members of their clan (extended family of kin). The word 'to write' in the ancient Roman language of east central Europe is 'chin', which means 'to carve'. *

Women would later carve their symbols on everything used in their daily round of activities: bowls, drinking vessels, spindle whorls, jugs for water, oil, wine, figurines fashioned in their own likeness, and their beloved full bodied Mother Goddess as well as in the Goddess' many animal shapes. These latter figurines and vessels are called 'anthropomorphic' or animals that are given human features. They were very common in the ancient world, just as they are today. Think of Mickey Mouse and other Disney characters.

Dr. Marija Gimbutas collected hundreds of these remarkable female animal figurines with writing incised on their surfaces. They demonstrate the language of the Goddess speaking to her earth children and her earth children's responses to her.

Dr. Marija Gimbutas led major archeological expeditions throughout 'Old Europe' (as she called the former Czechoslovakia, the Baltic area,

---

* In old English and Germanic languages, writ and writen, as well as reissen, may be the prehistoric roots of writing. These words connote scatching, incising, and cutting into a hard surface with a sharpened tool (before papers and pens were discovered).

Southern Poland, Western Ukraine, Macedonia, former Yugoslavia, Italy, Romania, Moldavia, Bulgaria, Hungary, Greece, and Transylvania).

Egg shaped stones were found carved into Fish Goddesses with a woman's head, Bird Goddesses with the beaked head of a bird, the body of a woman with perforations in her arms that probably held feathers, suggesting wings (Paleolithic 'Angels'?), the Bear Goddess holding her infant reminiscent of the much later 'Madonna and Child' religious images, snake-headed Goddesses with their young, pregnant Goddesses, pig-Goddesses, their bodies impressed with seeds of grain.

These are some of the creative ways in which the Paleolithic and Neolithic peoples (c. 8000 BC) imaged their deity, their Primal Ancestral Mother, and it confounds the imagination. They are not 'Barbie doll' pretty. They are powerful conveyors of meaning, incised on their little bodies with profound 'writings' that told the wonderful story of the Earth Mother who gave birth to all forms of life, sustained it, and at the end of life, received it back into her ample bosom.

The European Great Mother Goddess was a symbol of embryonic life (often imaged as a frog or tadpole or egg), regeneration (the snake or the egg or the butterfly), the supreme creatress who created new life from her own substance, (before male sperm were understood as a creative force). Life and death were intertwined.

As Mother Terrible, she was placed in graves to help facilitate the release of the energies of the dead - their spirits or souls or energy essences. The Sumerians called her 'Ninhursag', she who gave 'life to the dead'. Life and death were seen as a continuum by most ancient societies who lived closer to nature than we do today.

Neolithic Imagery

The life-death-life cycle was of great concern to the Paleolithic as well as the Neolithic agricultural societies. At first, the corpulent (pregnant) early Paleolithic Goddesses were associated with wild animals. By 8000 BC, the Neolithic imagery depicted her with domesticated animals, indicating that women had already learned how to tame the feral animals by bonding to them and nurturing the animal babies orphaned by predators in their environment. Animals became more and more associated with the Goddess as her 'familiars'. Thousands of years later, in this same area of Old Europe (Germany), women healers (Wiccans) would be murdered for befriending cats, their animal 'familiars', which made them heretics and heathens in the eyes of the Inquisitors.

Tartaria Tablets

Tablets found in Tartaria in the central Balkan Peninsula attest to an advanced civilization of the Neolithic Goddess culture in which a linear symbol script was used. This is the first known attempt in the prehistoric world of linear writing, c. 5500 BC. (5) This 'symbol writing' or picture writings were found on artifacts most probably made and used by women. This pictographic, prototypical writing thus predated the Phoenician alphabet by 4,550 years, the earliest Sumerian cuneiform writing by 2,000 years, and Egyptian hieroglyphics by 2,500 years.

Ceramics had already been fired in primitive kilns, c. 20,000 BC by the upper Paleolithic people of central and Eastern Europe; and on these clay ceramics, 15,000 years later, the early pictographs or symbol writing began. The first art objects believed to have been sculpted of clay and baked in kilns were small Mother Goddesses, with their legs close together forming a peg to be placed in the earth at the entrance to cave shelters. These are believed by many archaeologists to have served as protective deities. Other settings in which they have been unearthed include near the oven (hearth), beside grindstones where women ground grain to use as food, in burials, and as votive offerings in domestic shrines (naturally formed niches in the cave walls).

Almost all of these small 'Venuses' were inscribed with graphic designs symbolizing abstract spiritual ideas important to an agricultural society. This picture writing or pictographs were also found in polished black pottery found in a valley in central Bulgaria. (6) This black painted early European pottery was very distinctive and advanced for its time, c. 5400 BC, as compared to pottery found in Jericho in the Middle East dating from the same Neolithic period. This European pottery was so remarkable for its artistry 7,000 years ago that Professor M. Vlasic who first excavated Vinča (as the site in Bulgaria was known to archeologists) believed it had to be of Aegean origin. He believed that the Greeks had probably founded a colony in the Balkans. However, the mythical imagery incised on the elegant black and highly polished vessels and figurines reflects European, not Grecian origins.

The anthropomorphic figurines with distended belly of pregnancy, another with exaggerated buttocks, were typical of this time period,

(Neolithic) 4800 BC Vinča culture. Some scholars say the large buttocks are caused by a predominantly grain diet.

Some of the earliest continuously occupied sites are located on this 'prehistoric highway' including Sarajevo, Bosnia, and Macedonia. Dr. Marija Gimbutas excavated in Bosnia in 1967 and found the Butmir civilization, which flourished from 5000 BC to 4000 BC. The inhabitants occupied caves or open settlements surrounded by an irrigation ditch. Their economy was based on domesticated sheep and cattle, fishing, hunting, and cultivation of wheat and barley.

Contrary to former opinions of researchers, Dr. Marija Gimbutas did not find a 'cultural backwater'; but instead, a remarkable and distinctive culture with writing, art, clothing, jewelry, masks, and a sophisticated mythology passed on pictorially through symbols.

The Tartarian pendants with a Neolithic script found in 1963 in the Mures River valley of western Romania also attest to an advanced 'for its time' civilization.

The Vinča used a written script of symbols two thousand years before Sumerian civilization, and about three thousand years before the Linear A alphabet of the island of Crete, where a very advanced civilization existed in the Aegean area. These 'language fossils' of the Vinča culture of former Yugoslavia can lead us to the female origins of writing in the far distant past.

Neolithic symbols commonly incised on objects made and used by women in the female centered culture were the beginning of the alphabet.

Sketch by Pres Miranda

The development of the alphabet: the diagram shows how aleph, an ox, beth, a house, and nun or nahas, a snake, evolved into the letters A, B, and N of our alphabet. Neolithic era, c. 6000 BC

The first attempt at writing was actually a drawing of a picture, variously termed a symbol, glyph, pictogram, ideogram, or hieroglyph. These linear pictographs were painted on vessels, statuettes, and pendants like the Tartaria tablets.

These clay tablets from the Vinča culture of former Yugoslavia are probably the earliest form of human writing and have been carbon dated to 5500 BC. Other picture writings were carved onto a hard surface with a flake of sharpened flint stone. Can you imagine how laborious and tedious this process must have been? The Egyptians had not yet invented paper from the pulp of the papyrus plant. Eventually, the complex pictures were simplified into lines that just gave the suggestion of the former picture, and a new specialty arose in the ancient world, that of the 'professional scribe'.

Runes

In Northern Europe, women were traditionally the keepers of the runes, which were credited to the Mother Goddess, Idun, (who would later become masculinized as 'Odin'). Celts and Teutons used several variations of the runic alphabet.

As was usual in prehistoric cultures, a new technology, such as writing, was treated with a great deal of awe and fear. Runic letters were believed to have come to the female diviners from a deity; and the runes (symbols cut into pieces of wood or stones) were at first used in the practice of religion for divination, and after healing, trying to determine what the deities had in mind. This was called 'casting the runes'.

In 'The Woman's Dictionary of Symbols and Sacred Objects' Barbara Walker writes that this "was a special practice of female diviners and therefore inevitably became associated with witchcraft in the minds of medieval male authorities."

"Soon, all runic alphabets were forbidden, and women who were formerly the custodians of literacy were deprived of the very letters with which they had once written. However, the runes continued to be used secretly for casting spells and for divination." (7)

Druids

To become a Druid took twenty years of memorization and training. In Celtic society, these women, and men were magicians, poets, musicians, astronomers, teachers, and judges. They were greatly respected in Europe and feared and respected by the Romans who tried to conquer the Celts in the British Isles. Most of the Druids were ambushed and massacred by Roman soldiers during one of the sacred Celtic festivals where they had gathered on the Isle of Anglesea. To this day, their knowledge and practices remain largely unknown to us, because of the secrecy with which their oral traditions were passed on. Their runes can offer us but a tiny peek into the world of the Druids.

Readers and Writers

The one who inscribed, the 'scribe', would have had to be of exceptional intelligence to memorize many symbols and remember their meanings. In 3500 BC the entire society was illiterate, (or pre-literate), except priestesses or priests who were originally the only learned members. Others like the Druids had found a way to pass on their knowledge to their successors verbally.

The Druids (priestesses and priests) of the Celts communicated with each other in a secret sign language, probably the precursor of the Runic alphabet of the northern tradition. Runes are sometimes called the 'twig alphabet' because all of the letters can be made with pieces of twigs. They were angular. There were no rounded letters in the original Runic alphabet of northern Europe and Scandinavia.

Writing, The Chronicles of Barbarism

During the Bronze Age, c. 4000 BC, when the restless nomads from the north were de-stabilizing the more settled, Agrarian societies of the Balkans, Near East, the Middle East, and India, the written word proved invaluable in glorifying their massacres for all time. Some of these earliest written accounts of devastation became the 'Holy Scriptures' of certain countries, (8) as improbable as this might seem.

In these ancient mythologies, the conquerors of the indigenous peoples appear to be superhuman, godlike heroes, while the unfortunate, less aggressive original occupants of the territories are painted as less-than human, sinful, and unfit to live. 'Abomination' is a word I frequently encountered in my study of ancient literature. The murderous conquerors always wrote that the indigenous populations they were eliminating were 'abominable' or their customs were 'abominations'. By thinking of other human beings as non-humans, it probably became a lot easier to destroy them.

I remember this happening in my own country during World War II. Our government through the media demonized the Japanese, who had shocked us in a very clever surprise attack on Pearl Harbor. While I was only ten years old at the start of the war, I still remember vividly the ugly caricatured faces of 'Japs' that stared out from every poster put in every public place during the war effort in 1942 to rally support against the enemy.

This also happened during the Vietnam War, when the Vietnamese (most of whom were innocent) were dehumanized as 'gooks' in order that our soldiers could kill them without guilt. This was exactly what was done in the ancient world as well, with the introduction of writing.

This wonderful 'new' technology (c. 3000 BC) was used primarily for propaganda purposes; as well as accounting, taxation, record keeping, etc.

Imagine the disappointment of dedicated scholars like M. Champillon (who deciphered hieroglyphics) or Michael Ventris (who deciphered Linear B of Crete) when they were able to read a carefully, painstakingly, beautifully engraved steatite plaque found in an ancient temple, and all it said was "three liters of olive oil were brought to the Temple of Isis or Knossos by ... (name illegible)". One would have hoped for a revelation of deep and profound spiritual significance. Instead, one found mostly bureaucratic account ledgers.

Of course, these clay tablets with their mysterious symbols provided valuable insights into the daily workings of these ancient cultures. Because writing was invented at the same time (approximately) as the destructive invasions were taking place, we tend to think that humans have always been violent and aggressive; when in fact, for the first 500,000 years of human life on this planet, we lived together quite peaceably and cooperatively.

Before 5000 BC, there is no evidence of fortified towns, with the exception of Jericho, zealously guarding its water supply in the Near East. There were no huge caches of deadly weaponry of militarism, no mass graves of hundreds or thousands of neither human skeletons, nor anything else, that would have given archeological evidence of mass killing and destruction. There were not even any 'chieftain graves' found from this period, before 5000 BC. A chieftain grave is one in which a much wealthier or powerful leader is buried with horses, chariots, wagons, sacrificial wives, concubines, servants, and richly ornamented possessions.

The lack of chieftain graves in an area usually indicated a more egalitarian society, less warlike, in which no one was awarded extraordinary status. This is why many archeologists believe that early human societies were based on cooperation in order to survive, and not warfare, in order to expand and accumulate the wealth of other tribes. However, much is not known about these earliest societies because they were not able to leave a literary record due to the lack of writing.

Clay Tablet in Linear B Script

Clay tablet in Linear B script were found and dated from the 'Last Palace' (before the invasions) of Knossess, Crete. Words are divided by vertical strokes and each figure stands for a whole syllable. Many of the signs are ideograms, or pictures of the things they stand for. It is to the marauding invaders who burnt the palaces to which we owe the fire-hardened records that have been found, c. 1400 BC.

Tripod Tablet

The Tripod Tablet found in the 'Palace of Nestor' at Pylos, in the southwest Peloponnese, carried the Linear B inscription. It lists types of vases, including cooking vessels with three legs, and may date from as late as c. 1200 BC. It can be viewed at the National Museum, Athens.

The Roots of Writing in Female-Centered Neolithic Culture

Recorded history begins c. 3400 BC when the Egyptians and Sumerians were able to leave a written record of their existence, their politics, their economy, their values, and their religion. Of course we know that writing began much earlier, in the ancient woman-centered societies of the Neolithic era c. 6000 BC, when women left their marks (symbols) on everything they made themselves and used in their daily round of chores.

They used spindle whorls while making yarn for textiles, clay vessels for cooking, eating, drinking, serving, and storage. Female figurines were made in their own image, or that of their beloved Mother Goddess in her various animal, bird, or fish manifestations, and inscribed with the 'writings' that told her story of seeds, fields, rain, vulva, pregnancy, birth, and regeneration.

Sketch by: Pres Miranda

The inscription on the spindle whorls had long, complex writings that follow the circular movement of the tool and consist of glyphs with a specific identity recalling those on seals and clay tablets.

In Old Europe weaving is generally closely linked to myths and religious rites and the act of spinning is full of allegorical and sacred force. It is thus difficult to explain these inscriptions with their practical use. Spindle whorls are among the most significant votive offerings found in religious centers and female graves.

The whorls rotate when in use and it is thus possible that the geometric motifs represent writing. Perhaps to be read by the weaver, or the divinity, as the whorl turns? Is this a kind of prayer directed towards to the heavens like the Tibetan prayer wheels?

The inscription from Dikili Tash could be a prayer for expressing devotion, requests, or gratitude.

Culture depends on the ability to invent and use symbols with a shared meaning that everyone can understand. This may take the form of pictures, alphabets, words, and writing. This is the way knowledge is passed to each succeeding generation. This was almost always the task of the mother. She was the one who taught her children to speak, thus passing on the language of their culture and providing them with a useful tool with which to learn all that had been learned in generations before them. In this way, women were 'carriers of culture', passing on knowledge and craftwork from generation to generation. Instead of destroying what had gone before, women moved civilization forward, millennia after millennia.

Among the oldest known picture writing is a limestone tablet from Kish, Mesopotamia (present-day Iraq). On it appear signs for head, hand, foot, a threshing sledge, and numerals, c. 3500 BC.

It now is displayed at the Ashmolean Museum, Oxford

Incised Cucuteni culture pregnant figurines, with elaborate 'writing', reveal mystical insights of the Neolithic women's world in Northern Moldavia c. 4500 BC. A pregnant figurine with etched writing can be seen at Plovdiv Archeological Museum, in Bulgaria.

Chronology of Writing

For invention of the first written alphabet, (9), we are indebted to the Canaanites and Phoenicians (Semites) who first used an alphabetic writing to transmit their ideas to paper about 1500 BC in the Syro-Palestinian area. It is believed they were workers in the Egyptian turquoise mines on the Sinai Peninsula. Some of the letters were derived from Egyptian hieroglyphics, but many other letters are the earliest Phoenician alphabetic letters.

The development of the alphabet (10) was the culmination of a long, slow process that began with:

- Dot-like engravings on rock 75,000 years ago in Australia;
- Pictographs found painted on potsherds and figurines from matrifocal cultures in south central Europe, 6000 BC;
- Hieroglyphs of Egypt, c. 4000 BC;
- Cuneiform of Sumeria, (present-day Iraq), c. 3500 BC;
- Paper made from pith of the papyrus plant in Egypt, c. 3200 BC;
- The development of a more rapid, cursive, pen and ink script in Egypt, c. 3200 BC;
- Linear A and B alphabet of the island of Crete, c. 2500 BC;
- Chinese characters burned into the shoulder blades of an ox and breastplate of a turtle, c. 1000 BC;
- The Phoenician alphabet of 1500 BC;
- The Greek alphabet (derived from Phoenician), c. 720 BC;

- The Runic (twig) alphabet of Northern Europe;
- The Ogham (parallel lines) of Ireland, date unknown;
- The Mayan glyphs of Yucatan peninsula, Mexico, c. 500 BC, perhaps one of only four truly original scripts of the early world.

There were many variations of these ancient 'alphabets', including: Mexican glyphs (hieroglyphs, or pictographic symbols) of the Aztecs, c. AD 300, and the Sanskrit of India, c. 250 BC.

Humans of every era, from the very dawn of civilization, have exhibited a deep-rooted need to leave their mark for posterity:

- The Australians of the Pleistocene period, c. 75,000 BC engraved designs/symbols on rocks with dots.
- The Paleolithic Stone Age people of Europe and Africa painted on cave walls and rocks.
- The Neolithic Europeans incised their pottery and (mostly female) figurines with ideograms and symbolic signs.
- Ancient Egyptian priestesses and priests and royalty wrote hieroglyphs on every stone available until they discovered the art of making paper.

From *The Dawn of Civilization*, there has been an innate drive to communicate, to leave a more permanent, more lasting, record than the spoken word. The signs were at first pictures of the objects, animate and inanimate, which played an important part in their lives.

A pregnant woman, the 'Venus of Laussel' incised in limestone at a Paleolithic cave entrance, was an early attempt by prehistoric people to tell all those who would later enter that cave,

"Look, pay attention! This woman is most sacred and holy; value her highly!"

Unfortunately, by the time I was pregnant and birthing my six children from the 1950's to the 1970's, pregnancy had not been the 'holy, magical' state for many millennia. Only maleness was highly valued; and the word 'pregnancy' was never mentioned in the Catholic churches I attended up until 1980. Since that time, I am happy to relate, I have heard the word 'pregnant' uttered by a Catholic priest, in a respectful tone of voice, in a Catholic Church.

Cave Art, a Form of Writing

The next most important message left for posterity by people of the Stone Age, c. 25,000 BC, was the importance of animals. The beautiful cave art paintings they left for us in the limestone caves they used for dwellings, tell us that they studied closely the animals in their environment and tried to understand what their relationship should be to these magnificent, sometimes huge, creatures. Perhaps they prayed to the spirits of the animals, and tried to figure out how to get the meat and furs they needed to survive in the harsh winters of northern Europe.

Females were also pictured in the cave art, dancing, observing, feeding, and playing with their babies. Later, the Neolithic (agricultural age) people of Europe would paint their symbols and images on pottery and figurines (mostly of pregnant women and animals merging into women). *

Still later, the ancient agriculturists of Mesopotamia (present-day Iraq) and Egypt would make small pictures of objects and inscribe them onto thin clay 'tablets' or bricks. Again, they pictured animate and inanimate objects, (11) which played a major part in the life of their communities.

Sheep, cows, cereals, milk-pails, agricultural implements, the facade of a temple, the human head, the act of eating or drinking, the human foot, the act of walking or going, even the reed standard of the Goddess Inanna were obvious pictograms, the meaning of which was self-evident to everyone who lived in the society. The entire population would have known what these picture symbols meant. They were the signs used for star, Goddess, God, and heaven, for earth, foot, and so forth.

These 'temple economies' as the ancient civilizations came to be known, first used writing to record religious transactions, because these early countries of Sumer, Egypt, Assyria, Mesopotamia, and Anatolia, were theocracies. The Queen or King or Pharaoh was also the chief

---

* ARCHEOLOGIST DEAN SNOW REPORTED IN JUNE, 2009, NATIONAL GEOGRAPHIC, that by analyzing stencils of hands adorning the walls of El Castillo, pre-historic cave art of 26,000 BC many of the artists were women suggesting their position in Stone Age culture may have been greater than previously thought.

High Priestess or High Priest. In this way, the population was easier to govern and control.

This system reached its apex in Egypt, where Pharaohs (some were women, like Hatshepsut and the Cleopatras) were worshiped as Goddesses and Gods as themselves. In other words, they were not seen as incarnations of a deity; but they themselves were the deities.

Writing, in these theocracies, was very much a mystical, magical tool, which only a chosen few could understand. Only priestesses, priests, and scribes taught by them, could read or write. Writing was used to record the transactions of the temple, as the bureaucracy and administration became more complex.

Small clay tablets inscribed with crude pictographic signs, dating from 3100 BC, have been found at Sumer, present-day Iraq. The simple pictures represented objects, which (12) gave rise to the association of ideas with the pictures. The 'picture writing' later evolved into cuneiform, a stylized, but vague outline of the former picture. Thus, the symbols (cuneiform) could be rapidly impressed in wet clay with a wedge-shaped stylus, or pen. 'Cuneiform' means 'wedge-shape'. The tablets were then baked to preserve and harden them. In this way, there arose a complex civilization that was able to record its activities and thoughts in writing.

Thousands of these cuneiform 'tablets' have been found at temple sites throughout the Middle East. Some of the clay tablets even had their own clay envelopes.

Cuneiform has not yet been completely deciphered, as some of the concepts are quite obscure to us even today. However, the earlier picture symbols have been more easily deciphered. For instance, the (13) sign for mons veneris or female pubic area **'V'** also meant 'maid of the mountains' or 'slave girl' because the ancient Sumerians often abducted their slaves from the mountainous areas surrounding Uruk, one of their major cities. Thus the same sign came to have several related meanings.

Sumerian Pictographic Writing

The association of writing with religion was an ancient one. The picture symbols used in the earliest pictographs of Sumeria and Egypt were deeply rooted in the prehistoric past and no doubt had long been associated with protective magic. The similarities between the picture symbols of the Neolithic, Matrifocal European farmers of 6000 BC, and the later Sumerian and Egyptian city-states of 4000 BC are recognizable.

Water, snakes and snake-shaped wavy lines, pubic triangles, suns, stars, moons, rain, vertical broken lines, spirals for pregnancy, meanders, chevrons, swastikas, circles, and crosses, all have an ancient lineage. These symbols were used, along with animals and humans (almost always females in the beginning) to memorialize our ancestors' most profound insights about the spiritual and natural worlds. It appears that they viewed these worlds as one and the same; nature was also imbued with divinity.

Goddess Figurines with 'Writing'

Many of the 'Goddess figurines', often called 'fertility symbols' by archeologists, were completely incised with symbols, as if repeating the picture/sign/symbol/word over and over would multiply the figurines' magical power.

The Goddess figurines have been found in wall niches of caves and shelters, at hearths, (recognizable from charcoal deposits from ancient hearth fires), and also at entrances to caves and shelters.

The earliest use for writing then was religious; an appeal to a deity for protection for the clan and its crops, supplication for pregnancy, or the hope for good crops from fertile soil. The earth's fertility was closely correlated to the women's pregnancies in the symbolism of the earliest food growers.

Hieroglyphics: Sacred Writings

The Egyptian 'hieroglyph' means 'priestly writing', so called by the later Greeks who tried to decipher the inscriptions on temple walls, tombs, and papyri. Many of the earliest Egyptian writings contain incantations used in healing rituals, magical formulas for protection from scorpions, illnesses, etc., and prayers to be said at religious festivals and for the dead. Women seem to have had equality in ancient Egypt, (14) as most of the medical papyri deal with gynecological ailments and protective charms for women and children.

It is also well known that women practiced medicine, from surviving literary evidence c. 3000-2000 BC. A lady of the house who could read probably did the doctoring for her large household of staff, family, and friends. Those who could read and write in any ancient society were rare and considered magical. Often the ones who could 'read' in prehistoric societies were female, as they invented most of the symbols in the first place. They were the ones planting the seeds, becoming pregnant/fertile, gathering the herbs for medicinal use, healing the sick, and easing the death throes of the dying. This is not to denigrate the contributions of men. They often faced death in hunting to make sure the tribe survived.

Priestess, Oracle, Psychic, Seer

Priestess, scribe, oracle, medicine woman, shaman, huntress, prophetess, seer, diviner, doctor, teacher, carrier of culture - women as well as men, filled these roles and made use of reading and writing for sacred purposes. This role of oracle or visionary healer is memorialized in the word 'reader' often used to describe a woman who 'reads the cards' and gives spiritual as well as practical guidance. This was an ancient function of women in all societies for millennia. Our present-day psychics are following an ages-old female vocation and deserve our respect (though not necessarily our money; as we have many more avenues of self-knowledge available to us than did the ancients).

Tarot: Holy Cards

Tarot cards were one of the early symbol systems of writing used to gain spiritual insights. The Tarot symbols on the cards in a Tarot deck are still useful for gaining insight, self-knowledge, and guidance; but they need to be studied in depth, not superficially. In this way, they can lead us toward creative thinking and problem solving. The Tarot system of knowledge was on the 'forbidden' list of the Catholic patriarchs for hundreds of years, probably because of female associations with the Tarot. These divination cards were the inspiration for the 'holy cards' of Catholicism.

Pictures of saints and multitudes of religious symbols were depicted on cards as devotional aids, as most converts could not read in the Middle Ages and earlier. (Much of the world's population is illiterate).

Runes (25 BC-AD 450)

Runic alphabets had twenty-one angular letters cut into pieces of wood or wood chips. These were shaken, then thrown on the ground, (called casting) and read for hidden messages, meanings, and solutions to conflict. Because the Celtic, Teutonic and Scandinavian runes came to be associated with women's religious and magical skills, all runic alphabets (there were several) were eventually forbidden when northern Europe was Christianized, on the grounds that those who could read the runic alphabet were practicing witchcraft (women's wisdom). Thus women were once again denied an avenue of knowledge and helpfulness to the community at large.

Another ancient alphabet used for divination and religious purposes was the I-Ching of China. Complex word signs were carved on sticks. They were 'thrown' at random and then read for guidance. The child's game 'pick up sticks' is derived from these early divining practices.

By the time written records first appeared in Egypt and the Near East, c. 3500 BC, patriarchy was well established. Earliest accounts are mostly bureaucratic record keeping and pronouncements of the ruler or pharaoh concerning his own greatness and his identification with the local deities.

In *Women in Prehistory* Margaret Ehrenberg wrote, "Most early written records were written by men about unusual events rather than about everyday lifestyles, and they usually referred to the lives of a small number of wealthy or (privileged) people, few of whom were women. The everyday lives of the majority of women were never considered worth describing". And with the advent of writing, history begins and prehistory ends. The scribes, as well as the rulers who paid them, were men; and they mostly described topics of interest to themselves, such as violence, warfare, and conquest. Egyptian hieroglyphs survived in the 'Pyramid Texts' of Egypt, so called because they were written repetitively and hypnotically on the walls of the pyramids.

In Egypt, as well as many other ancient civilizations, one of the primary topics of writing was religion. Many texts were religious; such as the 'Book of the Dead', which contained spells and incantations to help the recently deceased navigate safely through the underworld.

- **'Execration Texts'** were ritual spells that cursed the enemies of the state (neighboring countries); and called down upon them nasty plagues and horrible misfortunes.
- **'Instructional Texts'** explained the incredibly complex religious-mythological basis of Egyptian society.
- **'Magical Texts'** invoked deities of healing and protection, and,
- **'Coffin Texts'** contained funerary spells and blessings for the dead, meant for the inscription on coffins.

Before 3200 BC in Egypt (as well as in many areas in the ancient world) all knowledge had to be passed orally from generation to generation. The verbal transmission of information required a vast repertoire of memorization skills on the part of those passing on the instructions (elders), as well as those receiving the knowledge (usually younger members of the family, clan, tribe, culture).

Mnemonic Devices

Some of the learning methods used to aid the mind to retain knowledge were: teaching songs, rhymes, telling facts in groups of two or three sentences, tattoos, poetry, stories, tying knots of string on fingers (still used today), drumming, dancing, chanting, and pain.

The latter method is still used in excruciatingly painful initiation ceremonies of some tribal cultures in which mutilation is employed. The theory is that what is told to a person while in unbearable pain will never be forgotten. The rationale used in many of these secret societies' initiations, such as the Sande of W. Africa, is that survival of the person to adulthood may very well depend on her/his remembering what is told to them during their initiation at puberty. The dangerous, demeaning initiation ceremonies of today's college sororities and fraternities are a remnant of this tribal practice. The basic training of the military also falls into the category of pain and dehumanization to learn survival skills.

The value of writing, so easily taken for granted by recent generations, must have indeed seemed magical at first. There was now a way to solve civil disputes, record property rights, give receipts for taxes, document marriages, and divorces, (yes, ancient people got divorced). They could record their lineage and kinship ties.

Since human memories are notoriously fallible, there was now a way to create a permanent record of a transaction instead of a series of knots on a piece of cord, or beads arranged in sequence on a string. These methods still survive in the abacus, an ancient calculator, and the rosary, (an early bead counter). The knots used in prehistory for the recording and storing of information are memorialized in jewelry designs as well.

Writing then, the permanent recording and storage of information, brought about major changes in the control and dissemination of knowledge. The scribes proved to be invaluable to pharaohs, queens and kings c. 3400 BC, as they set about to expand and consolidate their nations. Religious ideas, carved in stone in a public place, were one of the methods used to unify thoughts and belief systems of large diverse populations. The 'Narmer Palette' is an example of writing and religion used together in the service of the state.

Narmer Palette

Egyptian Pharaoh Narmer was credited with bringing together politically, Upper and Lower Egypt and forming it into a powerful unified state with a dynasty that was to last thousands of years. He did this through the use of Egyptian symbol writing, hieroglyphics. The Narmer Palette was one of the first known royal edicts, a monumental inscription on a slate palette with the head of the ancestral Mother Goddess, Hat'hor, carved on both sides of the top of the palette. She was shown as a 'Sacred Cow' (a long cherished maternal animal sacred to Eastern matrifocal societies) with a human face, continuing the Neolithic Goddess-manifested-in-animal-form tradition of 6000 BC in the Balkans and Near East.

In this way, by depicting one of the most important deities with a human face on the same royal edict that contained his own likeness, and with hieroglyphs proclaiming him as the 'King of the Two Lands', he cleverly began the merging of the Goddess into the King; and so began the long tradition of the Goddess-Queens and God-Kings of ancient Egypt. (15) From now on, rulers had the ultimate tool with which to control their subjects: the royal word of the deity carved in stone along with the deity's image.

The royal scribes wrote pronouncements made by the pharaoh on everything: walls, pillars, coffins, pyramids, ostraca, shards, pottery, papyrus, linen, pectoral, jewelry, statues, pendants, bricks, stellae, obelisks, amulets. The dissemination of knowledge and information worked very well. Egypt remained a powerful, magical, mystical kingdom for three thousand years more. *

---

* Evidence of an Egyptian Presence in Israel:

As I was writing about King Narmer, a news item released by the Associated Press, revealed early evidence of Egyptian colonization in southern Israel, c. 3200 BC. A serekh (palette) belonging to King Narmer, as well as official seals and the tomb of a young Egyptian woman with her hieroglyphic wall inscriptions and standing stones were unearthed at Halif in the Negev Desert. It is believed by archaeologists from the University of California and Jerusalem's Hebrew Union College that the newly unified Egyptians were attempting to expand, in order to procure items of prestige for their elite, such as wine, olive oil, and slaves.

Goddess of Writing

Female origins of writing can be traced in attributes historically associated with ancient goddesses. Athena, the queenly ancestral Goddess of Libya and Greece was known as (16) inventor of the alphabet and other civilized arts, and guardian of the forbidden mystery of 'wise lunar blood' or reproduction.

India's Goddess Vac (whose name means 'voice') (17) was known as the Mother of Creation who "spoke the first word 'OM' to bring forth the universe". Biblical writers may have been influenced by this legend, when they attributed the first words of creation to their male god. Goddess Vac also invented the alphabet whose letters were called 'matrikas', the mothers. Females throughout time have proven the truism that "Necessity is the mother of invention." Goddess Kali Ma is usually depicted wearing the 50 letters of the Sanskrit alphabet of ancient India on her necklace of skulls.

Goddess Inanna, the supreme divinity of ancient Sumeria (present-day Iraq) (18) was depicted always holding two reeds, called her 'standards', on hundreds of clay tablets incised with pictograms. While the reed was her agricultural symbol of abundance, it was also a stalk used by women to paint the pots they made for use in their homes. The reed was later cut in a new way to serve as a stylus (pen) with which to write more easily on the rounded pots. Pottery was originally modeled after the rounded belly of pregnancy.

Mesopotamian seal: her foot on a Lion, her head crowned with a horn rimmed hat, and caduceus with the star (her seal) in the background.

Mother Goddesses Ma'at and Isis of Egypt were credited with giving Egyptians the knowledge of writing. In Rome, Goddesses Carmenta and Fata Scribunda (Scribe of Fate) were credited with the invention of writing. In Scandinavia, the Goddesses of the alphabet were called the Norns, and 'Schreiberimen' or 'Writing-Women'.

Bibliography for Writing

1. *The Dawn of Civilization*, Mellaart, James, et al, London, McGraw Hill, 1961
2. *Mythologies of the Ancient World*, Kramer, Samuel, et al, NY, Anchor, 1961
3. *Goddesses and Gods of Old Europe*, Gimbutas, Dr. Marija, CA, U of CA Press, 1982
4. The Politics of Women's Spirituality, "Blood, Bread, and Roses", essay, Groden, Judy, NY, Anchor, 1982
5. *Goddesses and Gods of Old Europe*, Gimbutas, Dr. Marija, CA, U of CA Press
6. Ibid
7. *The Women's Dictionary of Symbols and Sacred Objects*, Walker, Barbara, NJ, Castle, 1988
8. *Mythologies of the Ancient World*, Kramer, Samuel, editor, NY, Anchor 1961
9. *The Dawn of Civilization*, Mellaart, James, et al, London, McGraw Hill, 1961
10. Ibid
11. *The Dawn of Civilization*, Mellaart, James, et al, London, McGraw Hill, 1961
12. *Archaeology of the Bible*, Magnusson, Magnus, NY, Simon & Schuster, 1977
13. *The Dawn of Civilization*, Mellaart, James, et al, London, McGraw Hill, 1961
14. *Magic in Ancient Egypt*, Pinch, Geraldine, London, British Museum Press, 1994
15. *Women in Prehistory*, Eherenberg, Margaret, University of Oklahoma Press, 1989
16. *The Woman's Dictionary* of Symbols and Sacred Objects, Walker, Barbara, NJ, Castle, 1988
17. Ibid
18. *The Dawn of Civilization*, Mellaart, James, et al, London, McGraw Hill, 1961

Gloria Bertonis, with Carol Miranda

References:

The Sacred Paw, Sanders & Shepard, NY, Viking, 1985

The Wisdom of the Serpent, Hutchinson & Oates

Saudi Armco World, Aramco Services Co., Houston, TX, Sept-Oct 2001, Vol. 52 #5

Mars/Earth Enigma, Emerson, DeAnna, Lakeville, Mn Galde Press, Inc. 1998

CHAPTER V:
Textiles - Women's Work

She-Comes-Who-Is-Beautifully-Robed

Women have long been associated with textiles, as the first textiles originated in the plant world, the traditional domain of the female. Weaving, sewing, knitting, crocheting, embroidery, quilting, tatting, patchwork, appliqué, beadwork, lace making, dressmaking, rug braiding are traditional women's craft work; not only for utility but also for creativity, artistry, survival, and self-expression. Even before the first woman spun the first thread by rolling it around on her thigh, women were piecing together animal hides and furs artistically to wear as clothing.

Five hundred-year-old female mummies found in an indigenous Inuit settlement on the West Coast of Greenland were wearing beautifully handcrafted fur anoraks that showed a genuine flair for style while worn even in death. The tight-waisted coats were sewn of the light belly fur skin of seals for the sides and shoulder pieces; while the ornamental back piece was taken from the back of the ringed seal. A surprising attention to what we would call 'high fashion' was apparent in many of the mummies' garments. Shorts were made of multicolored patches of fur, joined together by sinew stitching in an elegant pattern. The fine stitches were perfectly symmetrical.

It is impossible to look at this exquisitely preserved 500-year-old clothing and not be impressed. The indigenous Eskimo Inuit women who made their own clothing from natural findings in their environment had no fashion industry to provide patterns or styles, and no Paris runway on which to model their stunning creations.

Why then, did they take the time and effort to make clothing of the finest workmanship? Why spend long painstaking hours designing and sewing everyday clothing that was probably worn to do mundane chores in a harsh isolated section of the planet? Perhaps the reason lies deep within the human psyche, in which there probably exists an urge to create beauty, a finely-tuned aesthetic sense, an enduring appreciation of beauty whether found in a piece of fur, a flower, a feather, or a seashell. For not only did these Inuit women fashion extraordinary clothing, they also decorated their faces with tattoos. Married women tattooed themselves by drawing a needle with colored thread through the outermost layer of skin, perhaps as a permanent sign of status.

Early women knew that hot ashes from their hearth fires would staunch severe bleeding from an injury. Today we would call it 'catheterization', a technique use by my gynecologist when he performed a D and C operation on my cervix for excessive bleeding. It stands for 'dilation and cauterization', or burning of the tissues. When the women performed this minor surgery on a face, arm, or leg, etc., they would have noticed that a permanent design was left inside the scar as it healed. It would have had a bluish tint, and they may have decided to use the ashes on artistically designed, deliberate cuts in the skin, as a form of beautiful personal decoration. This may be the origin of tattooing.

Beauty is a deeply ingrained desire in most females, still today; and we will suffer almost any torturous procedure for the sake of beauty, just as the Stone Age Divas did.

An account of women and their fine art of sewing and textile weaving began long before the discovery of the Inuit mummies of Qilakitoq. (1) It began about 20,000 BC in the Gravettian culture of Lespuque, France during the Stone Age. There, archaeologists unearthed a small, plump (possibly pregnant) 'Goddess' figurine carved in bone and wearing a skirt of twisted strings suspended from a band around her hips. What is peculiar about this first woman-made skirt of a textile that was NOT skin or fur, is that it would appear at first glance to have absolutely no useful purpose. Covering only the middle of the buttock area, it left the frontal genital area completely exposed and unprotected. The loose strings comprising the skirt would have easily opened when the wind blew or when the woman walked or moved.

Another possibility for the use of the string skirt in the Paleolithic era would have been for protection from the flying embers of her hearth fire. It would have served as the cave woman's apron. Yet the string skirt was worn in the rear, not in the front, apron style. Wearing her strings over her buttocks would certainly not have offered her any protection while cooking, as an apron is meant to do. After ruling out modesty, warmth, protection, what is left for the string's purpose? As early as 40,000 BC, which is the date given by some researchers for the invention of string, our Paleolithic ancestresses took pieces of short, weak, organic fibers and twisted them into longer, stronger lengths of string for their micro-mini skirts.

Why take the time and trouble to twist strips of bark, grass, or vines into longer strips, attach them to a band, and wear them jauntily over the middle of the buttocks? The only answer can be, of course, for decoration. The movement of the women's hips as they walked would have made the supple string skirts sway to and fro in a scintillating motion. This surely would have been an attention-getting device to catch the eyes of nearby males, just as the swaying tassels of the go-go dancers of yesterday had an erotic effect on males in the audience.

Sketch by: Pres Miranda

Illustration: String skirt worn by women in
Egtved, Denmark burial c. 1800 BC
Source: Copenhagen National Museum

Another reason offered by Dr. Elizabeth Wayland Barber, is that the string skirts may have designated the wearer's status, indicating that the wearer was ready for mating and childbearing. (2) The oldest surviving string skirt is from Egtved, Denmark and is preserved at the Copenhagen National Museum. The Danish skirt is dated from a Bronze Age burial, c. 1800 BC. The skirts depicted on the Paleolithic 'Goddess' figurines of France are much older, c. 30,000 BC.

The Goddess figurine which was found in France was carved in mammoth ivory with such precision that the twists in each piece of string are clearly visible, even after 20,000 years. (3) Only five and one-half inches high, this extraordinary masterpiece of antiquity has been named 'Venus of Lespuque', and was found in the foothills of the Pyrenees Mountains in France.

Another 'Venus' figurine found in the Ukraine is believed to be the earliest carved representation of a human female. Carved out of mammoth ivory, and dating from the Gravettian culture c. 30,000 BC, she is pregnant, with pendulous breasts, and looks down at her distended abdomen. She is wearing a girdle or belt of fringe. Many of these 'Venuses', as archaeologists call them, were found over a wide area from southern Russia to Italy. They were called 'Venuses' because their sexual characteristics were emphasized.

In 'Dawn of Civilization', James Mellart described the figurine as having "full breasts, prominent buttocks and signs of pregnancy. (4) Heads might be represented in conventional fashion. Very rarely were any facial features indicated. Thighs were shown as plump, but legs were tapered and feet merely indicated."

Some authorities (Michener, Auel, Gimbutas), (5), (6), (7), believe the legs and feet were pegged to enable the figurine to stand alone in the soft earth floor of the Paleolithic cave shelter, perhaps near a hearth.

Mellaart adds, "In the rare instances in which the figurines were not entirely naked, their clothing was confined to a girdle or fringe. We do not know what purpose these figurines served, but they did far more than reveal primitive men's (sic) concerns with fertility and reproduction of their own kind. They epitomize the ability to give expression to this concern in three-dimensional works of art that remain effective despite their small size." (8)

Stone Age Divas

Carved of mammoth ivory and very exquisite, this female statuette shows a string skirt carved under the buttocks.
Pyrenees, France c. 19,000 BC
Source: Musée de l'Homme, France

When we describe these tiny little 'Goddesses' with their string skirts, we think of the most rudimentary of human inventions, a piece of string. Yet it is impossible to imagine the magnitude of this humble object in the lives of Stone Age peoples.

Our earliest ancestresses would undoubtedly have had many good motivations to create lengths of string. These would include reasons such as: to tether a wandering toddler to their side as they foraged for food and medicinals or to secure bundles of grain grasses, barks, branches of berries, and twigs as they gathered fuel and edibles during their daily gathering forays.

Perhaps they used them to string shells, teeth, or pieces of bone for a necklace, or to knot the string into nets for catching birds, fish, and small animals. With string, our Stone Age foremothers could have tied preserved food high on a rock or a branch to protect it from the animals. With string, she could tie back her hair as she did her daily chores. She could make knots of different sizes of string to serve as memory aids in her medicine pouch, perhaps to help her remember which herbs were more toxic than others. By 500 BC knots on string were being used in India as rosaries when praying to Hindu Goddesses.

Because women's ancient cultural artifacts were usually organic and did not survive over millennia, we must remember that we have little archaeological evidence for the vast array of women's contributions to the survival of our species.

However, one piece of neatly spun cordage has survived from about 15,000 BC. Although fossilized, it was obviously a heavy cord twisted from three two-ply fiber strings. (9) This fossilized cord was found in the painted caves of Lascaux, France by archaeologists. Rolling pieces of fibrous plants on their thighs, humans learned to make soft, flexible strings of any length they desired.

Dr. Elizabeth Wayland Barber wrote, "So powerful, in fact, is simple string in taming the world to human will and ingenuity that I suspect it to be the unseen weapon that allowed the human race to conquer the earth, that enabled us to move out into every eco-niche on the globe during the Upper Paleolithic. (10) We could call it the String Revolution".

Women had long used vines, long stringy plant stems, strips of bark, animal guts, sinews, veins, and tendons to secure their children and belongings; as well as fasten hides into winter wraps. Now they had a way to spin and twist thinner string into thread to sew together smaller pieces of fur, suede, and skin into garments with the use of ivory or bone needles.

We tend to forget that women formed an important pool of innovators; and that they constantly moved culture forward, often in long-forgotten ways, or in ways that seem insignificant compared to the dramatic and oftentimes deadly adventures of the males in their society.

Yet the women had their own tools often overlooked by untrained archaeologists of previous centuries whose main focus was the search for weapons, bronze, gold, and silver antiquities, or jewelry with high resale value. In their bag of tools, besides knives and scrapers, prehistoric women would have carried needles, string, flints for carving, combs, scoops, paints, medicinal herbs, glue, and perhaps a whistle or hollow reed for making music, or summoning a wandering toddler.

Words can be fossils too. The only way we know the ancients used glue is because there was a word for it in their root language, Finno-Ugric, which extended into the modern languages of Finnish, Lithuanian, and Latvian, Lapp, and Hungarian, among others. In fairness to women, it is fitting to remember their important, life-changing contributions to civilization - and one of their major contributions were textiles.

Weaving Textiles: Women's Work

It began with a piece of string; with learning how to twist and roll short strands of plant fibers on their thighs or in their hands, to make a longer strand of thread, string, or twine.

This was the necessary first step: to make the lengths of thread that would then be woven in and out of each other to create a piece of fabric. Paleolithic woman would already have known how to weave as they probably had made baskets by peeling the bark from birch, willow and linden trees. They had probably entwined grasses and other pliable natural material into containers for their gathering and scavenging activities, as well as for carrying their infants while nursing and working at the same time. They had also experimented with their own hair for thousands of years creating unusual artistic hairstyles long before they had clothing, as we know it.

Because they were nomads, always on the move in their never-ending search for plant and animal edibles, they would have needed a container to tote their meager possessions from one encampment to another. The !Kong of Southwest Africa still live a nomadic existence. The need for a way to tie together and carry things on the spur of the moment made string an important invention. In fact it was probably the second most important human craft. The first craft being making blades from flint stone for carving containers from wood, stone, bone or ivory and making art objects, possibly religious female figurines.

This was the way human societies existed for hundreds of thousands of years all during the Paleolithic era, which covered a vast time span from 200,000 BC to about 10,000 BC. With the dawn of the Neolithic (agricultural) age, sometime after 10,000 BC, our ancestors were able to settle down and make the food grow around their settlements. The earliest remains of such Neolithic habitats have been unearthed in the Middle East, Mesopotamia (present-day Iraq), Anatolia (present day Turkey), and the Balkans, (southeastern Europe).

While no one knows for sure which gender did what task, it is probably safe to assume that women spent much of their time performing chores that were compatible with child rearing.

Making thread and string, and weaving them into textiles would have been activities that could be performed while keeping one eye on busy toddlers. These tasks (spinning and weaving) would not have presented any danger to the children.

We already know that the first human made articles of clothing (excluding animal skins) was a skimpy string half skirt worn low over the woman's buttocks in the rear. Eventually, she turned her flirtatious stringed skirt to the front; and later, made it wider (though not longer in length) so that it covered her entire hip area, slung low on the hips, and attached to a wide waistband. The loose, swaying, open strings could not have had much practical use for warmth or modesty; or even for wiping hands, as the strings swayed open constantly. These were undoubtedly the early aprons which are the quintessential symbols of maternal caretaking, and efficiency.

My best guess is that the women tied their most often used articles to the strings to keep their tools close at hand, as pockets were not yet invented. The archaeological records contain many female figurines wearing the non-functional string skirts, over a wide time span and a broad geographic area. One such female figurine is wearing a string skirt and offering her breasts in a typical Middle Eastern gesture of nurturance, c. 2553 BC.

The woolen string skirt found on the preserved body of a young woman who was buried in a peat bog at Egtved, Denmark, c. 1800 BC, was so wide that she was able to wear it wrapped around her waist twice. Stone Age figurines showing women wearing these skirts were found in Gogarino, Russia (c. 20,000 BC), the Pyrenees, in settlements of the Vinča culture, Serbia (c. 4500 BC), western Ukraine (c. 3500 BC), Yugoslav Macedonia (c. 3000 BC), and (10) Anatolia, present-day Turkey (c. 2553 BC).

Stone Age Divas

Sketch by: Pres Miranda

Lower half of figurine wearing string skirt slung low on hips found in Southeastern (former) Yugoslavia. Dated to c. 4500 BC.
Source: R. Galovic, Archeoloski Pregled (1960), after Gimbutas

The first miniskirt, shorter even than the Stone Age string skirt, was worn in the Bronze Age. The remains of a young woman were found in Olby, Denmark. She was wearing only jewelry and a minimal string skirt with the ends of the strings encased in little tubes of bronze. European archaeologists were scandalized that their ancestresses were so scantily clad, wearing nothing at all except a see-through, very, very short string skirt and jewelry. With the addition of the metal tips to the swaying strings, the skirts would have jangled as the woman moved.

In Northern Europe, the additional embellishment of metal tips to the ends of the strings would have reflected light, making the woman even more noticeable. Where metal wasn't available, women often fringed the ends of the strings stylishly, or else knotted the ends in order to keep them from fraying. Serving no practical purpose that can be discerned the skirts may have served as an attention-getting device.

Ancient societies almost always used special techniques or 'markers' to designate the position of the individual within the society. With little in the way of personal possessions or wealth, to mark status in the Stone Age, Neolithic and Bronze Age societies, one's ranking within the family, clan, or tribe would have been shown by a status symbol. The string skirt may have been such a marker, proclaiming that the wearer had reached puberty (11) and now 'possessed the mysterious ability to create new life.'

In another part of the world, Polynesia, the women's swaying grass fiber skirts and hip movements became ritualized into the sacred dance called the 'hula'. String skirts, in addition to being worn by Polynesians, were worn by ancient Nubians (12) and Egyptians as well. Terra-cotta figurines found in Egypt show Nubian female captives wearing string skirts c. 1900 BC. Nubia, a neighboring country, (13) was traditionally a rival of Egypt in antiquity, as were Syria and Libya.

Other markers besides the string skirt used to denote rank or status in the remote past were tattoos, hairstyles, rare feathers, stones, bones, seashells, and jewelry, especially gold, because of its highly reflective capacity. Gold was used to attract the opposite sex, as well as to symbolize wealth, power, and marital status just as it does today. Gold is easily worked into exquisite designs, is durable, and has been highly prized since the beginning of time.

In Greek mythology, the Goddess of Love and Beauty, Aphrodite was said to wear a girdle of gold, which made her irresistible to all males. While we think of a girdle today as a solid, confining, utilitarian garment, in 600 BC it may have been a glamorous wide belt that girded the loins: the 'skirt of a hundred tassels' worn by a Goddess in Homer's Iliad. Instead of bronze tips, Aphrodite's string skirt was tipped in gold, as befitted a Greek Goddess.

Even today, string skirts, worn as aprons, are part of the folk costume of the Mordvins of Russia, Bulgarians, Serbs, Romanians, Macedonians, and Albanians. The women decorate the front band by weaving patterns of lozenges, that ancient symbol of women's wombs and fertility/pregnancy.

Sprang weaving of Greece and the Netherlands is similar to braiding and dates back to the Neolithic era. (14) Greek women lived near the shores of seas, and rivers, so they may have invented it to catch fish, small birds, animals like rabbits, etc. Sprang is a red knotless netting also called 'zostra' in Greece and used as a spiritual aid in difficult childbirth by young women fortunate enough to have inherited one from their mothers as ancestral heirlooms. Some women consider the zostra sacred as it is passed on from generation to generation giving it a feeling of holiness. They place it on the abdomen of the woman in a difficult labor and maintain that it does work wonders.

In both Greece and Lithuania, traditional aprons, called 'zostra' and 'zurstai' respectively, had great significance, as did the mothers and grandmothers who wore them. In Lithuania, this apron called a 'zurstai' was always given particular attention in the women's traditional outfits. These aprons are the most richly embroidered and decorated piece of clothing worn for special ceremonies, like weddings. In earlier times in some villages it was considered improper for a woman to appear in public without her 'zurstai' apron.

Etymology, the study of word origins, is one of the few ways that women have of searching for their historic roots. (15) 'Clotho' was the name of an Athenian Goddess. She was the 'Spinner', the oldest of the Moirae or Fates. The word 'cloth' may derive from this female mythological figure, just as the words 'vest' and 'vestment' are derived from Vesta, Roman Goddess of hearth and home and warmth. A vest was worn for added warmth and vestments were sacred robes 'invested' with the Goddess power of Vesta herself. The word 'rob' derives from the word 'robe', the most precious possession, and often the only possession of many in the ancient world. Your female-woven robe would therefore be the only thing of value a thief could steal or rob from you.

Similarly, the word 'spinster' originally meant 'a female spinner' and was not used to designate an unmarried woman until the 18th century. 'Spinster' derives from an Indo-European root word, 'spen', to stretch, which also produced the Lithuanian word, 'pinti', to weave. (16) I remember the Lithuanian women, newly arrived from the old country, setting up their large handmade looms in the cellars and garages of their homes in the Blue Mountains of Pennsylvania. They wove carpets, tablecloths, blankets, bedspreads, and mats as if by magic in my eyes. As a small child I watched their complicated, steady, patient maneuvers. If you gave them your rags (bits of old clothing) they would cut them up, piece it or even just knot it and use it on the loom to make kitchen rugs.

Lithuania and Finland left archeological evidence of 'well-made hunting and fishing nets composed of fiber stripped from the bark of elms and willows' (17) in the Mesolithic era, c. 15,000 BC. Dr. Elizabeth Wayland Barber's research (18) led her to conclude that women in Europe may have already invented weaving by 20,000 BC as a way to strengthen the original string skirts. Dr. Wayland wrote that making string was such a rudimentary skill that it was known worldwide. Weaving, however, is much more complex and was not even known in some world cultures at the beginning of this century.

One of the reasons, besides need, utility, and artistic expression, that women excelled in the textile crafts (which later became huge wealth-producing national industries), was that it was something they could do while also tending to babies and small children. A loom would not have been a threat to the child's safety. It is basically a lightweight wooden frame to hold pieces of string (thread) taut while they are pulled over and under each other to form a solid piece of fabric. At first the looms were small, just a frame easily held in the hand or carried while living a nomadic, food-gathering lifestyle. Once women began farming and settling in one area permanently, the looms became larger and stationary. The women were then able to weave large pieces of material instead of just the narrow waistbands they had been weaving; and hip belts that held up their little string skirts could now be enlarged into dirndl skirts.

The earliest archaeological evidence of a piece of woven, human made fabric came from Jarmo, Iraq, in the form of two little clay balls with textile impressions on them. (19) The weaving was precise and neat, in two different patterns, showing that the weaver had been at it for some time before 7000 BC, the radiocarbon date of the find.

Jarmo was a Neolithic Kurd village in ancient Mesopotamia (present-day Iraq). There was also evidence of weaving in another Neolithic village, Catal Huyuk in prehistoric Anatolia (present day Turkey). It is believed that prehistoric weavers used the ground loom, which is still in use by Bedouin (nomadic Arabic) women in the Near East. Because these ancient looms were made entirely of wood, they did not survive through millennia (as was the case of many ancient artifacts created and used by women). We know these looms were used in antiquity because carvings of women using them survive in Egypt and also from vase paintings and other representations of their use. (20) The Egyptian representation shows women processing flax, spinning it into thread, measuring warp threads on wall pegs, and squatting while working the ground loom. The use of this loom spread south all the way to the east to India.

Another type of loom used by Neolithic women, c. 5,000 BC, was the warp-weighted vertical loom. This one was still in use twenty-five years ago by women in rural Scandinavia, according to Dr. Barber. European women possibly in Hungary probably invented it, and its use spread to northern and Western Europe.

While the wooden frames of these looms did not survive the last 7000 years, the clay weights did; and we can trace the use of the vertical looms through archaeological findings of the baked clay weights that kept the warp thread tight.

Before inventing the loom, a Paleolithic and Neolithic woman probably tied the warp threads 'to her own waist, and the far end to something else like a tree or her big toe'. (21) She would have been very limited in the size of the piece of cloth that she could weave - probably just a waistband, headband, or belt. (22) Many European descendants of these Neolithic weavers, including my Lithuanian relatives, still create magnificent headbands, sashes, and borders for their native ceremonial dresses. They also weave large tablecloths, rugs, coverlets, bedspreads, and afghans on their home looms. *

In addition then, to providing food for her family, planting and harvesting grain grasses, grinding the grain into flour for bread, baking the loaves, gathering fruits, tubers, nuts, berries, eggs, and meat from small birds and animals and fishing, women now had another task. That was, providing the fabric to clothe their families. Women first had to find flax or hemp, or cotton or clumps of wool in their environment, then learn how to grow it, harvest it, and dry it. To make linen, they had to place the dried flax in water long enough to rot the useless part of the stem away from the fibers. This was called 'retting'. Then they combed the fibers till smooth and free of debris.

Just as they worked together in the fields to grow food, so the women probably worked cooperatively to grow and prepare the flax. It is believed they sang 'call and response' songs to set the rhythm of the endless

---

* Our cousin, Bronė Bernatonis Nenartavich, known for the artistry and perfection of her weaving, was featured in the booklet Dienos-Darbeliai and was still weaving until her death at age 90 in 2009 in Silinai, Lithuania.

repetitive motions of the hard work in the fields. (23) "The slow, droning chants also had the interesting effect of blunting one's awareness of the pain of aching muscles, hunger, and the length of time spent."

Dr. Marija Gimbutas said that the songs she heard the women singing in the fields of her native country, Lithuania, aroused her curiosity about the Goddess cultures of the past, which they recalled in their ancient work songs. Determined to find the origin of the songs called 'dainos', she chose a career in archaeology and led several major expeditions in 'old Europe', the area around the Balkans where much Neolithic evidence has been unearthed. *

With their children, playing close at hand and observing, the women passed on their skills to the next generation. Women traditionally have worked together and bonded in sisterhood by organizing work projects such as sewing circles and quilting bees. (There is the prehistoric Bee Goddess again, resurrected and making her presence felt in pioneer America.) My own Mother had a sewing circle of friends that met regularly for more than thirty years during which they created masterpieces of crocheting, tatting (using a bobbin to make lace), embroidery, and quilting. Mother, at eighty-nine years young when she died, was still crocheting exquisite afghans, sweaters, booties, doilies, scarves, hats, slippers, shawls, pillows, and other articles of usefulness and beauty.

The 'bog burials', the wonderfully preserved, fully clothed bodies found in the peat bogs of Denmark and Switzerland, offer archaeological evidence of beautifully woven wool clothing from 4000 BC. (24) It is hard to imagine that Neolithic European women would have had the time and energy to make decorative fabrics. Just the daily work of survival and childbearing and rearing would have filled their days and evenings. Yet evidence shows that the Neolithic lake-dwellers of Switzerland wove complicated patterns of stripes, triangles, and checks; and added finishing touches of braided fringes, beadwork, and fancy edgings.

The homespun fabrics in their natural earth tones would probably appear drab to our twentieth-century eyes, used to brilliantly colored fabrics of every color of the spectrum. Most Neolithic (c. 4000-1000 BC) textiles would have been brown, beige, ivory, and white, as are the natural fibers of cotton, flax, and wool found in nature. However, dyes were already beginning

---

* Today, these 'dainos' holy songs, have been incorporated into a fusion rock band in Lithuania called, 'Zalvarinas'.

to be made from plants, minerals, murex shells, etc. producing the colors of blue, yellow, purple, and red. Patterned textiles from this period have been found in central Germany, as well as all over the rest of Europe.

The long winters of northern Europe probably contributed to the quantities of cloth woven in the colder areas. Many spindle-weights were found in the archaeological remains of the huts of the Tripolyte culture near Kiev, south Russia c. 3000 BC.

Sheep may have been tamed and herded for their wool as early as 4000 BC in Mesopotamia (present-day Iraq and Iran). (25) Other researchers state that 10,000 years ago, the nomads of southwest Asia realized that by herding sheep, they could survive and even prosper on the windy mountains there. At first the sheep provided food for the nomads; eventually, they learned to make yarn (string) from the heavy clumps of hair that fell off the sheep's bodies every spring.

A woolen pile rug dated to the fifth century BC was found inside the frozen, preserved tomb of a nomadic tribal chief at Pazyryk in southern Siberia. A woolen felt wall hanging also found in the tomb depicts a well-dressed horseman approaching a Goddess.

Felt (compacted wool) may have been 'discovered accidentally' (as so many innovations in the prehistoric era probably were), by the women using clumps of wool to kneel on while grinding grain or performing other household chores.

By 700 BC, Asian nomads had developed felt houses called yurts, which were easily folded and carried as they roamed China and central Europe.

The felting process of shrinking and pounding to create a smooth fabric is called 'fulling', the origin of the English surname, 'Fuller'. (26) It was a very time-consuming process done by hand by entire families. In Scotland, it was called 'waulking' because the wool was more quickly compressed by walking on it. In early days, the wool was first soaked in stale human urine collected in tubs. The ammonia in the urine sterilized the fibers and made them more pliant. Families sang together to keep the rhythm of the 'fulling' going smoothly and to relieve boredom.

The designs of Irish fisherman's woolen sweaters knitted by their womenfolk in a distinctive family or village design were said to help identify bodies washed ashore after accidents at sea. The origins of the patterns themselves are said to be rooted in Celtic history, perhaps even harking back to the female symbols of the Stone Age. The sweaters are usually called 'Isles of Aran' fisherman's sweaters.

Although linen fibers (made from flax) existed before wool, it is thought that wool may have been spun into yarn first since it could probably have been spun right off the backs of the sheep. These strands would have been noticed when the sheep rubbed their backs against something. This repetitive rubbing turned their coats into tight strands, which then could be cut off and spun into longer lengths. (27) Author Nina Hyde saw women seated on the curb in Ladakh, India, "twisting armfuls of loose wool onto a wooden spindle using a technique known since the Stone Age". She believes that Joseph's multi-colored coat of the Old Testament was wool, and that Jesus' cloak, for which the Roman soldiers drew lots, was probably woolen also.

These Biblical stories give us some idea of the high value placed on clothing in ancient times. People had so little clothing they may have owned only one coat/cloak/cape that had to last an entire lifetime. If this garment were of quality "work-woman-ship", (as the one worn by Jesus, as it would have been most likely spun and woven by Mary, his Mother), it would have been highly desirable to the soldiers who may not have owned one of their own. Joseph's cloak, because it actually had colors woven into the fabric, would also have been worth noting by biblical scribes as a garment of high value.

This was brought home to me very poignantly in Bath, England at the public baths dedicated to Minerva-Sulis, the Roman-Celtic Goddess of the sun and health. Devotees of the Goddess often threw lead curses into the waters or attached them to wooden posts and doors. One of the preserved curses inscribed on a small leaden rectangle, and dated to about AD 100, implored the Goddess to punish "the thief who carried away my cloak". That may have been the one and only cloak the victim would have owned; and we, with our closets full of colorful, warm, well-made clothing of every fiber and fashion, can hardly imagine the enormity of such a loss to the average person living two thousand years ago.

Native Americans also loved woolen cloth from Europe, as it was more comfortable to wear than the leather skins they were used to. A length of woven cloth was the most frequent item of trade used by the Europeans to trade for the furs that were highly valued by European royalty. It is sad to contemplate, but textiles from Europe helped seduce the Native Americans away from their millennia-old tribal values. (28)

They eventually altered their ancient life styles, and their sensitive relationships with animals and their environment.

This is not to imply that Native Americans did not know weaving. Many tribal women had been weaving extraordinary basket containers from the split roots of evergreen trees, from strips of the inner bark of basswood, willow, and cedar trees, from cornhusks, hemp, and many other natural fibers. Dr. Harrington wrote about the Lenni Lenape who lived in Bucks County, Pennsylvania and also in New Jersey. "Holding the ends (of hemp) with her left hand, she could roll two strands of fiber at the same time on her thigh with her right hand, the forward motion twisting them separately, the backward motion combining the two into one strong cord. She kept adding more fibers on the left and winding the finished cord in a ball on the right. It looked almost magical." (29)

Bowstrings were made by rolling sinew on the thigh, twisting two strands into one for extra strength. The women of the Lenape created extraordinary ceremonial outfits made of embroidered deerskin. The embroidery was done with strands of red deer hair and sometimes-small shells were incorporated into the symbolic designs. Yellow quills were also used for embellishment, as well as appliquéd motifs such as a large turtle all done in oval white shells sewn onto the softened deerskin.

Many Native American tribal women were skilled weavers. (30) The Chilkat of the northwest coast wove elaborate ceremonial robes of mountain goat wool and cedar-bark twine. Each cloak took a year to weave. The Hopi tribal women of northern Arizona are skilled weavers, as are the Navajo. The blankets woven by Navajo women were prized throughout the world even in the eighteenth century just as they still are today. Weaving, for contemporary Navajo women, is a tie to their past.

Typical archaeological evidence for rug and blanket weaving in antiquity includes bone needles, shuttles, bone weaving combs for pushing down the weft threads, bronze awls and loom weights of baked clay. These items were often found in female burials. A mummy preserved in the desert sands of the Paracas Peninsula of Peru appeared to have been buried with her favorite backstrap loom. Her shroud was a beautiful, ornate blanket that she herself had probably woven. Wool has been used in Peru for centuries, the brilliant colors, and ancient designs woven into the very fabric of the Peruvian women's lives.

Each village had its' own distinct colors and symbolic patterns, reproduced by the women as they wove. (31) The Maya of Guatemala, indigenous Amerindians, prized woven textiles so highly in AD 535, that walls of tombs painted with a weaving design symbolized royalty. Besides the glyphs (word symbols) on the tomb walls, the entrances often featured a braided-woven mat design painted on the walls; which indicated a royal burial.

Unfortunately, tomb robbers were well aware of these royal tombs such as those found in Rio Azul, Guatemala. (32) When tombs are looted, fiber remnants are often thrown away as trash and lost forever to historians.

Much of women's work in tribal cultures was of this organic, non-permanent variety; and it has been difficult (but not impossible) to trace women's contributions through the millennia.

Women were the food gatherers, growers, preservers, servers, and the spinners of thread, weavers of cloth, nurturers of children, animals, and the men of the family (who also worked long, hard hours). Women were the caretakers of the needy members of the clan: the children, the sick, the crippled, the elderly, the dying, and the birthing mothers. It is important to realize that a huge proportion of women's time was spent in creating the next generation, as well as caring for those already here. In spite of the demands on their time, women of antiquity learned the crafts necessary for survival, practiced them, perfected their skills, and passed them on to the next generation without benefit of reading or writing.

The women of the Mayan culture were skilled weavers, (sometime before) 900 BC, to about 600 AD, when it reached its peak as one of the world's great civilizations. Each Mayan village had its own traditional outfit, distinguishable from the others by its colors, styling, design motifs, and type of weaving. More than one hundred traditional outfits, all different styles, were woven in an area the size of Pennsylvania. Even today, in the high Andes, a woven hatband design can identify the weaver's village.

Partially fossilized fragments of textiles were found in a Mayan tomb in Rio Azul. Examination under an electron microscope revealed the textiles were 1000 years older than any ancient Mayan fabrics previously found. The outer shroud on the body was fine cotton open-weave brocade. The ancient weavers had used red tint made from cochineal insects. Cinnabar was also used to create an orange shade; and other flowers and vegetation were used as colorants. To use plants in this way requires a knowledgeable population of women artisans, who also knew the medicinal properties of the plants in their environment. (33) Medicinal herbs, identified and gathered mainly by the woman, were a major export of the Mayans in trade.

Mayan Moon Goddess, Ix Chel, was known as the Patroness of the Art of Weaving. Her domain included southern Mexico, the Yucatan Peninsula, Central America, and El Salvador. She was probably worshipped for about 1000 years, up to the conquest by the Spanish conquistadors, AD 1517. By learning the attributes of the ancient Goddesses, we can trace the female origins of many arts, crafts, and sciences. Goddess Ix Chel, the Weaver, is sometimes shown seated, with her bird companion perched on her outstretched foot, a warp thread wrapped around her big toe, and a hand-held loom on her lap. She is shown absorbed in her weaving, as women, and many men have been, for millennia, creating textiles, the fabrics of our lives.

photo Peter T. Furst

The weaver with her bird companion on her feet
weaving textiles on a hand-held loom.
Source: Museo Nacional de Antropologia, Mexico,

Gloria Bertonis, with Carol Miranda

Oriental Rugs

For 12,000 years, wool fiber has been spun on women's looms, creating works of art called 'rugs'. Tribal women of the Kurds, Berbers, Uzbeks, Afghanistans, and many others, made mats first, which were used as doors (flaps) for their portable homes. Because they led a nomadic lifestyle, all household goods had to be carried from location to location, often with very short notice. (34) Woven carpets were ideally suited for their lifestyle. They provided privacy by serving as a door, hung over the opening of the yurt or tent. They also served as floor coverings and as blankets when needed on cold winter nights in the mountains of Asia, Turkey, Iraq, and Iran, (formerly ancient Persia, after which the rugs were named).

Rug making was a very complex activity that required a high level of intelligence and a great deal of labor and time. First the sheep had to be grown, then shorn, then the clumps of hair spun into long threads, then dyed with dyes the woman had to prepare in her kitchen, from the plants she herself grew in her garden. Then plan a design, make a loom, and patiently sit for hours carefully weaving the design into the pattern of the weaving. Fortunately, it was an activity the women could do while minding their children, which was always a consideration in every female endeavor and accomplishment.

One historian, Stuart Piggott, reported that the oldest carpet ever discovered, lay beneath a Queen and King buried together in a tomb at Dorak, Turkey, near the Marmara coast. (35) In ancient times, c. 2339 BC, the date of the burial, this area would have been known as Troy. The Kurds are an ancient indigenous people who live there still.

While their homeland, Kurdistan, no longer appears on the map, they are an industrious tribal society spread out over several countries, which all treat them badly. The invaders who usurped their homelands treat all indigenous peoples harshly. Our own country's treatment of its Native Americans is an example.

The invaders probably assumed that the original inhabitants were of a lesser intelligence. Yet that is hardly the truth. The Kurds, for instance, make fine rugs, as they have done for thousands of years, which are highly prized all over the world. Not only are they of superb quality and beautiful, they also will last forever. The style is called 'kilim', with mostly geometric tribal designs, which are the woman's symbolic language.

As the symbols evolved through the ages, they became more and more stylized, and more ornate, so that only a trained eye could probably 'read' them today. Women all over the world, and throughout every time period, have used the symbolic language of art (ideogram, pictograph, glyph, etc.,) to tell their stories, to pass down their wisdom, to leave a lasting impression of their existence. With the advent of reading and writing (for most of the world's population, only about 100 years ago) the symbolic language has fallen out of use, so that most weavers today probably do not remember the meanings of the ancient symbols woven into the intricate designs. But somehow, I feel, these designs still speak to our subconscious; because that is most probably where they originated, in the mists of antiquity.

Kurdish kilim rugs are flat woven and tribal in style and design. They are very durable, made of wool mostly, and very lightweight, because the Kurds were nomads and needed their household goods to be portable.

The kilims are truly nomadic cottage industry rugs made for their own use; and therefore, with a lot more heart than mass-produced textiles. They are ornate and fanciful, highly collectible if one can be found. We have had an embargo on Iranian products for many years. The age, the dye, and the quality determine the price for a kilim rug. A rug that is 6 feet by 9 feet could sell for $3000. Some oriental rugs (including Chinese and Persian) could cost up to $10,000.

The oldest woolen carpet in the world was discovered inside the frozen tomb of a nomadic Tribal Chief at Pazyrk in southern Siberia, c. 500 BC and was documented in the National Geographic Magazine of 1988.

Villagers in Turkey that have an ancient weaving tradition still weave rugs using old patterns found in mosques. Natural dyes from plants were used; and they mellowed with time to a lovely soft subtlety. Madder (the root of the madder plant and is a deep reddish-purple color) was used to make red dyes, wild chamomile provided yellow, black came from acorn shells, tree sap, provided orange, and the combinations could be extensive, depending on the woman's time and creativity. Even without an identifying signature, the rug would have been her singular subjective world-view, her interpretation woven into it with love and care, and still recognizable today as incomparable art of great utility and value.

Bibliography for Textiles

1. The Mummies of Qilakitog, Nordquist, Jorgen et al, National Geographic, Feb, 1985
2. *Women's Work: The First 20,000 Years*, Barber, Dr. Elizabeth Wayland, NY, Norton 1994
3. Ibid
4. *The Dawn of Civilization*, Mellaart, James, et al, London, McGraw Hill, 1961
5. *The Source*, Michener, James, NY, Random House, 1965
6. *Clan of the Cave Bear*, Auel, Jean, NY, Crown, 1980
7. *Goddesses and Gods of Old Europe*, Gimbutas, Dr. Marija, CA, University of CA Press, 1982
8. Dawn of Civilization, Mellaart, James et al, London, McGraw Hill, 1961
9. *Women's Work: The First 20,000 Years*, Barber, Dr. Elizabeth Wayland, NY, Norton 1994
10. Ibid
11. Dawn of Civilization, Mellaart, James, et al, London, McGraw Hill, 1961
12. *Women's Work: The First 20,000 Years*, Barber, Dr. Elizabeth Wayland, NY, Norton 1994
13. *Magic in Ancient Egypt*, Pinch, Geraldine, London, British, Museum Press, 1994
14. Mt. Athos, Greece, Village from the Past, Karenikolos, Maria, National Geographic, December 1983
15. *The Women's Dictionary of Symbols and Sacred Objects*, Walker, Barbara, NJ, Castle, 1988
16. *Dictionary of Word Origins*, Ayto, John, NY, Arcade, 1990
17. *A History of Pagan Europe*, Jones, Prudence and Pennick, Nigel, London, Routledge, 1995
18. *Women's Work: The First 20,000 Years*, Barber, Dr. Elizabeth Wayland, NY, Norton 1994
19. Dawn of Civilization, Mellaart, James, et al, London, McGraw Hill, 1961
20. *Women's Work: The First 20,000 Years*, Barber, Dr. Elizabeth Wayland, NY, Norton 1994

21. Ibid
22. Home video produced by author's cousin, Ethnographer Alma Bernatonis, and her husband, Prof. Anthony Bernatonis of Kaunas, Lithuania 1990
23. *Women's Work: The First 20,000 Years*, Barber, Dr. Elizabeth Wayland, NY, Norton 1994
24. Mysteries of the Bog, Levathes, Louise, National Geographic, March 1987
25. Dawn of Civilization, Mellaart, James, et al, London, McGraw Hill, 1961
26. *Wool, Fabric of History*, Hyde, Nina, National Geographic, May 1988
27. Ibid
28. *Man's Rise to Civilization*, Farb, Peter, NY, Dutton, 1968
29. *The Indians of New Jersey*, Harrington, Dr. M.R., NJ, Rutgers University Press, 1963
30. *Indian Tribes of North America*, Copeland, Peter, NY, Dover, 1990
31. Rio Azul, Lost City of the Maya, Graham, Gordon, National Geographic, April 1986.
32. Ibid
33. Ibid
34. Dawn of Civilization, Mellaart, James, et al, London, McGraw Hill, 1961
35. Ibid

CHAPTER VI:
Women as the First Doctors

She-Who-Causes-Us-To-Breathe

The very word 'medicine' contains a mother syllable, 'me'. Because the primary syllable, 'ma', can be traced farthest back into Indo-European prehistory than almost any other word in our language, I have used it to trace female origins. (1) The word 'mamma' simply imitates the sound of an infant suckling at its mother's breast. In Latin, 'mammatis' means 'of the breast'; and nearly every language in the world contain a similar 'mother' word. The word for 'father' shows no such ancient lineage, telling us that paternity itself was not clearly understood for many millennia; and that, in fact the concept of 'fatherhood' is a relative newcomer in terms of human evolutionary thinking.

Mother Syllable

Even after the development of complex, diverse languages, there was no standardized spelling for the simple reason that there was no reading or writing, as we know it today, until about 3000BC. When writing began, the words were written as the scribes heard them. Therefore, each word had many possible spellings depending on the dialect of the speaker; just as in our own country today, the same word will sound quite differently depending on where the speaker lives: New England, Philadelphia, Tennessee, New York, Oklahoma. The speakers might all sound differently although saying the exact same word.

The mother syllable can also sound differently in different areas of the world; and can be written (because it was used before standardization) as ma, me, mi, mo, and mu. The German word for 'mother' is 'mutter'.

The word, 'medicine' then, comes from the mother syllable and the

Latin 'medere' which means 'to heal'. The earliest healers and doctors were Mothers: Medicine Women, Wisewomen, Shamankas, and Wiccans. They were the 'foragers', and the 'gatherers' of the Paleolithic Age. Everything organic in the immediate environment came under their scrutinizing eyes. Through trial and error and by observing the animals' feeding behaviors they learned what was good to eat and what was poisonous. They learned which plants could heal and which could kill.

They also learned about hallucinogens: mushrooms, cacti, roots, and seeds that could produce a trance-like state when ingested. In a trance, they believed they could travel freely between worlds: animal, natural, supernatural. This is probably where the common image of a witch riding a broomstick originated. Moldy rye bread eaten in extreme hunger may have contained a hallucinogenic mold called 'ergot', which gave the psychedelic sensation of flying. Since white bread was as yet unknown in the Middle Ages, Martha Corey of the Massachusetts Bay Colony and millions of women like her, may have been burned at the stake for merely eating moldy rye bread during the mass hysteria of the witch hunts.

As Shamankas, or Shamanesses, women in antiquity were responsible for re-opening the supposedly blocked energy channels of the sick person. My Chinese acupuncturist doctor uses this same principle today: she unlocks the vital 'chi' energy as it follows certain meridians (pathways) in my body. (2) The meridians were charted thousands of years ago by sages who very well may have been women. There are no written records found from this period in China, although the Chinese were already using ideograms (symbolic writings) in antiquity.

Many indigenous peoples have the belief in a cosmic energy that permeates the universe as well as each individual. Ancient Egyptians called it 'Heka', the strong spiritual force that was later deified by the invading Greeks and personified as the Goddess Hecate. Belief in the healing 'Hecate'- power spread to the Romans and northward to many Germanic tribes.

Because the letter 'C' had many pronunciations, such as k, sh, ch, s, or x, the powerful Goddess' name became 'Hexate' in Germany. The women doctors who healed in her name became known as 'hexers'.

As a child, I lived near Germans who had settled in Pennsylvania and were called the Pennsylvania Dutch erroneously (a corruption of

'Deutsch' which meant German). They practiced the folk medicine of their foremothers and used 'hex' signs on their barns to protect their animals. These were highly stylized symbols used by the women healers of the Stone Age. The symbols of the Goddess Hecate were believed to contain potent healing magic; thus the name, 'Hex' signs. The German settlers in Berks County, Pennsylvania were excellent farmers, herbalists, and veterinarians.

This same healing energy (which pervaded the universe and was believed to be especially concentrated in certain plants) was known as 'huna' in Hawaii. Hindu yogis called it 'Kundalini'.

Medicine women, priestesses, 'yoginis', as well as later priests and shamans, all healed, transferred, and balanced the life force often transferring their more abundant supply to the sick person, whose life energy was believed to be depleted. In this type of healing, the tribal belief system (religion) and medicine were closely aligned for millennia. This is what today we call 'holistic' healing: that individuals and their mind, body and environment form a seamless whole or holistic system. This alignment of mind, emotions, beliefs, and body has made a comeback in recent years in the charismatic movements of many churches, as well as in the field of alternative medicine.

This healing system utilizes natural plants and herbs, oils and massage, and many other ancient techniques from various cultures. So, in effect, medicine has come full circle returning to its prehistoric roots in the plant world at the very dawn of humanity in the Old Stone Age or Paleolithic phase c. 200,000 BC and earlier.

By the time homosapiens were living in Africa, Israel, Syria, China, Hungary, Spain, France, Algeria, England, Java, Burma, Malaysia, Thailand, and Vietnam, they were nomadic; but seemed to stay (3) "within a certain territory whose resources they knew intimately and thus could exploit with maximum effectiveness." These early humans were gatherers and hunters. The women left the campsite daily to search the surrounding area for edibles.

There are still primitive hunters and (4) gatherers living this way today in Australia, Africa, Japan, Panama, Central America, the Andes, the South Seas, the Himalayas, the Arctic, the Philippine Islands, and Brazil, although their numbers are almost depleted.

The plant world was always the domain of the women; and their tools were a sharpened stick or antlers for digging in hard soil and a sharpened stone for cutting apart roots and tubers. In the course of their daily foraging expeditions, the women came to know the habitat, growing cycles and composition of every growing thing. So it is not surprising that they also discovered the medicinal, healing properties of the plants they handled every day and brought back to their hearth fires. Nothing escaped their scrutiny; for their observations and efficiency as providers of food and medicine determined whether or not they and their children survived.

To women of the Stone Age, knowledge of the difference between edible and non-edible vegetation meant life or death. They often traveled great distances in search of food, usually with an infant and toddler in tow. For even though they spent a great deal of time planning and preparing for a hunt, there was never a guarantee that they would find an animal, or that the men would have the skill and the weapons needed to catch and to kill it. We don't even know for sure that the hunters carried their prey back to the campsite and shared it with the women, children, and elders. They may just as well have eaten it on the spot like most male animal carnivores do.

Therefore, even in societies where hunting was believed to have been practiced, the women's food-gathering still provided as much as eighty percent of the clan's food in many cases. There would hardly have been any driving motivation for the men to feel responsible for the children and the women who birthed them; for there was no concept of paternity or knowledge of the male's role in impregnation.

Because the survival of the clan or tribe often depended on the women foragers' skills in seeking out the edibles in the local environment, the women had to memorize a great deal of oral knowledge passed down from mothers to daughters before the advent of writing. The women had to develop keen eyesight and accurate discriminatory abilities in choosing the plants they would carry back to the campsite while also carrying a child. Through close observation, experimentation, and an accumulated store of knowledge passed on orally down through the generations, female foragers also became familiar with the medicinal properties of the plants they knew so well as foods.

Once again, it was the mothers who would have had the greatest incentive to find a way to lessen pain. The agony of childbirth was surely apparent to those early gatherers, hunters, and foragers. Screams of pain can go on for hours, even days, as is the case of problem births; and this most likely would have upset the equilibrium of the entire clan, making everyone tense and anxious.

Women would have been highly motivated to experiment with pain relievers or hallucinogens available in the natural environment to overcome the pain of childbirth. This may have been how narcotic substances were first found and exploited. Relieving the pain of injured hunters would also have been a priority; as well as relieving the suffering caused by accidents and aging such as a broken leg, impacted tooth, burst appendix, arthritis, kidney stones, etc.

We know that hallucinogens have been found and used by every indigenous tribe; and this may have been their first use; that is, relief from intractable pain. Substances like marijuana, pulque, peyote, hallucinogenic mushrooms, fermented beverages of all kinds (saliva was the first 'yeast') were the first drugs that induced a trance-like state or stupor in which pain was not present. Later, these hallucinogenic drugs became part of religious rituals, pointing to the early connection between healing (medicine) and religion.

The earliest known doctors were also the practitioners of religion. They were the priestesses of the (5) earliest possibly known religion, the religion of the Bear Goddess. They were also the witches and wizards of Wicca, the ancient household religion of the Stone Age, and priestess-physicians of the old Fertility Cult religion of the Neolithic, the 'wisewomen' and 'cunning men' of Paganism. They include the shamankas and shamans of indigenous tribal religions, medicine women and medicine men of Native Americans. All functioned by combining religion and the healing ceremony in a single whole worldview. These medico-religious ceremonies are still to be found today in many indigenous cultures including tribes in Africa, the Philippines, Chile, Brazil, and Siberia. To this day the dress donned by a male Siberian shaman for a healing ceremony includes attaching 'ornamental, symbolic breasts' to the front of his robe, (6) pointing to the female origins of medicine in Siberia, as elsewhere in the ancient world.

The medicine woman of the Mapuchi Indians of Chile is called a 'machi', a mother-syllable word (as is their tribal name Mapuchi, in deference to their clan mother) derived from the mammary glands of mothers, who were perhaps the very first doctors and nurses.

Medicine in Ancient Egypt and Mesopotamia

In ancient Mesopotamia (present-day Iran and Iraq), charms, religion, and magic were often used as parts of a healing ritual. Because germs were unknown before the invention of the microscope, due to their invisibility to the naked eye, the cause of illness was often attributed to 'bad air' or malevolent spirits present in the home or village. The 'bad air' concept was amazingly perceptive five thousand years ago, as we now know that many viruses are airborne and indeed make the air 'bad' for us to inhale.

Ancient Egypt provided a wealth of information about early medicine because the Egyptians kept meticulous records, many of which survived to this day. From the existing papyri we know that there were many female doctors in Egypt before 2000 BC. The Edwin Smith Surgical Papyrus (named for its' finder) contained magical incantations that were probably part of a much earlier oral tradition. (7) The voice and the hands, as well as the mind, may have been the first medical 'tools'. Women, especially mothers, may very well have first practiced this type of ancient medicine.

Surely each of us can recall an instance in our childhood when a mother or grandmother soothed our injury with her voice and hands and made the hurting stop; or at least lessened it a great deal. The healing hand was an important part of ancient medicine and survives today in jewelry as a stylized open hand worn as a pendant. I have one in my own vintage jewelry collection. It is a small gold filigree open hand made in the Middle East. This type of hand 'fetish' or 'charm' is also called the hand of Fatima or the hand of God; and is meant to offer protective magic to the wearer.

Biblical authors who described Jesus practicing 'faith healing' two thousand years ago in the Holy Land documented the 'laying-on-of-hands', as this healing modality is known. Today we might call it a 'healing touch'.

The voice was also used extensively as a healing 'tool' in antiquity. In ancient Egypt, the voice of the priestess/priest, local wise woman/doctor, or magi/magician would be called upon to give a command to the patient in an authoritative voice. As 'magical' incantations, these verbal commands invoked powerful Goddesses and Gods to rid the patient of disease. Preventive medicine, c. 3200 BC, was mainly magical. Ancient Egyptians believed 'bad air' or 'an evil wind' caused infection as the people of Mesopotamia did. Airborne viruses often cause pulmonary diseases, and the magical spells used to counteract the ever-present 'bad air' viruses were a combination of prayers, chants, blessings, affirmations, visualizations, role-playing, and invocations. All of these techniques invoked a supernatural deity; that is, the authoritative command brought the deities 'into existence and also controlled them' to provide, for instance, the cure for a stomachache. (8)

Egyptian healers/magicians/priestesses also used the homeopathic principle of fighting 'like with like'.

Scorpion Goddess' name, Sarqet, means 'she who causes one to breathe'. She would thus be persuaded to use her strong power against scorpion bites, which were an ever-present hazard and often fatal. But other, more practical remedies were available to the patient as well. The first line of defense most probably would have been the local wise woman. She would have used all of her senses to make a diagnosis and determine which bodily organ or system was causing the problem. For instance:

<u>Touch</u>: she would have taken the patient's pulse, and in the case of a wound, felt to see how hot it was and whether there was fever.

<u>Sight</u>: the skin, eyes, tongue, nails would have been closely examined, as well as any obvious injury or discoloration.

<u>Hearing</u>: by the sound of a baby's cry, a midwife would be able to tell if it would live or not. The cough or wheezing or the congested chest of a sick person, as well as the heartbeat, also give clues.

<u>Smell</u>: infections always have an identifiable smell to a trained nose.

After a diagnosis the patient would then have had access to both practical medicines as well as magico-religious rituals; what we would call traditional medicine and alternative medicine.

Magic was only one part of the interrelated knowledge that a well-to-do Egyptian matron would have had in her library of scrolls, rolled up, and kept in jars. Egyptians saw everything as connected; and magic would have been connected to religion, as well as connected to medicine, nature, and animals.

A 'lady of the house', who could read, probably would have done the doctoring for her large household staff as well as for family, friends, and neighbors. The 'lady of the manor' in Medieval Europe did this as well. Those who could read and write were rare in pre-literate societies and were considered magical for their ability to understand the enigmatic markings that we know today as writing. In her book, *Magic in Ancient Egypt*, Geraldine Pinch wrote that "literate European housewives compiled household books on remedies for a wide variety of ailments", as well as recipes for cosmetics, from the early 16th to 19th century AD. (9) It is probable that housewives in Egypt did the same.

Affirmations in Ancient Egypt

Affirmations were also used in ancient Egyptian healing rituals, just as they are today in holistic or alternative healing sessions. Three thousand years ago priestesses, nurses, and/or priest-physicians would affirm to the patient that the desired effect was already achieved, in a firm and convincing tone of voice, repeating the affirmation over and over to convince the deity as well as the patient.

The officiates in magico-medical papyri of the earliest Egyptians were often identified with the Goddess Isis, which could point to women as the earliest physicians in Egypt. It is logical to assume that women doctors would have been the ones most likely to align themselves with the female deity, in this case, the well-loved Goddess Isis.

Other deities frequently mentioned in later texts, as 'divine sponsors' were RA, Horus, and Thoth. (10) The "ideal medical practitioner had the authority to speak in the name of the gods and goddesses". The practitioner's magico-religious affirmations were probably used to impart authority and confidence to the patient taking medicine. Today, affirmations are still used as part of a holistic health regimen. "Every day, in every way, I am getting better and better" is one that I have used and found helpful.

In the ancient Leiden Papyrus, the mother giving birth was identified with the Goddess Hathor and affirmed that it was Hathor herself giving birth. This affirmation chanted over and over again, gave psychological support to the mother who may have been experiencing a particularly prolonged or difficult labor. How I wish my own doctor had addressed me as a Goddess during my own prolonged and difficult labors in birthing my six children! Adding a mythological dimension to a woman's labor and delivery would certainly have had an ennobling effect on my self-esteem in those early years of young motherhood.

Other 'magico-medical' aids used in Egypt were amulets made of special minerals, in special shapes, inscribed with special words. Many were found in children's graves indicating an increased concern for their welfare and survival. There seems to have been great concern for the health of women also; many of the recovered medical texts dealt with gynecology. Women also faced enormous risks in childbirth in the ancient world and would have needed extra protection. The amulets signified medicine in the form of that protection.

The 'heka' (spiritual force personified by the Goddess Hecate) that created and protected life, was thought to reside in rare and unusual objects: shells from the Red Sea, river pebbles shaped like a pregnant woman, cowry shells shaped like the female vulva. A steatite figurine of a young girl wearing a cowry shell belt is believed to date from the eighteenth century BC in Egypt. Cowry shells that resemble vulvas were worn in many areas of the world in antiquity, strung on cords and worn as girdles: possibly to promote fertility or ease menstrual cramps and the agony of childbirth. They are still worn today in parts of Sudan; and some even survive from antiquity, strung on leather strips. Some amulets were made of semi-precious stones in the shape of the Goddess Taweret (the hippopotamus) and other deities.

Still reproduced on jewelry today is the most well known of all Egyptian amulets, the scarab beetle. My antique scarab bracelet of jasper, jade, lapis, amber, and turquoise is one of my most cherished pieces of jewelry. The scarab design represented the deity 'Khepri', the God of Becoming; and retained its popularity and power well into Roman times, circa AD 380. Actually, it has never gone out of fashion; it is still treasured as one of the most widely identifiable symbols of the ancient world.

Amulets also took the form of knots tied in linen or leather cords to bind up/stop negative energy (spirits). Cord has always been valuable to humans; string or thread was sometimes a sacred ritual object. Strings or cords were often depicted with Goddesses, symbolizing fate or human destiny to the Egyptians, Romans, Germans, and Greeks.

Knotted cords are still used as a fetish worn by teenagers today as 'friendship' bracelets, perhaps in the same amulet-protective sense that they were worn thousands of years ago. Catholic nuns and monks wore ropes around their waists to symbolize they were bound to God by their religious vows.

Amulets in the shapes of eyes were also used to counteract the 'evil eye' of negative persons who tried to harm superstitious believers.

Curved horns, pagan symbol of the Horned God, the male generative principle, is still used as a fetish or protective amulet in agricultural areas like rural Italy, Sicily, Turkey and Greece. Belief in the 'evil eye' also persisted well into this century in rural Europe and the Middle East.

In Egypt, 'the protective power of the fearsome goddess who was the Eye of RA' was behind the wearing of eye amulets or pendants. Pendants were thought to serve as shields against evil spirits (germs). These were made of stone, carnelian, amethyst, jasper, limestone, faience, feldspar, gold, silver, turquoise, glass, linen, and papyrus. They were shaped as Goddesses, Gods, animals, fingers, hands, falcons, turtles, feet, faces, arms, pillars (phalluses), ears of corn, pairs of eyes, and scarabs, as well as other shapes that were blessed in the temples. The medical-religious practice survives today in the miniature body parts that are placed at the feet of Our Lady of Guadalupe in Catholic churches all over Mexico.

The ancient Egyptians loved symbols and invested them with much power and meaning. Perhaps the equivalent today would be religious medals blessed by a priest in church and rosaries worn by the sick or troubled. Religion seems to have been linked to medicine since time immemorial.

The Egyptian deities most often appealed to, on behalf of the sick, were Amun-RA, Thoth, and Goddess Hathor, 'who listens to prayers', as well as the all-powerful, beloved Goddess Isis. Catholics of today might pray to St. Jude (patron of hopeless cases), St. Teresa, Our Lady of Lourdes, (Mary) who is reputed to perform miracle cures, Our Lady of Fatima, (another apparition of Mary and miracle cures), Our Lady of the Snows (Mary), Our Lady of Knock, Ireland, (Mary) and the Mesoamerican Virgin of Guadalupe, (Mary).

Because the ancient Egyptians left a legacy of written records reaching far back into prehistory, I have used their civilization as an example of the types of services ancient doctors may have provided in the late Stone Age. Mothers may have been the first doctors because of the need for ways to make their babies well when they were sick. A crying, unhappy, uncomfortable infant in pain was certainly an effective incentive to cure the baby, just as it is today. The mothers would have needed substances to pacify a sleepless baby, to ease the pain and itching of insect bites and rashes, to reduce a fever, to halt diarrhea and vomiting, to kill body lice, mites, intestinal worms, and parasites, to cure constipation and colic, and the myriad other irritations that make babies cry to get our attention.

The mothers' intimate knowledge of their own bodies during menstruation, pregnancy, childbirth, and lactation; as well as their intimate knowledge of the bodies of their infants and children, and the plant world from which the first medicines derived, led me to believe that women would have had the strongest motivation to discover and practice medicine.

Because I am writing of women's contributions to the human race, I will not include men's involvement in medicine, which has been well documented and highly respected. So well respected in fact, that physicians have attained god-like status in almost every society. This is well deserved; but the time frame of which I write did not include much of the scientific knowledge we have today, especially the knowledge of the male's role in reproduction.

It is quite possible that, in humanity's infancy, women were seen as god-like or even as Goddesses because of their ability to create new life, bleed at will (men weren't able to menstruate), and produce a life-sustaining beverage (milk) from their breasts. Mothers and their infants may have been central to the clan; having a baby was probably the most admirable feat that anyone (man or woman) could perform. Later, killing would come to be seen as the most incredibly brave act.

But for millennia, women would have been held in awe for their magical ability to create new life and breast milk to sustain it. The mother-doctors would have known from information passed down to them orally from previous generations of mothers, how to survive the serious risks of childbirth. They could have transferred this inherited knowledge to the curing of men's illnesses as well.

Today we refer to this instinctive female knowledge as 'old wives' tales' or folk medicine. Even though we may dismiss these old-fashioned remedies, from our lofty perch of 20th century science, it is well to remember that much of it worked, or we wouldn't be here today to question it. There was a hidden world of female magical, religious, and practical medicine that has not been well documented in standard literary texts because the medicines themselves did not survive, being organic; and because our ancient ancestresses did not leave written records.

All societies were still pre-literate; but the women practitioners of the healing arts had their own system of memory aids (such as knots in string, beads, symbols, pebbles) to help them remember one herb from another and its use. Masks, female figurines, sistrums (tambourine drums), charms, amulets, textiles, pieces of knotted strings and cloths are found frequently in archaeological digs; but the written texts that would validate the medicinal use of such objects have not been found since there was no writing as we know it before the Bronze Age.

However, we do know that someone was performing successful cranial surgery in the period preceding the Bronze Age, the Neolithic (farming) Age of 5100-4900 BC. In the French region of Alsace, the skeleton of a fifty-year old male was recovered showing the removal of a rectangle of bone from the top of the cranium using 'flint or metal blades by drilling a series of small holes, making intersecting incisions, or scraping through the bone.' This operation is called 'trepanation' (11) and is still performed today in certain African communities including western Kenya where it is done to relieve pressure from skull fractures.

In the magical-religious context of the ancient world of medicine, in which women played the central part, it would have been done to cure headaches, epilepsy, tumors, or mental illness.

Women may well have been surgeons seven thousand years ago. In removing babies through emergency cesarean operations, Neolithic midwives may have learned a great deal about surgical procedures. We know that the cranial surgery of at least one patient in the Neolithic Age was successful, because the skull showed evidence of long term healing, meaning the patient survived the ordeal, was cared for by other clan members, and lived several years longer.

Medieval Medicine

In this chapter I will attempt to list some of the natural remedies that were recorded in the medieval period, c. AD 1400, and which were probably used centuries earlier. Peasant women in Medieval Europe, besides tending the fields, weaving the textiles, caring for the animals, and bearing children, had the added responsibility of caring for the sick. A widow might be hired as a nurse, 'to gather herbs, brew them, and care for a sick wife.' (12) Dressed in black 'widows weeds', these impoverished, helpful, practical nurses came to be vilified as 'witches' during religious persecutions.

Women were the pharmacists, nurses, and physicians for their families. They used the plants, savin and rue, to sweeten the air and to keep away the fleas and lice that plagued the family during the long winter months when they could not bathe. Peasant women knew how to mix the juice of the houseleek and sage with water to ease the itching and pain of the insect bites. While they did not have access to diagnostic tests, they knew which diseases to treat by the presence of certain symptoms: that is, fever, cough, cloudy eyes, headaches, abdominal pain, swelling, bleeding, discharges, rashes. They relied on intuition and knowledge passed from generation to generation. They could, like the women in thirteenth century France, call on the services of the village wisewomen, an elder acknowledged to have special skill with herbs, "who knew rituals and prayers that could cure." (13) Medical wisewomen (also called 'witches') were respected for their vast knowledge of plants, herbs, and palliatives. Before there were pharmacies, people turned to nature to cure every ailment.

Healing was a specialized art, and the wisewoman 'doctor' had to have a wide range of practical solutions to every physical (and often spiritual or psychological) problem. Of course, the archetypal feminine therapies of tender care, gentle healing touch, massage, and empathy were useful as well. Midwives were especially valued for their specialized knowledge of childbirth with its attendant hazards. Midwives and wisewomen healers were usually paid using the barter system before money came into common use among the peasantry. A blanket, length of woven fabric, eggs, cheese, wine, a metal pot, anything metal (such as a tool), might have been the method of payment. Sometimes an animal would be given in payment for medical services. Often the services were 'gratis' as the peasant population worldwide often existed at the barest subsistence level.

But all of this changed drastically when the universities began educating men in the science of medicine and its practice became financially rewarding. By denying women access to the universities and by forbidding anyone but university-trained physicians to practice medicine in Italy and later throughout Europe, the wisewomen were effectively barred from servicing their country folk and even their animals.

Medicine-women, 'witches', and 'hexers' were the earliest veterinarians, serving animals as well as people in their ancient, time-honored ways. Animals were essential to human survival; as they were killed and eaten in the long winter months when there were no crops and farmers had limited resources for preserving food.

In Western Europe, November was known as 'Blodmonath' or 'Blood Month' when the household animals were slaughtered so that they wouldn't die of starvation in winter (before it was known that cattle could survive on hay and other dried grasses). The tradition of feasting in November, which we call 'Thanksgiving', comes from this ancient ritual, as there would have been plenty of fresh meat available for neighbors and kin when an animal was butchered.

Midwifery and doctoring was essential for the animals' health; for it would have meant that the family would survive as well. The ironic twist of fate is that these same 'witches' (wisewomen, midwives, medicine-women, hexers) were forbidden to practice the very science they had discovered and shared freely (by writing manuals of their herbal remedies and techniques).

Trotula, a physician from Salerno, Italy wrote the first published European medical guide, 'Concerning the Disorders of Women', which was widely used in both manuscript and printed version into the sixteenth century. She had very good advice for women, like sewing tears in the vagina with silk thread and using poultices for breast abscesses. "But having written such excellent texts, midwives had given over their last advantage." (14)

The 'new' medical specialty of gynecology was created but excluded women by effectively barring them from the guilds, academies, university degrees, patronage, and licensing. Church and state, working hand in hand, systematically excluded women from all but the least prestigious areas of medicine. Only in the late nineteenth century would a small number of women again be admitted to the practice of medicine.

The Church, during the Inquisition of the Middle Ages, decided that the 'witches' or medicine-women who had inherited the art of making 'simples' (herbal remedies) from the Stone Age, were 'heretics' and no longer qualified to practice their ancient skills. With the cooperation of the rulers of Western Europe, the British Isles, Ireland, and Scandinavia, medicine became an exclusive brotherhood, and an extremely profitable profession.

Midwives especially were the targets of the wrath of the Medieval Inquisitors. Because of their knowledge of reproduction midwives were able to help women regulate the size of their families by the use of contraceptive herbs, spermicides, and cervical barriers. As a last resort, they could perform abortions. (15) Peasant women in Europe used "douches, purges, spermicides like salt, honey, oil, tar, mint juice, and cabbage seed." Some abortifacients like lead and ergot (moldy rye grain) were effective but dangerous. With enough lead ingested, a woman became permanently sterile.

As Anderson and Zinsser writes in 'A History of Their Own', "desperate pregnant women tried douches or teas of rosemary, myrtle, coriander, willow leaves, balsam, myrrh, clover seeds, parsley, and animal urine." It is doubtful if any of these substances succeeded in dislodging the fetus; but one can get a feeling of the level of desperation in peasant women of the Middle Ages whose meager two-acre land allotment could not possibly support many children and also pay the wealthy landowner's taxes.

Vaginal barriers such as beeswax and linen rags were hardly more effective. Many actions to prevent impregnation were also tried: jumping up and down after intercourse, drinking cold liquids, boiling herbs and letting the hot steam enter the cervix, opening the cervix with a spindle, drinking vinegar, and also massaging the abdomen strenuously.

Contraception in Ancient Egypt, Greece, Rome

The oldest records of contraceptive techniques are found in the medical papyri of nineteenth to eleventh centuries BC. There were vaginal barriers in use (tampons) that were used to prevent the sperm from entering; and 'when the tampon was saturated with acacia gum, honey, or crocodile feces', it was believed to kill the sperm.

Greco-Roman women relied on many contraceptive potions. All prescriptions were originally women's recipes, prepared at their hearths. One such recipe called for "a concoction of rue, which was a widely used abortifacient, attar of roses and aloe." This was certainly an improvement over crocodile feces: but it may not have been as effective. Another mixture called for panax juice, rue seed, and cyrenaican juice blended with wax and served in wine. Still another recipe/prescription consisted of wallflower seed, myrtle, myrrh, and white pepper dissolved in wine, to be drunk for three days. Another mixture called for sour honey with gillyflower seeds and cow parsnip. All were used both to prevent conception and to induce abortions. They were said to lead to severe irritations in the head and digestive tract as well as to vomiting.

While these recipe prescriptions may seem ridiculous from our twentieth century vantage point, we can plainly see that the women of 330 BC in Rome and Greece, women of 1800 BC in Egypt and Mesopotamia (present day Iran and Iraq), as well as women of AD 1400 in Europe, had the same concerns as women of today. That is, how to control conception so that the children brought forth would be welcome and able to survive in a frightening world full of hazards. Hazards such as infant mortality, starvation, fatal insect bites (scorpions and spiders in Egypt), pestilence and plagues, were prevalent in those times before antibiotics.

Unfortunately, many of these early contraceptives and abortifacients did not work, and infants were born to single mothers as well as to married women who were forbidden to keep their newborns as in parts of China today. Infanticide, the last resort, was practiced from earliest recorded history. It wasn't called 'infanticide' but went under the euphemism of 'exposure'. The newborn was placed on a raft of rushes and floated on water, which was believed to transport it to the local divinity in Egypt, Middle East, and Ireland in prehistoric ages. In areas with no rivers or streams nearby, the infant was abandoned on a hillside and could be rescued by infertile couples.

In China, it was said that midwives prepared a box of ashes to be placed next to the birthing bed. If the newborn was female, she was placed face down in the ashes. In many countries, females were less desirable than boys because of economic conditions. Girls would eventually require marriage dowries, which could bankrupt a poor family living on the edge of survival. (16)

Another drastic measure taken in the Middle Ages in England and Europe was to pay a wet nurse in the country to breast feed the newborn; and then stop the payments. In this way, the birth parents were removed from the death and the loss was less profoundly felt.

Unwanted pregnancies have plagued women from the beginning of time. It is only recently that medicine has been able to offer a foolproof (almost) contraceptive, as in the birth-control pill. Perhaps if women's experimentation with herbal spermicides had not been rudely interrupted by the witches' holocaust of the fourteenth to the seventeenth centuries AD in the western world, when almost every woman with medical knowledge was killed, women today would have a much healthier alternative for their reproductive choices. They would not have had to resort to hotly debated abortions, which are always done as a last resort and with a very heavy heart.

The Book of Simple Medicine

In Medieval Europe, AD 1151, the Abbess (the superior) of a convent in Bingen, Germany, an extraordinarily gifted Catholic nun by the name of Hildegarde, wrote treatises on medicine and natural science. In her *Book of Simple Medicine* "she listed almost three hundred herbs that were useful for healing, telling when to pick them, and giving their medicinal uses" writes Anderson and Zinsser in 'A History of Their Own'. "She described animals, plants, and rocks in her natural science book." In the 'Book of Simple Medicine', "she catalogued forty seven different diseases speculating on their causes and possible cures."

Although German was her native tongue, she wrote in Latin, the universal language of the Roman Catholic church and the sciences. She used ancient as well as twelfth century AD texts as her sources, explaining that "disease came from disruptions to the body's equilibrium, and suggested insightful remedies centuries ahead of her time, including the circulation of the blood, the ties between sugar and diabetes, nerve action to the brain, and contagion". Her medical treatises were in addition to songs, symphonies, poetry, and "illuminated manuscripts describing her visions of the harmony of the universe, including the inter-relationships and interactions between human beings and the cosmos". She was widely acclaimed and traveled long distances to lecture to nuns, monks, priests, popes, and emperors.

But clerical attitudes to women in the Catholic Church became more rigid and repressive by the twelfth century and religious women were advised to keep silence and remain cloistered behind convent walls, according to Anderson and Zinsser. So, one of the few avenues of learning and accomplishment open to Medieval women; the abbeys, priories, and convents of the Catholic world, effectively shut them up for hundreds of years until the sixteenth century when once again, educated religious sisters would be awarded the title 'Doctor of Letters' but not the power that went along with it.

Other Medieval nuns who are remembered for their keen intelligence are Mechtilde of Magdeburg and Julian of Norwich.

Nature's Medicine Chest

Women whose domain was always the plant world since the beginning of time, learned to exploit every organic substance in their environment for its healing, curing and pain killing potential. Women were highly valued for their medical expertise in ancient societies before medicine became a highly paid male specialization. Women used nature's own medicine chest, the natural world all around them. Even insects were used if they could be of help in treating disease. Leeches are walking chemical factories that are still used today to eat infectious blood in a wound that is resistant to antibiotics and penicillin.

In days of yore, people would go into streams barelegged and let the leeches cover their legs, then knock them off into containers and sell them to patients, physicians, midwives, etc.

Tree fungi were used as an antibiotic for treating bladder ailments and tuberculosis. Pieces of birch fungus threaded on fur strips were found with the remarkable preserved body of the 'Iceman', who lived during the Copper Age, 3300 BC, and whose body was found in the Alps several years ago. He is believed by scientists to have been a traveler or hunter caught in a blizzard in the Alps fifty three hundred years ago, carrying the fungus strip in case of injury. His body was encased in ice for over five thousand years, and has provided researchers with a wealth of information. My companion and I traveled together to the great museums of the western world to study archaeological remains, and goddess figurines, and we observed the iceman in the British Museum.

Fungus Mycelium is a leather-like layer under the bark of certain dead trees. It was also used by the aboriginal Ainus of Japan as an antibiotic after surgery.

Sphagnum moss has also long been noted for its healing properties. The Inuit of Alaska and other Native American tribes used it. Native Eskimo/Inuit religious healers of today (17) use a falsetto voice, high pitched like a woman's, to reach the realm of the supernatural, perhaps in imitation of earlier times when their women evoked the Goddess of Sea Mammals who alone had the power to ease human suffering.

In England, bathing in peat bogs was believed to alleviate rheumatism. Warm springs were used by Native American warriors who bathed in them to heal their wounds, hundreds of years ago. The water in Warm Springs, Georgia, was thought to cure polio and many patients went there to bathe in the curative springs, including President Franklin Delano Roosevelt.

One of the best known medicines, aspirin, is derived from the bark of the willow tree, which was probably chewed for pain relief in antiquity, although there has been some evidence that ancient medicine women knew how to make pills and rolled them by hand. Today the willow bark is chemically reproduced in laboratories as aspirin, a substance with many beneficial uses.

We know that Neolithic people chewed gum made from the sap of the birch tree, c. 4000 BC. Pieces of gum with tooth marks were found in an alpine community on Lake Zurich, Switzerland, where a Neolithic village prospered.

The word, 'birch', derives from 'bear', possibly indicating that the early lake-dwellers of the Swiss Alps observed bears chewing the tree bark in spring. When the bears awakened after the winter hibernation, they often ate greens like dandelions and tree bark to jump-start their digestion and elimination. There is some evidence that Neolithic mothers regarded bears with respect as 'nurses' or bearers of the knowledge of medicinal plants.

Digitalis, a heart regulator, was derived from foxglove, a common garden flower; and belladonna provided hyoscyamine, both still in use today. The sap of the aloe plant, a succulent, was known to relieve burns and I still use it today on skin rashes or burns. I keep an aloe plant on my windowsill in the kitchen and I can have instant pain relief by snipping off a piece of leaf and letting the juice soothe a burn.

Marigolds are still used in lotions to soothe the skin. The well-known drug Valium derives from the root of the valerian flower. Ancient women knew that it paralyzed the nervous system and could be used in small doses to ease the pain of childbirth. They also knew that in small doses it had a tranquilizing effect, the purpose for which valium is used today.

St. John's Wort is another common garden weed used for centuries by healers. Today it is used to treat depression and anxiety in .3% extract sold in drugstores. Researchers are also looking into its possibilities for postponing Alzheimer's disease. Its Latin botanical name is 'hypericum'.

One-fourth of all drugs manufactured today come from the plant world and long-term studies are beginning in the United States to test the efficacy of many more plant derivatives.

"Twentieth century scientists are gaining respect for the peasant women's knowledge of when to pick, where to cut, and how to preserve the many herbs, roots, and blossoms that she used. Changes in temperature and light from day to night, from season to season, alter the chemical properties of many plants" write Anderson and Zinsser, "for example, the yield of poppies is four times greater at nine AM than at nine PM". (18)

For every ache or illness there was a remedy to be found in nature, before the Age of Science. Childhood illnesses were especially threatening because infant mortality was very high and the children who survived infancy needed to live. A cough, fever, sore throat, or congestion were very serious and mothers or the village wisewomen needed to know what worked.

Calamine tea, saltwater gargles; lemon juice mixed with honey, even 'inhaling the smoke of burning coltsfoot leaves' might be used as the first line of defense. Ginger or mint might be used for stomachaches. Mother always kept a small jar of honey and lemon juice in the refrigerator, which mercifully soothed a sore throat; a practice I followed while raising my own six children.

My mother used to make a nasty preparation of a hot mustard plaster applied to my little girl's chest with a warm flannel cover. While the medicine was disagreeable, her loving ministries were the 'healing touch' that always worked. The very fact that I am here today is a tribute to her tender, loving care and knowledge of natural remedies.

Oil of cloves would be soothingly applied to a throbbing tooth, warm camphor oil to a painful ear. A whiff of ammonia stopped a dizzy spell or faintness. In a pinch, lavender would also work. Gentian blue, derived from flowers, or wormwood, killed pinworms when we played in the dirt and forgot to wash our hands, and then ate the tiny parasites that took up lodging in our intestines and itched unmercifully during the night.

For diarrhea, tansy leaf tea might offer relief from painful cramps. For menstrual cramps, a thimble full of rum or brandy was the preferred remedy before Lydia Pinkham's 'Little Pink Pills' for women's monthly problems appeared on druggists' shelves.

Of course many 'cures' were silly and may have worked simply by the power of suggestion. For instance, the day I rubbed a raw potato on the warts on my hand and then buried it. I swear it worked when I was twelve. And so did many other folk remedies. Though we may chuckle at them today with our superior scientific knowledge, we need to remember humans and animals were kept alive and their sufferings eased for millennia by medicinals or 'simples' prepared and administered by housewives.

Without their knowledge and skill none of us would be here today. For this at least we owe them a wholehearted - Thank You!

It is with a sense of delight that I scan the shelves of 'nature's remedies' now filling more and more shelves in the pharmacy and food store. It seems we are coming full circle (to use the metaphor of an ancient female womb symbol); back to an awareness of the potential health benefits of the plant world, an area our foremothers knew extremely well and used to full advantage for their families and communities.

Women's kitchen gardens were the first pharmacies, their recipes were the first prescriptions, their kitchen stoves (or earlier hearth fires) were the first research laboratories, the women themselves were the first doctors, chemists, scientists, veterinarians, herbalists, pharmacists, naturopaths, midwives, and surgeons.

The First Hospitals

Women who became nuns in the Catholic Church of Europe, c. AD 900, may have opened the first hospitals. Hotel Dieu, (House of God), was begun by nuns in Paris AD 1240. Nuns often set aside rooms in their convents to house the sick, the homeless, unwed mothers, the orphaned, the dying, and the elderly. From the thirteenth century on, in Italy and France, nuns received permission from the Pope to serve in public hospitals for the poor. Nurses are still called 'Sisters' in England even though they are not members of religious orders; probably a carry-over from early times when priestesses were also physicians and religion and medicine were one. (19)

In AD 1600, the Sisters of Charity had seventy convents in France and Poland; and were the principal nursing and charitable order of France. They nursed in hospitals as well as on the battlefields. Europe was constantly at war in the Middle Ages as independent principalities fought over territory and resources. Women of the French court c, AD 1616 sometimes used their own manor houses as orphanages and as centers for feeding the poor, much like our soup kitchens of today. Noblewomen founded monasteries and homes for the poor. Sometimes they used their fortunes to found a religious order, as did the Baroness de Chantal, Foundress of the Order of the Visitation, AD 1622. By the time of her death in 1641, she had founded eighty-eight convents throughout Europe, dedicated to nursing the sick and to teaching. (20) In *Causes et Curae: Book of Medicine Carefully Arranged*, AD 1151, The German nun Hildegarde catalogued the 47 most common diseases of her day and suggested mind-body connections centuries ahead of her time.

In my personal music collection, I have tapes of Hildegarde's music as interpreted by Richard Souther and sung by soprano Emily Van Evera at St. Andrews Church, Toddington, England. The tapes, "Vision" and "Feather on the Breath of God" have a haunting spirituality and other worldly feeling that is communicated to the listener. In her own words, Hildegarde wrote, "Underneath all the texts, all the sacred psalms and canticles, these watery varieties of sounds and silences, terrifying, mysterious, whirling and sometimes gestating gently, must somehow be felt in the pulse, ebb, and flow of the music that sings in me." To listen to Hildegarde von Bingen's music is to have a profoundly healing experience.

Later nuns were forbidden to travel long distances, as they sometimes did in order to make religious pilgrimages to sacred sites in the Holy Land and elsewhere. They were not allowed to teach boys, and were forbidden to attend the universities.

Since physicians were by this time required to be university trained, women were effectively precluded from practicing medicine, even midwifery which had naturally been a specialty of women. However, wealthy noblewomen still continued to join the convents, abbeys, and priories; and the women of Europe's royal families continued to found monasteries, convents, poorhouses, and hospitals. They were Margaret of Bourgogne, Blanche of Castille, Queen of France, Elizabeth of Aragon, Queen of Portugal, Isabella, Queen of Spain, and Margaret Beaufort, mother of King Henry VII. (21)

By AD 1850, over one hundred thousand sisters nursed in prisons, military hospitals, and their own Catholic hospitals as well as public hospitals. Noble women and Catholic nuns may well have started the first infirmaries, clinics, hospitals, orphanages, old age homes, hospices, and abused women's shelters, homeless shelters, sanctuaries for political refugees, and schools. (22)

Women as Surgeons

Although 'surgeon' had a quite different meaning in the Middle Ages, as 'one who specialized in bloodletting', it was definitely a very skilled specialty. Surgeons' guilds (unions) were open to women in France, Italy, England, and Germany from the thirteenth to seventeenth centuries. Female surgeons removed tumors, amputated limbs, and removed fetuses that had died during labor and were stuck in the birth canal. (23)

In Paris, by AD 1292, women were listed as 'barber surgeons', (barbers sometimes performed medical functions as well). The French government allowed widows to perform as barber surgeons if this had been their husband's profession and they had been their husband's assistants. When the London Parliament licensed surgeons in AD 1511, there were thirty-seven English women listed as surgeons. During and up to this timeframe, thirteenth to seventeenth centuries AD, women practiced more than one medical specialty. (24)

Contemporaries called such women 'dochters' or 'doctors' which has a female origin and means 'daughter' in German. As her mother's right hand, the daughter of the family would often be called upon to 'doctor' family members when their mothers were busy. Some were trained by their university degreed husbands or fathers to set bones, act as midwives, and serve as physician's assistants. In the seventeenth century Lady Anna Halkett acted as surgeon, midwife, and doctor to the King of Scotland. But as the universities graduated more men, guilds established regulations, and cities required licensing of doctors and women were eventually excluded from professional certification. (25)

The women doctors found themselves marginalized, even though they had much practical experiences of the vast knowledge of the curative powers of plants, and first hand knowledge of gynecology and obstetrics. Their cures were attested by the townspeople. A palliative hands-on treatment of poultices, purges, and salves, and other practices built their reputations as healers. To be a physician, to receive the degree of Doctor of Physick would eventually become an impossible dream for European women who had always taken primary responsibility for the medical care of their families as well as caring for the soldiers injured in wars and tending to the sick of the villages.

Housewives consulted their books of 'Physick' or the village wisewomen. Eventually even the wisewomen were eliminated. They were called 'witches' and burned at the stake and their knowledge of medicine burned with them. The Papal edict that outlawed Wicca as heresy, also outlawed surgery. This may be why surgeons called themselves 'barbers'.

Not until the nineteenth century would women of even the highest rank have less hazardous experiences of childbearing. Queens and commoners alike, until the late 1800's, along with their infants, would begin to die in unprecedented numbers in childbirth and its' complications. The chain of knowledge, forged in the Stone Age, and passed on from mother-to-daughter for millennia, had finally been broken and silenced by the patriarchs.

Goddesses of Medicine

Aja

She is the African Goddess of Health of the Yoruba tribe of Nigeria. She is a benevolent forest goddess who teaches her followers how to use medicinal herbs. The Goddess Oshun is also revered by Yorubans as a bestower of health on her devotees. As a Water Goddess, she cures the sick and imparts fertility with her sweet water. Healing waters have a long association with health. Today we call healing by water, 'hydrotherapy'. 26)

Anna Perenna

This Roman Goddess of Health and Medicine was known as the 'Giver of Life, Health, and Abundance'. (27) Her name, 'Anna', contained the sacred syllable 'an' which always signified 'abundance'. 'Anna' is also the feminine of 'annus', or year, from which the word 'annual' is derived. As 'Perenna', she personified the 'past year', or the 'perennial'. She was the bringer of health through an abundance of good food and herbs. She was already ancient in Roman times, and may have been an indigenous Etruscan deity of Italy. The Goddess Anna Purna or Anapurna of India has an identical legend, suggesting ancient contacts between India and Indo-Europeans.

Bona Dea

Her name means Good Goddess and she was the 'Goddess of Healing' in the religion of the Roman women who were the only ones allowed to perform her rituals. However, men were able to receive healing from her through the efforts of the women in their lives. (28) As was typical of Earth Mother Goddesses, the serpent was her symbol. It is indicative of medicine's long female associations that the serpent, that ancient guardian of the women's grain fields, is still used today as the symbol of medicine, the Caduceus.

Corn Mother

Many Native American corn-growing tribes personified the corn as a woman probably because women, the food-gatherers, also became the food-planters or farmers.

It was believed by the Cheyenne, Pawnee, Hidatsa, and Plains Indians that the Corn Mother Goddess taught her people many things. She taught them how to plant corn, how to study the sky, and how to make medicine bundles. The study of the movements of the sun, moon, and stars was of crucial importance to farmers; and the one who was able to compute these cycles mathematically, achieved high status in the tribe. This person would have been an astrologer-priestess, or 'medicine-woman'. She would also have known which herbs to carry in her 'doctor kit' or 'medicine bundle', as it was called by Native Americans.

The legend of the Corn Mother clearly points to female origins of agriculture, astrology, math, and medicine in these cultures.

Corn Mother was also known as Cherokee Maize (corn) Mother, Creek Maize Mother, Natchez Maize Mother, and Tewa Corn Mother. To the Hopi, Kachina Mana is the Corn Maiden who gave them white corn, which is the 'most sacred of the corns'. In the Greco-Roman world, Goddess Demeter was the Corn Mother. (29)

Demeter

'Meter'- the Greek word for 'mother' is also a root word for 'medicine'. We can deduce that mothers in the dawn of humanity were the ones most likely to administer medicine or health (in its widest sense) to their infants and children. Mothers would also have been the ones most likely to have intimate knowledge of the physical body because of the close observation of their own bodily processes: menstruation, copulation, pregnancy, childbirth, and lactation.

Because of the women's food gathering skills they would also have been familiar with everything growing in their environments; and would most likely have been motivated to use plants medicinally in the care of a mother in labor pain, a sick infant or other clan member (injured hunter or elderly person). The Greek Goddess Demeter, 'the Mother', is thus associated with the entire life cycle, from birth, through time, to death, and back to life again in the typical agricultural life-death-life cycle.

In 600 BC, Goddess Demeter in a Homeric hymn was portrayed as nurse of the Queen's son, an indication that women were known as caretakers and healers of the sick in classical Greek culture and earlier. (30) (Homer drew on earlier oral sources for much of his writings.)

Drude
(Druide)

This Germanic Goddess of Northern Europe was associated with trees that were believed to have their own individual souls or spirits. These spirits, called 'dryads' by the Greeks, were believed to be female in most cultures. They were thought to be incarnated in a bark body, and the bark of trees was known to have many healing properties. (31) Aspirin was derived from the bark of the willow tree originally. It is now chemically reproduced in laboratories.

There are many scientists at work with computers today, trying to artificially duplicate the chemical compositions of plants and trees, especially those found in the Amazon Rain Forest.

The Druidesses and Druids were the highly respected medical practitioners, mathematicians, and astrologers of the Celtic tribes of Europe, British Isles, and Ireland.

Eastre
or Eostre

Eostre was the Anglo-Saxon Goddess of Spring and new beginnings, and also the Greek Goddess of Dawn. (32) She gave her name to the direction from which the sun begins each new day (East), as well as the spring festival of rebirth known as Easter. She was an agricultural Goddess of health whose name survives in the Jewish Passover as 'Esther'. The northern Germanic tribes of antiquity knew of the strong influence of the sun on health and wellbeing. Thus Eastre, She-Who-Brought-Back-The-Sun-Each-Morning was associated with health, that is, the healing power of herbs and sun. Goddess Eostre/Esther also gave her name to the springtime mating cycle of female animals, estrus, and to the female hormone estrogen.

Erzuli

A Caribbean Moon Goddess who was brought to Haiti by slaves from West Africa. She was revered as a bestower of health and beauty. She sometimes showed herself as a water snake, as symbolized on the universal symbol of medicine, the Caduceus. Erzuli was mistress of the waters of health of the Yorubans of West Africa. (33)

Ganga

To Hindus, this Goddess was the personification of the beloved River Ganges that flows through India. She was probably an ancient animating spirit of water. (34) The tributary at Benares is the most sacred spot of the Ganges River. Indians still make pilgrimages to her there, as 'Mother' Ganges has promised to wash away all sins of devout Hindus who immerse themselves in her purifying, healing waters. Women bathe daily in her waters, fully dressed, for health benefits such as freedom from emotional suffering.

Hexe

The name of this Germanic Goddess was also used as a nickname for 'hexers' (healers) who were able to use herbal remedies as well as affirmations and incantations to restore health and 'nullify spells of enemies'. (35)

Professional hex practitioners of Germany and Pennsylvania used very ancient formulas probably derived from Egypt originally, as was their name, which was taken from the Goddess Hecate. The 'hexers' were also very highly regarded as the earliest veterinarians in the farmlands of Eastern Pennsylvania.

Hygeia

Hygeia was the Grecian Goddess of health and healing, from whom we derived the word 'hygiene'. Medicine was closely aligned to religion in the ancient world. Even our English word, 'health', derives from a German word, 'heiliq', which means holy. Hallow, hale, heal, health, holly and holy are words derived from this German root. The holly tree was considered sacred by the ancient Celts and is memorialized in a British Christmas carol, 'The Holly and Ivy'. My mother's maiden name was Holley, which was fitting, for she had a soothing, healing touch, and an aura of holiness about her person. I named my youngest daughter, Holley, to honor our mother. Holley entered the healing profession as a highly trained Nuclear Technologist. She inherited her Grandmother's soothing manner and compassion.

In prehistoric times to be 'heiliq' also meant to be 'without impairment'. (36) Hygeia, the Greek Goddess of Health is portrayed in Victorian scrip art.

Isis

Goddess Isis of Egypt, the Savior, was closely associated with medicine. There was a hidden world of female magic, religion, and medicine that was not well documented in the standard literary texts of ancient Egypt. Many artifacts found in burials and archaeological digs, such as masks, statuettes of dancers, sistrums (tambourines), enigmatic amulets, pieces of knotted string, and cloth have not been associated with any written documents; but may very well have been used by women doctors, especially midwives and temple priestesses.

Goddesses Hathor and Isis were probably the most frequently called upon by women. Seventeen hundred years <u>after</u> her worship was supposed to have died out, Isis retained her reputation for helping women with fertility problems. (37)

Goddess Isis, frequently depicted as nursing her 'holy child' Horus, was the protectress of birth and nursing. Just as today, women in ancient Egypt risked death when giving birth. Some of the hazards of childbirth were: miscarriage, a deformed child, stillbirth, difficult prolonged labor, hemorrhage, multiple births, birth canal trauma, sickness, injury, and/or death from childbed fever. Before antibiotics and sterilization, this infection called sepsis was a long agonizing death of the new mother. It is small wonder that incantations, amulets, charms, and spells were invoked by nurses, midwives, priestesses, and doctors in the birthing chambers. My own life was almost lost twice from hemorrhages after prolonged, difficult births.

Ix-Chel

The Mayan (Mexican) Goddess of Magic, Health, Healing, Love, and Sexuality was known as Ix-Chel. In her benevolent aspect she was the Goddess of weaving, curing, childbirth, and sexual relations. In art she was sometimes 'depicted with eagle claws and crowned with feathers'. (38)

In the ancient Mayan belief system, however, good and bad were not clearly separated; but were intertwined in every person as well as in deities. In her malevolent form, Goddess Ix-Chel could also cause destruction with water, as well as healing.

Kwan Yin

She is the Buddhist deity who is much loved wherever Buddhism has flourished, especially India, Japan, and China. As China's most powerful Holy Mother of Compassion, she hears those who cry out to her in pain. The Goddess of mercy, education, and knowledge, she protects the health of women and children especially by giving them the knowledge of healing herbs. (39)

Macha

This Goddess was known as the ancestral Mother Goddess of Family and Tribes in Celtic Ireland. Many non-Christian deities were three-fold or trinities (three persons in one). Reciting facts in sets of three was a time-honored device to help pre-literate societies remember their oral histories. Macha became a trinity known as the triple Morrigan; and turned into a frightening death Goddess by the warlike Celts. In her death-bringing aspect, she turned herself into a raven. The 'curse of Macha' was greatly feared in Irish legend.

Before the arrival of the Celts, Macha was the Great Mother Goddess of Ireland. She may have been a Queen of the Galioi (Gaela or Gaelica) a group of aboriginal peoples of Ireland whose successors deified her. Known as the Macha of the Red Tresses, (a red-haired Queen), who was credited with establishing the first hospital in Ireland. Because Ireland was isolated and virtually 'timeless' for almost 1000 years, it is difficult to date events and deities there.

Until c. 485 AD when Patrick brought with him the Roman alphabet in his attempt to Christianize the Celts, there was no written literature. We know, however, that Goddesses were prominent in Irish belief, probably because the arts of civilization were the women's domain and they would naturally appeal to female deities for help with their problems. Celtic Ireland was a warrior chieftain society, and the men were engaged mostly in feuds, cattle raids, tribal warfare and the like. St. Patrick called them his 'warrior children'.

Goddess Macha was warrior, queen, and deity. As a legendary athlete/warrior, she was said to have been able to outrun all the kings' horses.

As a deity, she was credited with bringing the healing arts to women. As Macha of the Red Tresses she was said to have been 'the seventy-sixth monarch of Ireland who built the first hospital in Ireland four-hundred years before the first hospital in Rome'. (40)

Originally, as fertile Earth Mother, the entire landscape of Ireland was sacred to her and her people. These were river, forest, mountain, spring, hill, tree, and lake divinities. These were revered long after Christianity was introduced. Trees were especially sacred to the Celts and were carried in festivals as the abode of the Goddess of Vegetation. Trees growing on ancestor's graves or beside a sacred well of the Goddess were especially venerated. A rag or article of clothing was hung on the tree by someone who needed healing; and the healing power of the Goddess then passed from her sacred well to the tree and to the sufferer. Springs and wells were equally divine, especially if they had medicinal value, such as hot springs or sulphur springs. The Goddess of such a watery site was considered beautiful 'and their personality was deeply impressed on the people'.

Macha's shrine was Emain Macha, the capital of Ulster. With the arrival of Christianity, the 'spirits of places' were gradually stripped of their divinity and trivialized, becoming the 'fey or faeries' of nature who still survive in 'Fairy Tales'.

The beloved Irish Goddess Brigid was also credited with medicine from the plant world. She was usually shown holding a cauldron in which she prepared the 'magical' recipes (prescriptions) that cured all human ills.

Masai Moon Goddess

She is the Goddess of Health and Healing of the Masai Tribe of eastern Africa. In prehistory, the moon was known as a benevolent female energy source that lit up the night for lovemaking. Thus came forth the long-held notion that the moon herself caused pregnancy, before any knowledge of the male's role in reproduction. Pregnant women of the Masai throw a stone at the new moon to 'request an easy birth' and a long life. (41)

Meditrina

Our word for 'medicine' comes from the Roman Goddess of Healing, Meditrina. All the English 'medical' words have their root in the Latin 'medere', to heal. Roman Goddess Meditrina was said to make use of herbs, wine, and magic formulas (prescriptions) in the form of recipes. (42) The Mediterranean Sea is probably named after her. Meditrina's recipe of herbs and wine and tomatoes is still regarded as a healthy diet.

Mesuk

This Goddess' name literally means 'Our Grandmother' to the Cree, Algonquin, and Ottawa Native American tribes. (43) She is the primal ancestral grandmother who taught her people the knowledge of medicinal plants. When medicinal roots are removed from the earth, she is given a symbolic offering of thanks for her 'giveaway'- the plants that were needed to heal illnesses.

Momoy

She is the patroness of Health and Healing of the Chumash of California. She was also credited with bringing education and all knowledge to her people. It is believed she gave the hallucinogenic datura plant to humans to ease the pain of suffering. 'She has medicine that can cure the sick and revive the dead. It is said that if you drink water that she has bathed in, you will avoid death'. (44) This is very similar to the Hindu belief in the healing waters of 'Mother Ganges', the river that flows through India.

Salus

She is the Roman Goddess of Health and Healing who corresponds to the Greek Goddess Hygeia. 'Salt' may have been named after her; as women who found layers of salt in their environments probably first used it for medicinal purposes. Salt has a salutary effect on wounds and infections. A salt-water gargle is still my first line of defense against a sore throat.

When we make a toast and say "Salud!" which means, "to your good health!" we are invoking the Roman Goddess of Health and Healing, Salus. (45)

Sekhmet

Goddess Sekhmet was associated with healing. This lion-headed deity of ancient Egypt was associated with stopping the epidemics called 'plagues' in antiquity. These epidemics could take the form of pulmonary (lung) infections and were thought to have been caused by an 'evil wind' or 'bad air'.

Tuberculosis, pneumonia, and other viral infections are indeed airborne and are caused by invisible droplets of infected mucous in the air. Thus the ancients were quite correct in supposing that 'contagious air was bad for you.'

The priestesses and priests of the fierce and powerful Lion-Goddess recited prayers to her during patients' treatments; and they were as integral to the healing as were the physical treatments performed by physicians. The Eber Papyrus (medical text) of ancient Egypt attributed specialized knowledge of the heart to Goddess Sekhmet's priestesses and priests. (46)

A black statue of Goddess Sekhmet from Thebes, Egypt, c. 1300 BC can be seen in the Metropolitan Museum, New York City, where my daughter Patrice and I were mesmerized by her enormous, larger-than-life beauty!

Sunna or Sulis

This Scandinavian and Northern Teutonic Sun Goddess is believed to have given women the secret knowledge of how to heal others. We know now that the body usually heals itself under ideal circumstances; but in antiquity, the medicinal herbs administered by the first female doctors may indeed have seemed 'magical'.

Goddess Sunna's namesake is the sun, whose health-giving benefits were acknowledged by ancient peoples. In Norse mythology, stones were sacred to Sunna and her worshipers carved deep stone circles across the Scandinavian landscape as part of her sacred (healing) rites. Almost all indigenous people carried stones painted with their Goddess' magical symbols as healing-stones, talismans, or amulets. Sick animals have also been known to rub themselves against large stones in the countryside.

In England she was known as Sulis, the ancient British Goddess of Healing Waters. Her health spa was located at Bath, England, where my companion and I saw her hot spring still bubbling up from the earth's core. We drank a toast to her under the name the Romans had carved in stone two thousand years ago, 'Medica Minerva Sulis'.

'Sulis' also means 'eye'; the spirals carved in stone by the ancients may have honored her also as an Eye Goddess, the sun being her all-seeing eye. The Scandinavian version of Goddess Sunna's name is Sonja.

Spider Woman/Thought Woman

In some Native American societies the creatress was female. Some of her names were Spider Woman, Thought Woman, Changing Woman (Navajo), and White Buffalo Woman. Just as the Lord of the biblical Genesis story spoke the world into existence with his Word; so the Thought Woman of the Keres tribe sang the world into existence and brought into being 'the firmament, the lands and seas, the people, the deities, plants, animals, minerals, language, writing, mathematics, architecture, the kachinas, the pueblo social system', and everything else. In these old Pueblo texts, female power is not confined only to maternity; but is recognized as a creative process that can bring great advancements to civilization including medicine and the knowledge of healing plants, herbs, flowers, roots, and barks that can be carried in a medicine woman's sacred bundle. (47)

Tlazolteotl

The Aztec Goddess of Health and Healing in ancient Mexico was portrayed in the glyph writings of the Aztecs with spindle whorls in her hair, pointing to the female roots of weaving textiles, as well as health and curing remedies. Mesoamerican medicine-women are called 'curanderas'; and the Virgin of Guadalupe, Mary, has replaced Tlazolteotl as their patroness. To the Huastecs, descendants of the ancient Mayans, Goddess Tlazolteotl was the transforming agent who heard their confessions, forgave their transgressions, and allowed them to be 'born again', healed and holy. (48)

Bibliography for Medicine Section

1. *Dictionary of Word Origins*, Ayto, John, NY, Little, Brown & Co., 1990
2. Personal communications with Dr. Rui Lian He, Acupuncturist and Herbalist, trained in Canton, China
3. *The Emergence of Man*, Pfeiffer, John, NY, Harper & Row, 1969
4. *Primitive Peoples Today*, Weyer, Edward, NY, Doubleday, 1959
5. *The Roots of Witchcraft*, Harrison, Michael, NJ, Citadel, 1972
6. *The Great Cosmic Mother*, Mohr, Barbara, & Sjöö, Monica, San Francisco, CA, Harper, 1983
7. *Magic in Ancient Egypt*, Pinch, Geraldine, London, British Museum Press, 1994
8. Ibid
9. Ibid
10. Ibid
11. Archaelogy Magazine, Walker, Amelie, NY, Sept. 1997
12. *A History of Their Own*, Anderson, Bonnie & Zinsser, Judith, Vol. I, NY Harper & Row, 1988
13. Ibid
14. Ibid
15. *Eunuchs for the Kingdom of God*, Ranke-Heinemann, Uta, NY, Doubleday, 1990
16. *The Woman Warrior*, Kingman, Maxine Hong, NY, Harper, 1985
17. *Primitive Peoples Today*, Weyer, Edward, NY, Dolphin, 1959
18. *A History of Their Own*, Anderson, Bonnie & Zinsser, Vol.I, NY, Harper & Row, 1988
19. Ibid
20. Ibid
21. Ibid
22. Ibid
23. Ibid
24. Ibid
25. Ibid
26. *Goddesses in World Mythology*, Ann & Imel, NY, Oxford Univ. Press, 1983
27. Ibid

28. Ibid
29. Ibid
30. *The Faces of the Goddess*, Motz, Lottie, NY, Oxford Univ. Press, 1997
31. *The Celtic World*, Green, Miranda, et al, London, Routledge, 1995
32. *Goddesses in World Mythology*, Ann & Imel, NY, Oxford Univ. Press, 1993
33. Ibid
34. Ibid
35. Ibid
36. *Dictionary of Word Origins*, Ayto, John, NY, Little, Brown & Co. 1990
37. *Magic in Ancient Egypt*, Pinch, Geraldine, London, British Museum Press, 1994
38. *Goddesses in World Mythology*, Ann & Imel, NY, Oxford Univ. Press, 1993
39. Ibid
40. Ibid
41. Ibid
42. Ibid
43. Ibid
44. Ibid
45. Ibid
46. *Magic in Ancient Egypt*, Pinch, Geraldine, London, British Museum Press, 1994
47. *Rise Up and Call Her Name*, Fisher, Elizabeth, Boston, MA, Beacon, 1994
48. Ibid

CHAPTER VII:
An Herbal Grimoire

She-Who-Makes-Us-Whole-and-Holy

For thousands of years herbs were used as safe medicines, and the persons who dispensed them were not always called "doctors". Often they were called shamanesses, shamankas (Siberia), witches, wise-women, medicine women, elderwomen, fenwomen (Ireland), cunning folk (Britain), hexers (Germany), and curanderas (Mexico). Shamanka is the Russian-Siberian pronunciation of a female shaman. Shaman is a mother-word (ma). Man did not mean male until the Middle Ages. Before that it meant 'human', or one who came out of a human mother.

Today many of our most widely used drugs are derived from ancient women's recipes: such as aspirin (as old as medicine itself) derived from willow bark and digitalis from foxglove. Every herb has its own biography, an ancient pedigree that may reach back two hundred thousand years to the very dawn of humanity.

Some nations, most notably China and India, have never stopped using herbal medicine. Even though they now use Western medicines as well, they still have faith in their traditional herbal prescriptions known for five thousand years, if not longer.

Before the nineteenth century all medicines came from nature until chemists began isolating and analyzing the composition of medicinal plants. The pharmaceutical industry was based on duplicating chemically what was already present in nature's living drugstore. Women's household herb or 'physic' gardens of the Middle Ages were the apothecaries of their day. Even today, one-fourth of all manufactured drugs still come from the plant world. Today there is a resurgence of interest in ancient herbal lore and most pharmacies, natural food stores, supermarkets, and department stores have an herbal section. The names on the bottles are meaningless to the consumer who has not had a legacy of herbal knowledge passed down through generations as was done in times gone by. For this reason, I have compiled the most common herbs and described how they were used in times past; along with the mythology associated with certain herbal remedies.

I prepared a 'tea' of Chinese herbs and drank it after every meal, as directed by the Chinese acupuncturist doctor who restored my body to vibrant health after an auto accident in 1990. But I do not advise the reader to use herbs on your own, since it is wise to remember that these medicinal plants release volatile compounds when prepared for use; and should be used only with the knowledge and consent of a physician.

This then, is a brief historical glimpse into the mythology of that ancient domain of the women, the plant world.

A

ALFALFA
This plant is available in tablets, teas, seeds, and sprouts and is said to have a detoxification effect on the body as well as nutritional, when the sprouts are added to a salad or sandwich. It is rich in vitamins and minerals and has a cleansing effect on the system. Alfalfa tea with honey or orange peel is a pleasant tonic that adds alkalinity to the body. Since many diseases are related to excessive acidity, alfalfa was used for long-term health.
(1)

ALOE
This is a bromeliad (a plant that stores moisture) which has been known since the days of ancient Egypt for its soothing and rejuvenating effect on skin. By breaking off a leaf, a jelly-like fluid is released which is rubbed on injured or burned skin for a cooling, soothing effect. My favorite face moisturizer contained oil of aloe. My mother also used it to keep her skin soft and wrinkle-free until her death at eighty-nine. Aloe is an ingredient in many high quality cosmetics. When mixed with attar of roses and rue it was known as an abortifacient in the Greco-Roman world. Recent experiments have shown the gel to be helpful for painful rheumatic and arthritic joints.
(2)
(3)

AMBER

Amber is a mysterious and beautiful fossilized resin from the sap of evergreen trees found especially in the Baltic area of Europe. In Lithuania and neighboring countries, pieces regularly wash up on the shore after a storm at sea. Until three thousand BC it was used for healing only in the Baltic area; but later was traded as far as Mycenae, Greece about sixteen hundred BC and ancient Egypt also. It was highly prized and has been found only in tombs with wealthy grave goods. Amber has a characteristic 'sticky' feel and was believed to possess magical healing properties as well as great beauty and longevity.

ANISE

The seeds of this plant have been used for centuries. It is known to have a calming effect on digestion and to soothe a sore throat. It is still an ingredient in throat lozenges. Several teaspoons of the liquor, anisette, in a cup of hot water can possibly ease bronchitis' racking cough. The seeds can be bruised with a mortar and pestle and seeped in boiling water for a tea that can be helpful for a temporary digestive aid, and to relieve gas or colic in infants. The tea should be strained to remove the seeds and fed by the teaspoon to infants after it has cooled, but only with a doctor's permission.

ARNICA

This plant was known to stimulate and increase circulation. It is named after the Greek Goddess Arne, daughter of Aeoluis, King of Winds, and was well-known to European 'witches' (herbal healers) and herbalists. This plant has yellow flowers and was known as 'leopard's bane' in Europe; but an almost identical arnica is found here as well. Known as a 'simple', or a staple in the home medicine cabinet, it was mixed with lanolin 'sheep oil' for use as a healing ointment. Mixed with a rubbing alcohol, it forms a tincture for first-aid treatment for sprains, dislocations, and swellings, and in another formula as a painkiller by homeopathic physicians.
(4)
(5)

ARTEMESIA

This herb was named after the Goddess Artemis, patroness of childbirth, and was used by ancient Greeks to ease the pains of labor. Women herbalists often named their medicinals after a Goddess, which points to medicine's female origins.

ASPIRIN

Aspirin is as old as medicine itself. It is derived from the bark of the willow tree and was probably chewed in antiquity to provide pain relief. Today it is duplicated chemically in laboratories.

B

BEETS

Red beets are common root vegetables that I think of as an herb also because they have medicinal use as a liver cleanser and stimulating tonic. Both the roots and the leaves are rich in vitamins and minerals. My Lithuanian Grandmother, Antanina, taught us to make red beet soup and it is still my favorite old-world soup. It is called 'boršcht' and 'salta birštai', when eaten cold; but I prefer the piping hot version with a dollop of sour cream floating on top and a thick slice of sour dough rye bread for dipping. The recipe is simple. Just sliced beets cooked in beef broth, with a dash of vinegar to 'pep' it up. Lithuanians always added a dash of vinegar to their wonderful variety of soups to 'wake up' the flavor. Pickled beets are another way to get the healthful benefits. Simply add vinegar, sugar, salt and pepper 'to taste' to the liquid of cooked beets. Place the beets in a mason jar, pour liquid over them for a pickling effect, place a few hard-boiled eggs (peeled) in the jar also; and enjoy the pickled eggs and beets the next day when they have absorbed the flavors. The fresh green leaves can be chopped and added to salads or used in an herbal tea.

BELLADONNA

It's name means 'pretty lady', probably because it was used as a sedative and dilated the pupils of the eyes. It may have been the 'date rape' drug of antiquity. A member of the nightshade family that includes potatoes, henbane, mandrake, and jimson weed, it can depress the parasympathetic nervous system when taken in large doses. In Europe, it was known by 'witches' (herbalists and medicine women) to produce hallucinations. It may be the reason they told Inquisitors they could 'fly';

as they may have ingested it before they were burned alive by Medieval Church authorities as 'heretics' for helping women control the size of their families with herbal contraceptives.

BLACKBERRY LEAVES
These were boiled into a tea by the Pennsylvania Germans and used for the pain of childbirth. The postpartum mother would then be served chamomile tea to relax her.

BIRCH
Ancient peoples enjoyed the flavor of birch beer, also called root beer, just as much as we do today. They used the sap of the birch tree as chewing gum, and may have found a way to brew its roots and bark into a type of beer, using their saliva (which contains enzymes) as an early type of yeast. Pieces of birch gum with tooth marks were found in an Alpine Neolithic community on Lake Zurich, Switzerland, dating back to 4000 BC. Many rural people as late as 1940 kept a barrel of root beer in their cold cellars to last all winter long.

C

CAT'S CLAW
This is a unique plant found in the Amazon rain forest in Peru and can be used as a gentle diuretic. It is extracted from the bark of the plant and thought by herbalists to have antioxidant properties, which makes it useful to strengthen the immune system. It is relatively new to holistic medicine in this part of the world.

CAMELLIA SINENSIS
This is the plant from which all teas derive. Whether the tea is black, green, or oolong depends on the method of treating the leaves after they are harvested. Black tea is allowed to ferment with its own enzymes that are released by a rolling of the leaves. Green tea leaves are not allowed to ferment. They are exposed to hot steam to destroy the enzymes that cause fermentation. Oolong tea leaves are allowed to partly ferment, then are lightly toasted over a charcoal fire to halt fermentation. Herbal teas are prepared by blending blossoms, fruits, spices, and aromatic roots with tealeaves and other botanicals. The Chinese may have been

using tea leaves medicinally in boiling water, as early as 2,800 BC. They called it 'ch'a' and it became an important part of Chinese culture. It was used also as an aide to meditation. The serving of tea became a stylized contemplative act and tea became a profitable export to Europe by AD 1600's, especially to England.

(6)

(7)

CHAMOMILE

The leaves of this flower are made into a tea that has been used for centuries for the calming, relaxing effect. It is also thought to ease a sore throat or a heavy cough. I have used this tea for my family, my friends, and myself for decades with very beneficial effects.

CHARCOAL

Rubbing charcoal into open cuts was done to relieve pain in antiquity. This left a permanent discoloration which later evolved into tattooing, a decorative art practiced by earliest human populations as a means of tribal affiliation and identification. While not an herb, it is the ash residue of willow, pine, and other soft woods; and it has been used medicinally as an absorbent, since it will absorb and oxidize internal fermenting gases when it is ingested as a paste mixed with water. Charcoal was also used as a poultice for gangrene and ulcer-like sores by traditional healers in the past. Today activated charcoal tablets can be used to maintain good intestinal health by absorbing the toxins that cause diarrhea. It is a natural product derived from vegetable sources; and it does not enter the bloodstream.

(8)

(9)

CINNAMON

This spice from the East was so highly valued when it first arrived in Europe in the Middle Ages that it was kept under lock and key in the manor houses. Aside from its wonderful taste, it is thought to have medicinal value as a stimulant and energizer. My cardiologist advised me that cinnamon can help lower blood pressure when ingested daily.

CRANBERRY
Cranberry juice has long been prescribed to flush out urinary tract infections. The berry contains the active ingredient 'which prevents E.coli bacteria from invading and sticking to the bladder'. Dr. Buchman suggests drinking eight ounces of un-sugared pure cranberry juice "at the first indication of burning urination", which is a symptom of cystitis. Cranberries are also high in Vitamin C. Cranberry juice can be soothing for asthma and bronchitis.
(10)

D

DANDELION
This is a common garden weed that has been a favorite herb of women healers for centuries. I remember the enthusiasm of the European grandmothers who searched for its tender shoots in the spring lawns. It can be used in salads with a hot vinegar and bacon dressing, which is how the Germans used it in the Blue Mountains of Pennsylvania where I grew up. It makes a delicious salad while the plants are young; however, later they become bitter. It is valued for its invigorating 'spring tonic' effect.

It was also made into a very tasty wine; but unfortunately I do not have the recipe. It was probably made in the usual way of mixing the leaves and roots with a sugar syrup and some yeast, then leaving it in a dark closet until it fermented. Later leaves of the plant can be brewed in an herbal tea along with freshly sliced pieces of the dandelion root for a tonic "to stimulate a sluggish liver". Dandelion coffee, similar to chicory, can be found in certain health-food stores and is used in folk medicine as a liver cleanser, tonic, and diuretic. Today dandelion root is available in 500mg capsules.
(11)

E

ECHINACEA
Formerly called 'purple coneflower', this herb was used extensively by Native Americans, "especially by the Pawnee, who chewed at the root all during the day". Echinacea is believed to stimulate the immune system

to counter the effects of bacteria-borne illnesses such as "colds, sore throats, and bronchitis, abscesses, and yeast infections". It should be used only during the illness rather than having it present in the system all the time. The body may become habituated to it and require larger doses with lessening of the effect. It was also used in times past as a blood tonic to rid the system of toxins during an infection.
(12)

ELDERBERRY
The elder plant is rich in B vitamins, calcium, rutin, and vitamins A and C. The flowers, berries, and bark of this plant have been used since antiquity for perking up a sluggish body. Today it is claimed that elderberry extract can cleanse the blood, strengthen the immune system, reduce inflammation, and stimulate circulation.
(13)

F

FOXGLOVE
This flower contains digitalis in its leaves, used since antiquity for heart problems. The leaves were seeped and drunk as a bitter tea that cured dropsy, the retention of fluid from a weak heart, liver, and kidney malfunction. The active ingredient in foxglove, digitalis, is widely used today in the formula for drugs prescribed for heart failure and related cardiac problems.
(14)

FUNGUS
Tree fungi have been used in antiquity as an antibiotic for treating bladder ailments and tuberculosis. Pieces of birch tree fungus threaded on a fur strip were found with the 'Iceman', the Copper Age traveler whose frozen body was found in the Alps several years ago. He was dated to 3300 BC. The fungus of rye grain, ergot, was known to 'witches' (wisewomen) as useful to relieve the pain of childbirth in antiquity. Recently it is being examined for usefulness in treating migraines.

G

GINGER

This aromatic root has an ancient pedigree as a flavorant, as relief from a gastrointestinal distress and flatulence, and as a mild stimulant that can replace caffeine for herb lovers. It has been used in the East for over two thousand years as a stimulant to circulation, blood vessel dilator, and arthritis relief. Ginger compresses can be used to relieve joint pain. Ginger tea with honey and lemon can also soothe a sore throat; and ginger added to bath water may relieve pain. I keep a ginger root in my refrigerator during the winter months because the tea made from it creates a feeling of warmth that is needed by people suffering from arthritis as I do. I slice a few pieces off the root and pour boiling water over it in a cup, and I have a fragrant, warming, stimulating cup of fresh ginger tea to ward off a chill and lift the spirit. Fresh ginger can also be chewed for nausea or indigestion, and the tea can be helpful for menstrual pain.
(15)

GINGKO BILOBA

This is a tree that is believed to be the oldest tree on earth, at least one hundred fifty million years old. These 'wonder trees' grow in China where the nuts have been part of Chinese traditional medicine for thousands of years. They were eaten for longevity, and prevention of strokes 'by helping the brain to increase its supply of blood and oxygen'. European doctors today believe that a daily dose of 40mg of 24% extract can help restore short-term memory, mental alertness, leg circulation, aging eyesight, even some hearing problems. This ancient plant is also thought to reduce edema caused by fluid retention from arterial pressure or menstrual cycles. It sounds like an herbal 'fountain of youth', and is used by twenty million people worldwide. As with most herbal remedies, it sometimes takes three to four months to notice the effects. Clinical studies have shown also that it may be helpful in delaying age-onset macular degeneration, probably by reducing free-radical damage. Ginkgo is also useful sometimes to relieve tinnitus, phlebitis, memory loss, and dizziness caused by circulatory problems. Be sure to consult with your doctor first.
(16)

GINSENG

Known for thousands of years by Chinese, Korean, Siberian, and Japanese herbalists, the ginseng root is probably the most widely used herb in the Far East. It has been celebrated as a stimulant (both mental and physical) and as an energy booster. The reason it is so expensive is that it takes six years for a root to mature under ideal forest conditions. It has been known to provide mental alertness during performances, as well as to impart a sense of well-being. It might be useful in small doses (a capsule in a cup of hot water) for special occasions when mental alertness and physical stamina are essential. It is available in tablets and capsules as well as powdered root and tincture (liquid concentrate). The active ingredient, ginsenosides, should be over 10 percent. One or two teaspoons of dried ginseng can be added to cooked food, salads, teas, etc. to relieve burnout from stress. Its main value to the Chinese is its toning effect on the nervous system, imparting possible increased resistance to stress, restoring strength after an illness like an allergy or sinus episode, relieving bad coughs, and decreasing an enlarged prostate in men while increasing testosterone. Of course, a physician should see a man with prostrate problem first.

This herb reacts differently in women and men depending on the body's needs. Ginseng, as a tonic for debility, has been used in China for five thousand years. Olympic athletes and astronauts have used Siberian ginseng extensively. It can also be used as a coffee substitute to keep awake and alert such as when studying for an important exam or while driving. Ginseng was the 'happiness plant' of the ancients.
(17)

GOLDENSEAL

The powdered root of this plant was used to seal wounds in past times and aid in their healing. It was used in small amounts as a tea that cleansed the system and invigorated many organs, by Native Americans and the pioneers in the West. The powder can be put directly on a cold sore to relieve the pain and possibly cure it overnight, if applied with a swab at bedtime. Poison ivy can also be soothed with compresses of goldenseal tea.

Berberine is the antibiotic agent in goldenseal that was isolated

in 1950; and which can be a defense against the winter cold and flu season.
(18)
(19)

H

HEMLOCK
Includes chemicals that can cause sensory paralysis, can depress the cardiovascular system, and cause delirium, hallucinations, or fatigue. European midwives in the Middle Ages may have used it in small amounts for the pain of childbirth, in combination with other herbs. This is the herbal infusion that Socrates had to drink when he was found guilty of corrupting youth in ancient Greece. It was easy to find hemlock in the hot climates in summer. Within minutes, paralysis would have set in, which would make Socrates unable to speak; and death would have followed soon afterwards.

HENBANE
(See Hemlock)

HEATHER
This flowering plant was often dried and hung upside down in the home to sweeten the air.

L

LAVENDER
This flower has been used for centuries for its clean, fresh, soothing fragrance. It smells so clean that is was named 'Lavabo', 'to wash', by the Romans. Inhaling lavender's slightly pungent aroma was also believed to stop dizziness. The flowers, steeped in a tea, were used to control nausea and as a general tonic for the body. Its main use today is in scents. I keep a crystal dish on my nightstand filled with fresh lavender. The fragrance has a calming effect as I drift off to sleep.

In France, the essence of lavender has been used for aches and bruises. It also makes an excellent insect repellent, kept in drawers, closets, and

tucked in pockets when outside in the summer, as the mosquitoes hate it.
(20)
(21

LEEK
A type of onion whose juice was mixed with the juice of sage leaves to ameliorate the itching of fleas and lice that plagued European peasants, as well as nobility, in the winter months when they could not bathe. Leek juice added to a hand cream may soothe chapped hands.
(22)
(23)

M

MISTLETOE
The Druids of Britain called this plant 'heal-all'. My ancestors in Wales probably gathered it from the sacred oak groves where it grew profusely. It was believed that if it was gathered at the winter solstice, it would retain its full charge of energy. When ingested, the berries are poisonous but Wiccan wise women probably had many medicinal uses for the leaves that were also called 'golden bough'. In traditional medicine it was used as a remedy for St. Vitus' dance, convulsions, delirium, and heart troubles.

MONKSHOOD
This plant includes chemicals that can cause sensory paralysis; depress the heart, cause delirium, hallucinations, and fatigue. In minute dosages, European midwives may have used it to relieve the pain of childbirth.
(24)

MUSTARD SEED
The seeds of mustard plants, when ground into a powder and mixed with water, have been used to induce vomiting. As a child, my mother often applied mustard poultices ('plasters') to my chest to relieve painful congestion. One part of the powder to four parts of flour with enough water to make a paste was rubbed on a piece of flannel and applied to the

skin. It was done carefully so blistering would not occur, as it generates a lot of heat.
(25)

N

NIGHTSHADE
(See Hemlock)
Nightshade and Hemlock herbs may have been used by female shamans for the altered state of consciousness that the herbs produced. They can cause hallucinations, giving the user a sense of being transformed into something else or of flying.
(26)

P

PARSLEY
The leaves of this common flavoring herb can be eaten raw as a gentle, cleansing diuretic. As a child I remember the mothers telling their children to eat parsley as a sort of natural antibiotic that would decrease the incidences of sore throats. It is also a breath sweetener. I always insisted my children eat the sprig of parsley on their plates. For mothers who have finished nursing, parsley in salads, parsley soup, and parsley tea will gradually decrease milk in breasts according to Dr. Dian Buchman. Parsley is a source of iron, potassium and vitamins A, C, and E; and was widely used throughout the ancient Greco-Roman world to accent the flavor of fish, just as it is today. The Greeks actually thought it too sacred to eat. It has value as a diuretic, deterrent to kidney stones, for liver detoxification, and possibly the prevention of cancer, as cancer cells do not thrive in a potassium rich environment.
(27)

PATCHOULI
This is an herb with the aroma of fresh soil and is slightly pungent. Its' oil was dabbed on a piece of cotton and placed in linen and lingerie drawers by my Grandmother and I have loved the fragrance ever since I was a little girl. It was probably used in past times to deter moths. Patchouli oil is an ingredient in many expensive perfumes, as it is believed to act as

a love potion as well as a protection against unpleasantness. It has also been used in the Far East in incense since antiquity. The highly prized cashmere pashmina shawls woven by the women of India were shipped with patchouli to protect them from moths along distant trade routes.

PEPPERMINT

The leaves were long known as a cure for indigestion. Peppermint is also soothing to the throat and is an ingredient in many lozenges. A strong tea of peppermint leaves mixed with a strong cinnamon tea has been used as a poultice (when a tea towel is saturated with the mixture) on an inflamed liver. A poultice of crushed peppermint leaves can also relieve muscle spasms. Peppermint tea, long known as an aid to digestion, can also alleviate a headache and quell the nausea of early pregnancy. The Chinese make a peppermint oil, 'Po Ho Yo', that is soothing to neuralgia pain. Peppermint oil was also rubbed on the sore gums of teething babies in days gone by. Peppermint also contains camphor that is useful to relieve pain. For the pain of sinus, a cup of peppermint tea can be enjoyed along with a warm peppermint poultice to the sinus area. Since peppermint is a natural source of menthol and camphor, care should be taken when giving it to infants and children.
(28)
(29)

R

RUE

This herb had several uses and European peasant women would have been sure to grow it in their kitchen gardens. Mixed with the plant savin, it was used to freshen the air and deter fleas and lice during long winter months indoors. These herbs were probably strewn on the floor and walked on to release the fragrance. Rue was also known as an abortifacient in the Greco-Roman world when taken in the proper dose. If an overdose was ingested it could be fatal to both the mother and the fetus. One recipe for a contraceptive was a concoction of rue, attar of roses, and aloe. Another recipe called for a mixture of seeds and panax juice blended with wax and served in wine. In my childhood I remember the women, newly arrived émigrés from Lithuania, tending the rue in their gardens. I wondered why they took such good care of it, as it is a rather nondescript plant with tiny round leaves and no flower. I have no doubt that it was most probably used as an effective means of birth control; and they needed to make sure they had a steady supply. The first contraceptives were probably potions (teas) that were drunk three or more days in succession by the women.

Rue is a medicinal herb that has been used from time immemorial as a tonic for the uterus, stomach, bowels, headache, to expel pinworms, and to relieve colic in children. Poultices were used for sciatic pain, arthritis, and gout. The usual dosage to bring on a sluggish menstrual period was one teaspoon of the chopped rue steeped in a cup of boiling water for one-half hour; and then sipped all during the day. However this should not be done without a physician's consent.
(30)

S

SAGE
Peasant women in Europe mixed the juice of sage leaves with water "to ease the itching and pain" of the bites of fleas and lice; and as a tea to dry up breast milk after the child had been weaned. It has also been used as a tea to aid a sluggish liver, cleanse wounds, improve circulation, ease a headache, and generally tone the body. The Chinese believed that sage tea kept them well.
(31)

SALT
The use of salt can be traced far back into prehistory where it was a 'primordial, sacred substance.' The Latin word for health, 'salus', derives from the word, 'sal' in Latin. Whenever we make a toast, "Salute, to your health!" we are saluting salt. The Celtic Goddess of Health was named 'Sulis'. Today it is one of the cheapest, humblest items in the grocery store and yet our language still reflects a time when salt was very precious. "The salt of the earth" is still the highest accolade. Romans offered salt to their deities, as well as using it medicinally, as a flavorant for food, and as a preservative for cured meats and vegetables. We still use it today for preserving foods such as pickles, ham, and many others. Today salt is still used mainly for its antiseptic function. My mother taught me to gargle with warm salt water at the first sign of a sore throat;

and I did the same with all six of my children. A salt solution was used by European women in the Middle Ages, and earlier as a spermicidal douche. Saline solutions are still used today in abortions. While not an herb in the usual sense, salt is a natural product with many uses in an herbal holistic lifestyle.
(32)

SAVIN
A plant used to freshen the air and to keep away fleas and mites that multiplied on the skin of Europeans during the cold winter months when they could not wash in streams and rivers. It has fallen out of use in modern times.

SLIPPERY ELM
This is a bark that can be useful for gastritis when seeped as a tea. It can also be used as a poultice, as Native Americans 'used it for wounds, boils, and skin diseases.' Today pure air-dried bark is sold in capsules to ease a cold, flu, and a sore throat.
(33)

SPHAGNUM MOSS
This mold or moss was noted for its healing properties, especially in the peat bogs of England and Ireland. Inuit Eskimos of the Arctic and Native American Indians used to bathe in it for rheumatism.

ST. JOHN'S WORT
This is a common garden weed used for centuries by healers. It has been used to relieve anxiety, depression, and insomnia. The active ingredient is hypericin, which promotes a sense of well-being and is a mood elevator, according to German researchers. It shows promise as an alternative to anti-depressants such as Prozac when used as an extract of .3%. When used in combination with ephedra, it is called 'herbal fen-fen' and used for weight loss; but this preparation is highly controversial and may cause seizures and even death. Known in times past as a blood purifier in cases of jaundice of the liver when a heaping teaspoonful of seeds were steeped in a cup of boiling water.
(34)

SULFUR

Burning sulfur was believed to drive away the evil spirits (germs) of disease in antiquity. Sulfur was believed to be sacred to the Goddess Athena of Greece, the patroness of healing and purification. Fire (burning sulfur) and brimstone date from this period, c. 600 BC and earlier. Brimstone was named after the Goddess' holy child, 'Brimus'; a bear name, which is another clue to the great respect earliest humans had for female bears and their wide knowledge of medicinal plants to eat when they were sick.
(35)
(36)

T

TEA
(See Camellia Sinensis)
Tea did not reach Europe until late Middle Ages; and it was originally used as a medicine, to create a sense of ease and wellbeing. It eventually became used more for its stimulating effect. It enabled factory workers to work longer hours on less food during the early years of the Industrial Revolution.

V

VALERIAN

Our modern valium pill is derived from the root of the valerian plant. In large doses it paralyzes the nervous system. It is useful in small doses, in tea as a tranquilizer, and is believed by herbalists to be one of the best tranquilizers known. Ancient wise women knew of valerian and used it to ease the agony of childbirth. Researchers are examining its usefulness for headaches, menstrual cramps, and indigestion. A valerian pill added to a cup of a favorite herbal tea might be calming after a trauma or for menstrual cramps or muscle spasms. Valerian root extract can be substituted for L-tryptophan, which can no longer be purchased in the United States as a sleep aid. Be sure to check with your physician before using any herbs or supplements, as they are volatile, even though natural.
(37)

VERVAIN

This is a fragrant herb that was believed to heighten psychic power in antiquity. 'Women have used it for centuries to help them sleep and be less nervous'. It has also been used to stimulate labor contractions in childbirth.

In the olden days, most housewives would have kept some vervain in their herbal pantry to reduce fevers, clear a cold overnight, ease coughing spells, asthma, and remove phlegm from the throat and chest. It would have been sipped as a hot tea and also used as a poultice on external sores.
(38)

W

WOLF HAIR

While not a botanical, the hair of a wolf (if you were lucky enough to find any) was carried in a pouch for protection in medieval times. The scent of it kept other animals away.

Y

YARROW

This is a very common weed that has been known to be useful since very ancient times as an insect repellent. "The flowers can be rubbed on the body to repel mosquitoes while you are in the country", writes Dr. Dian Buchman. Small amounts of the flowers can be chopped up and added to favorite herbal teas to help cleanse the liver. Midwives used it in antiquity to cause contractions that expelled the afterbirth of childbirth. Yarrow has been used in years past for its healing and soothing effect on mucous membranes, especially for the vaginal discharge of leucorrhea. Drunk as a hot tea, it is said to be useful to lower fevers and allay the misery of a cold.
(39)

Herbal Bibliography

1. *Herbal Medicine*, Dian Buchman, NY, Random House, 1979
2. *A History of Their Own*, Anderson & Zinsser, NY, Harper & Row, 1988
3. *Herbal Medicine*, Dian Buchman, NY, Random House, 1979
4. *Goddesses in World Mythology*, Ann & Imel, NY, Oxford Univ. Press, 1988
5. *Herbal Medicine*, Dian Buchman, NY, Random House, 1979
6. Republic of Tea, Lessons of the Leaves, 1995
7. Tea Time, M.King, Philadelphia, PA. Running Press, 1995
8. Bronson Pharmaceuticals, 1945 Craig Rd. St. Louis, MO, 84042
9. *Herbal Medicine*, Dian Buchman, NY, Random House, 1979
10. Ibid
11. Ibid
12. Ibid
13. Bronson Pharmaceuticals, 1945 Craig Rd. St. Louis, MO, 84042
14. *Herbal Medicine*, Dian Buchman, NY, Random House, 1979
15. Ibid
16. Ibid
17. Bronson Pharmaceuticals, 1945 Craig Rd. Louis, MO, 84042
18. *Herbal Medicine*, Dian Buchman, NY, Random House, 1979
19. Healthy Resources, Richard Carson, ed., CA, Pro-Health Inc. 1997
20. *A History of Their Own*, Anderson & Zinsser, NY, Harper & Row, 1988
21. *Herbal Medicine*, Dian Buchman, NY, Random House, 1979
22. *A History of Their Own*, Anderson & Zinsser, NY, Harper & Row, 1988
23. *Herbal Medicine*, Dian Buchman, NY, Random House, 1979
24. *A History of Their Own*, Anderson & Zinsser, NY, Harper & Row, 1988
25. *Herbal Medicine*, Dian Buchman, NY, Random House, 1979
26. *A History of Their Own*, Anderson & Zinsser, NY, Harper & Row, 1988
27. *Herbal Medicine*, Dian Buchman, NY, Random House, 1979

28. *A History of Their Own*, Anderson & Zinsser, NY, Harper & Row, 1988
29. *Herbal Medicine*, Dian Buchman, NY, Random House, 1979
30. *A History of Their Own*, Anderson & Zinsser, NY, Harper & Row, 1988
31. Ibid
32. *Tastes of Paradise*, Wolfgang Schivelbusch, NY, Vintage, 1980
33. *Herbal Medicine*, Dian Buchman, NY, Random House, 1979
34. Healthy Resources, Richard Carson, ed., CA, Pro-Health Inc. 1997
35. *The Woman's Dictionary*, Barbara G. Walker, NJ, Castle, 1980
36. *Goddesses in World Mythology*, Ann & Imel, NY, Oxford Univ. Press, 1988
37. *Herbal Medicine*, Dian Buchman, NY, Random House, 1979
38. Ibid
39. Ibid

CHAPTER VIII:
Goddesses as Sources of Women's History

She-Comes-Who-Is-Great

There are over twenty-eight thousand goddesses documented in the mythologies, religions, folktales, and legends of the world. Yet, ask any little girl in American today if she can name one and chances are, she would not know what you were talking about. This is very sad and shows the vacuum that exists in every girl or woman's psyche where her psycho-spiritual 'herstory' as a female should be readily accessible and available to her.

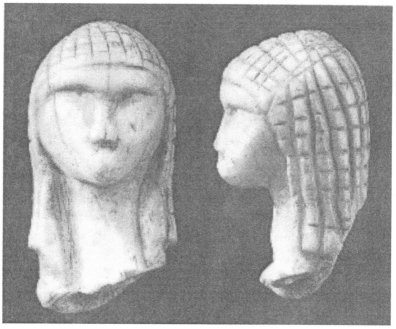

The miniature ivory female head with elaborate coiffure is one of the earliest attempts at human portraiture. The head was found in Landes, France and is less than an inch and a half long. c. 24,000 BC The Venus can be seen at the Musée des Antiquités Nationales, Ste. Germain-en-Laye, in Landes, France

The goddesses are every female's birthright and link her to lost history, role models of strength, power, and assertiveness; and affirmations of a link to divinity, through her very own female body.

Girls and women living in patriarchal societies are not encouraged to learn about the ancient goddesses because they would learn that divinity can also wear the face of a woman, not just a man's face: Jesus, Yahweh, Buddha, Allah, Shiva. No matter how softly tranquil their features are portrayed or implied, they are still the faces of men .

But the face of God was a woman's face for the first thirty thousand years of humanity's existence; and perhaps much longer, in the form of a female animal, Mother Bear for example. These female divinities were called 'Mother Goddesses' because humans knew that all new life enters the world through the body of a female, a mother, in both human as well as the animal world.

The earliest Mother Goddesses may very well have been clan mothers who actually existed. Their true names are lost to us in some cases; but not the love, respect, awe, and inspiration, they bequeathed to their children and the generations that followed.

It has actually become possible, as I write this, to trace any European woman's clan mother, to the country of her origin as far back in time as 30,000 BC or even earlier. I had my own clan mother traced through my own (maternal) DNA by simply swabbing the insides of my cheeks and sending the samples to a laboratory in Oxford, England. My individual DNA sequence was then traced to my ancestral mother through a computer program. What an extraordinary gift! I am connected to my very own 'Mother Goddess' by passing all the intervening generations, over millennia, backwards through time, to 28,000 BC!

In this chapter you will meet a few of the extraordinary divine women whose names may sound vaguely familiar; because they reverberate with your deeply intuitive self at a very primal level. I have found these goddesses very useful in retrieving women's lost history; as the attributes retained by these deities over the centuries, can tell us a great deal about women's contributions to human knowledge and advancement of civilization.

It is my fond hope that some day every schoolgirl all over the world will know their awesome divine names – the lovely, power-filled names of:

Al'Latte
Amaterasu
Aphrodite
Astarte
Athena
Bona Dea
Brigit
Demeter
Diana
Gaia
Hecate
Hera
Isis
Ishtar/Inanna
Juno
Minerva
Saraswati
Terra Mater

These names reflect the precious spiritual, psychological, and historical heritage of every woman.

For example, I have chosen Demeter (which means 'The Mother' in Greek) because she and Ceres (meaning grain or cereal) are credited with the invention of cereal, perhaps the greatest invention of humans.

Ceres statue of marble in Rome, Borghese Collection, is seen holding grain in her right hand. She possibly invented cereal.

Grain (cereal and bread) has enabled people to stay alive to create all the other technologies that give quality to our lives today. Without grains (including rice and corn) humans would have perished. Bread was what made all the difference and is aptly named 'the staff of life'.

Food was always first and foremost the focus of the world of women: how to hunt for it, gather it, grow it, collect it, serve it, cook it, preserve it, store it, and plant it. The entire burden of feeding not only themselves, but also their children, fell upon the women; for men probably knew nothing of their role in procreation until the Bronze Age or later. Males would have had little motivation to provide food for children they had no biological ties or emotional bonding with; although they may have bonded to the women and shared meat with the females and young.

However, meat was not a steady, predictable source of food because animals have very good survival skills and are not easily killed, especially with Stone Age weapons. Therefore, it was probably the female's life and death struggle to keep her young alive, that drove her to find a dependable source of food near her cave or campsite that led to the discovery of agriculture and domestication of animals.

She also needed to find a way to preserve food. By grinding grains into flour for bread, she found a palatable source of nourishment that could sustain life, long after the harvest and the last pieces of meat were eaten.

Each goddess is a treasure of information about women's probable inventions and technological innovations. As you read, you will come to appreciate, as I did, the magnificent gifts that women's intelligence, hard work, needs and creativity have contributed to human civilization and quality of life; as well as their bodies, that have created life itself.

Goddess Allat

The Goddess of the Sun, Allat, or Al'Latte, was worshipped as the Queen of Heaven by Arabic peoples before the male god Allah. The moon and the star, her heavenly symbols, are still used today on Islamic flags. Her name contains a hint of her ancient origins: 'lat' means milk, as in 'latte', and 'lactate'. Allat therefore meant 'the one who has milk'. She was worshipped in Babylon and her sacred stone (symbol of Mother Earth from time immemorial) was at Mecca.

She was masculinized by the later Islamic religion; and became

Allah, a patriarchal divinity. Her counterpart in India is Lakshmi, the Goddess of milk and female generosity.
(1)

Goddess Aphrodite

Aphrodite means 'born of foam' in the Greek language of the pantheon in which she originated. She was usually portrayed nude, arising from the primal sea, as the source of all life on earth. She stayed eternally young and beautiful, the symbol of female sexuality, desirability, love, and beauty.

Aphrodite was a love Goddess of the Titan generation of Greek Goddesses and gods, older than Zeus and his pantheon. She alone of the Greek Goddesses was depicted totally nude in keeping with her erotically irresistible nature. The classical Greeks usually draped the Goddesses and depicted only the males as nude. This was in keeping with their keener appreciation of the male body.

Aphrodite, motherless, born of her father Ournos' severed genitals, represents a transitional phase in human societal evolution. The Matriarchal era of mother right or mother worship was giving way to a shift in consciousness. Male semen (symbolized as the sun) had been recognized as the generative force in reproduction; and paternity was beginning to be highly valued. In the Paleolithic world, fatherhood was an unknown concept; but by the Neolithic era, c. 4000 BC, knowledge of the male's contribution to childbirth was becoming known due to cattle breeding.

Aphrodite, born of her father's foam (semen) without the help of a female (uterus) symbolizes the new importance that was being given to male semen and fatherhood. The male's contribution was in the process of being elevated to a new cosmic importance: the seed (semen) would eventually assume greater significance in mythology than the moon (womb).

Eventually, this over-valuing of the male would become known as patriarchy with all of its political implications for devaluing the female.

Aphrodite, as a transitional Goddess, mediated the forces of night (always more important in the Matriarchate when women were believed to be impregnated by the moon deity) and the forces of day (the sun's rays/semen) would now take on prime importance as the fertilizing force of the mater/matter.

Her temples were usually located on rock formations that overlooked the sea, the primal progenitor. Her moisture was the morning dew and mists, with which she could protect those she loved. The Irish also used the mythological mists as a poetic device to signify divine protection or intervention.

Goddess Aphrodite became known to the Romans as Venus, Goddess of fertility, love, beauty, sexuality, and erotic passion. "All who saw her felt that the instincts they shared with the beasts, they also shared with the gods".
(2)

Goddess Athena

One of the greatest cities the world has ever known was named after a woman, Goddess Athena, suggesting the female origins of civilization itself. Women founded many cities in antiquity, and also named them. Another such example is Carthage in N. Africa which was founded by Elissa, a brilliant tradeswoman.

As the Patroness of Athens and the Goddess who taught Athenians how to cultivate the olive tree, Athena is prominently depicted on the Parthenon relief, along with her olive tree.

Unfortunately, she has been portrayed since classical times in a militant pose, wearing a helmet and holding a spear and shield. This pose of Athena, as Goddess of War, was probably an invention of the Indo-Europeans from the north who displaced the indigenous Aegeans and Myceneans on the Greek mainland, and installed their own pantheon of violent deities, and militarized the original Nature Goddess, Athena.

The Goddess Athena's roots reach far back into prehistory, long before the classical Greek period of 600BC. She may have originated as the ancestral mother Goddess and household patron of the Mycenaean royal family; and was probably honored as the protectress of its citadel; just as she was later invoked as the protectress of her namesake, Athens. As a mother is fiercely protective of her young, so the mother Goddesses were protective of their mortal children.

Her warrior pose reflects her duty to protect her devotees; as well as her role of mentor, friend, and counselor of men.

Athenians credited her as the one who taught them to grow olive trees, a major cash crop of the entire Aegean area where the soil is very poor. This giving of credit to a Goddess often points to the female origins of agriculture as well as the weaving of plant fibers (flax and cotton) into fabrics, an offshoot of women's mastery of the plant world.

Athena is the Grecian Goddess of Weaving. Every year on her feast day she was dressed in a new peplos (shawl) which had been woven and embroidered in the previous year by the most skilled virginal weavers. More evidence for Athena's ancient origins lies in her name itself. The root of 'Athena' is the same as the words used for 'weaving' and 'spinning' among the indigenous inhabitants of the Balkans, who were skilled in weaving since 5000 BC. Athena thus may have originated in the Neolithic culture of former Yugoslavia.

Because she had no biological children, she was called Holy Virgin, or Athena Parthenia, 'she who comes from herself', and one who is complete unto herself. Her earlier mythological life as a nature Goddess is attested to by her association with the owl, her sacred bird. She may have been the Owl Goddess of the Balkans. Stone Age inhabitants of the area around former Yugoslavia frequently merged divinities with animal forms, much as the ancient Egyptians did.

Many ancient peoples believed birds contained, or perhaps were in contact with, Divinity. Birds, wings, and feathers always denote higher consciousness in religious art; thus birds are the messengers of the Goddesses and Gods.

Athena and her sacred owl were engraved on some of the earliest coins minted in the classical world. They are still admired and collected for their beauty and imagery. The owl is an ancient symbol of wisdom.

As a Goddess of the arts of civilization, Athena was credited with inventing spinning, weaving, pottery, the rake, the ox-yoke and plow for the women's fields, the horse bridle, the chariot, ships, arts and crafts, musical instruments, cultivation of the olive tree, sanitation, sewers, and engineering.

Most of her monuments depict her as a militant Goddess of Victory; but she is also represented domestically wrapped in a shawl and holding her spindle. Her most famous classical pose shows her as a Warrior Goddess leaning on her spear, helmeted head bent, mourning those

killed in battle, showing the suffering that even wars of self-defense can bring.
(3)

Goddess Coatlique

Great Mother Goddess of the Aztecs around AD 100-AD 1500, it was she who gave birth to the deities, the earth, to all life and death. The Aztecs borrowed from the earlier Toltec culture that was matrifocal; however, as the Aztecs became increasingly violent they moved more and more toward patriarchy.

Goddess Coatlique was depicted squatting in the traditional birth-giving position and was also shown with an infant in a cradleboard on her back. She was not only a maker of babies and the creative potential that a newborn represents, but also a death mother who wore skulls on her skirt. She closely resembled Goddess Kali of India in her death aspect, a common theme in Aztec culture. Besides skulls, her symbols were feathers (divine transcendence) and serpents (ancient protectors of women and their grain fields). Coatlique was also believed to devour the sun each evening and give birth to it the next morning, as the Goddess Nut did also, in the religion of ancient Egypt.

In her death aspect, the Goddess Coatlique was an agent of transformation. Since the earth herself was not only a producer of new plants, but also a receiver of all waste matter, including excrement, which she recycled into new vegetative growth; so also the Earth Mother Coatlique received the bones of all once-living animals and humans, and transformed them into new generations of people and animals.

Just as the earth 'ate' all wastes and transformed them into food; so did Coatlique 'eat' wickedness and transform it into goodness by creating a space for food to grow and flourish. In another sense, the earth (as visualized in the person of the Goddess) transformed putrid dead waste into life-sustaining foods and medicinal herbs and plants. Thus, Coatlique personified Karmic action at work in Aztec culture, just as Goddess Kali in India symbolized transformation of evil into good, reparation, forgiveness, and rebirth.

Coatlique was also the protectress of women; and was co-opted by the Spanish missionaries who transformed her into 'Our Lady of Guadalupe' in order to facilitate the conversion to Christianity of the reluctant Aztecs. Holy images and holy feast days of indigenous peoples were commonly incorporated into Catholic iconography and the liturgical calendar to ease the transition of the native Amerindians into the dominators' newly imposed religion.

Although the Virgin Mary was not as well rounded mythologically as the lusty Coatlique, she served the purposes of the conquistadors and missionaries. Many Latin Americans continue to have a fervent devotion to the dark-faced Lady of Guadalupe, a fervor that was very probably felt by their ancestors for their original Mother Goddess, Coatlique.

Goddess Cybele

Cybele (Si' ba lee) was the Great Mother of the Gods in the ancient religion of Asia and the Near East; especially Phrygia near the island of Cyprus and Lydia, a city in ancient Anatolia (present-day Turkey). By 280 BC her worship had spread to Greece and Rome where a temple was erected in her honor on the Palatine Hill. Roman soldiers and their families carried knowledge of her divinity to the far reaches of the Roman Empire, including Spain.

Cybele is still honored in Spain today as an ancestral fertility Goddess and symbol of Madrid. I witnessed her impressive bronze statue and fountain in the main plaza of Madrid, in front of the Palace of Communications, during my visit in 1997. She still sits, regal and beautiful in her chariot pulled by two lions, the animal symbols of royalty, power, and strength. She wears the royal crown of the builder of cities and holds an olive branch in one hand, the agricultural basis of Spain's economy, and a queen's scepter in the other. She was revered primarily as a natural Goddess watching over the wild things of the earth. She was also a Goddess of maternity and the fertility of humans, animals, and nature. Romans were sometimes protective of female fertility and introduced legislation to protect the rights of mothers under Emperor Augustus.

Unusually shaped stones were often revered in antiquity as a residence of divine energies just as the stones in the western wall of the temple ruins in Jerusalem are revered today; and Muslims revere the Dome of the Rock, as well as the holy meteorite at Mecca. In prehistoric times the 'Mother Rocks' on the Rhine were sacred power sources for the Germanic Tribes.

A meteor from Phrygia, on which it was believed that Cybele's image had appeared, was taken to Rome in 204 BC and dedicated to her as the Magna Mater, the Great Mother Goddess of the Roman pantheon. Later, as the Romans became more violent and patriarchal, she was given a consort, Vulcan, to limit her power.

Attis, Cybele's shepherd son, was tied to a tree, died an ignominious death, and was buried; and after three days in the tomb, arose from the dead and brought salvation to all believers. This belief is believed to have influenced the Christian religion developing in the Roman Empire at that time.

Cybele's annual spring festival, held every April 4th, was celebrated as the first festival of the year because Goddess Cybele, herself, came first.

The death and resurrection of her divine son, Attis, were enacted annually with great processions and festivals throughout the Eastern and Western world until AD 268. Priestesses, who honored her with lively music, dancing, and cymbal playing, attended her. She was sometimes shown holding a cymbal that may have derived its name from Cybele, God Mother, and Great Mother of the Gods. The very word, 'Godmother', is a survival of humanity's beginnings; when females were believed to be Mothers of Gods as well as Goddess Mothers in their own right.

(4)

Goddess EA

Ancient Greek Goddess of new beginnings, Ea, Eos, Eastre, East, Earth, and Easter. She gave her name to the direction from which the sun arises at the beginning of each new day. Easter, the Christian festival of new life and resurrection is also a derivative of her name. Her Hebrew cognate is Esther, the Prophetess. She is known as Ishtar, Goddess of the Morning Star, in Iraq (formerly Sumeria).

Eastre was her name as an early Anglo-Saxon spring Goddess. Estrus, the hormonal mood-swing suitable for mating is also part of her etymology, as is estrogen, the female hormone. Also known in Germany as Eostre, her devotees painted eggs in her honor. The rabbit, her traditional escort, also participated in her pagan fertility rites at spring festivals. Her followers greeted her on hilltops at dawn, singing, rejoicing, ringing bells, walking in processions, bringing flower offerings, baskets of colored eggs, and rabbits.

In various locations she was known as Astarte, Oestre, Ashareth, and Esther. Even 'estrogen' the female hormone, may be derived from her lovely name.

The present day Easter customs may very well be a carryover from Stone Age agricultural rites in which the Food Source was constantly placated by offerings of 'first foods' and sacrificial animals. Christian Easter services contain many references to Jesus as the 'sacrificial lamb' or 'Lamb of God who takes away the sins of the world', by his sacrificial death every spring. Leg of lamb was often eaten at the Easter dinner.

The Flathead Indians of Montana also saw the source of food as a primary focus of religion. Their beginning rite of the spring season was the 'First Roots Ceremony'. Two respected matrons led a small party of women to a fertile field where the oldest raised her arms to the sun, prayed for a successful planting, addressed the earth and pleaded for good crops, health and fertility, then dug up the roots. These were given to the Chief's wife who cooked them and served a meal symbolic of all food for the coming season, which were then eaten by all tribal members.

European women also brought baskets of eggs, bread, and other ritual foods to priests of the Catholic Church to be blessed for the Easter feast. Baskets of food, eggs, rabbits, are all symbols of women's ancient agricultural festivities with roots in the Stone Age.
(5)

Goddess Euronyme

'Euronyme' was the creatress of the world, according to a Pelasgian myth. Pelasgians were the original Greeks; an indigenous tribal people that lived there before the invading Dorians and others arrived.

In the beginning, Euronyme, the Goddess of All Things, rose naked from chaos, found nothing substantial for her feet to rest on, therefore divided sea from sky and rested on its waves.

Euronyme danced to warm herself, wildly and more wildly, until Ophion (the great serpent she created out of the north wind) grew lustful, coiled around her divine limbs and was moved to couple with her so she was with child.

This ancient myth, much older than the classical Greek mythology so familiar to us, dates from the intermediate period of the patriarchal takeover. The Mother Goddess (Creatress) was no longer giving birth alone; there was now the realization that she had to be 'fertilized' first by a male. Called the 'Inventor of Agriculture', she was also associated with sexuality and fertility.
(6)

Goddess Hecate

Hecate is one of the earliest Mother Goddesses known to us by name. She is believed to have originated in Thrace, (present day Bulgaria), which would place her in the area of Old Europe, the Balkans, where much of our civilization derives. By 4000 BC, she was known in Anatolia, (an area of present day Turkey), Egypt and Greece. Because she was older than the Olympic goddesses and gods, she was allowed by the patriarchal Greeks to share power with Zeus. Whereas she alone had ruled in the matrifocal social and religious order of antiquity, her powers were diminished by the time we encountered her in the Olympic pantheon of the Greeks.

As an Earth Goddess, her name means 'she who has power far off'. Because she looked after the fertility of the earth, she also became associated with the world of the dead, who were entombed in the earth. In this aspect she was called Queen of the Night, the moon, darkness, and the underworld. While this side of Hecate was only one of her many facets, it was the side that Medieval Inquisitors focused upon as they distorted her image into the ugly Queen of the Witches. It was the people most dangerous to the church's male power structure who Hecate encouraged: midwives, naturopaths, herbalists, psychics, family-planners, and learned women who could read and write.

In Germany, where Hecate was especially associated with the healing arts, millions of women were burned at the stake during a three hundred year period of persecution during which the wise women (wiccans, doctors, educators) of the villages were accused of heresy, tortured and murdered. Over-zealous ecclesiastics did this even though Pope Nicholas I prohibited torture of suspected 'witches'.

Hecate's name survives as the 'hex' symbol of the Germans who settled in Pennsylvania, known as the 'Pennsylvania Dutch'. They were well known as healers, and veterinarians, following the millennia-old tradition of Hecate, Goddess of Education and Medical Knowledge.

Hecate had counterparts in other pantheons: Goddess Kali of India; Heket of Egypt; Heq, the tribal matriarch of N. Africa; Morrigan of Ireland; Hekut of Nubia (present day Sudan).

Many Goddesses of the ancient world were often described as having three sides or 'persons': the virginal maiden, the all-giving Mother, and the elder wise woman.

Three phases of a woman's life were also seen in the phases of the moon, which were believed to influence the female's menses and fertility. Just as the moon waxed, became full, then waned - so did the woman's body. Hecate was the wise elder-woman of the female trinity. Roman Catholicism later borrowed the triple/trinity idea for its male godhead of God the father, God the son, and God the Holy Spirit.
(7)

Goddess Isis

Originally worshipped under her ancient Egyptian name, 'Au Set', the Goddess Isis (pronounced Eye-sis) was one of the most beloved deities in the history of humanity's religions. The earliest written accounts of her date from shortly after 3000 BC in Egypt where she had a male consort, Osiris, a youthful vegetation deity who ritually died every year and was reborn when Isis found his body and restored him to life with her magical mother power. Biblical scribes may have been inspired by the death and 'resurrection' of Osiris who was 'reborn' every spring when the seeds sprouted. Celibate priests called 'eunuchs' presided at the annual celebration of Isis' son who died, was mourned by her, and then reborn.

Isis was worshipped as the Great Mother Goddess of the Universe from Africa to Scandinavia for over 3000 years, until c. AD 350 when Emperor Constantine declared Christianity the official religion of the Roman Empire. As the female life force, she took the seed of Osiris and gave birth to Horus, the falcon-headed god. She was often depicted in a maternal pose, nursing her infant, the prototype of later Madonna and Holy Child iconography.

Symbolically her milk nourished all of humanity, her children. She was almost always shown with the round sun or solar disc on her head to indicate she was a solar, generative divinity, as the sun was, and still is, the origin of all life on the planet. The sun as a symbol of divinity has an ancient pedigree, as life cannot exist on earth without it. The sun disc was later borrowed by Catholic artists who used the solar disc as a halo to exemplify holiness of the saints.

As 'Isis Navigatum', she was the patroness of sailing in the Greco-Roman world and also Scandinavia. Prows of Viking ships were sometimes carved in her likeness.

Goddess Isis was also known as 'The Throne' and was often shown with a throne atop her head. Her name was written in hieroglyphs with a sign representing a throne, indicating how important she was to the bestowal of power on the kingship of Egypt. She usually held an ankh, symbol of eternal life, as well as the scepter of royalty.

Many researchers believe that Egyptian culture in the earliest periods of its history was matrilineal; and that it was the daughters, not the sons who actually inherited the throne. It was only from the 18th Dynasty, c. 1570 BC that the word 'Pharaoh' which literally meant 'Great House' came to mean 'royal male' of the household. By this time, Egypt had been invaded several times by Indo-Europeans; and had been heavily influenced by Indo-Aryan (Hittite and Hurrian) ideas of male superiority.

As a great guardian deity, she was invoked for healing and called 'Great of Magic', since Egyptian medicine was a combination of magic (amulets, invocation, hieroglyphs on papyrus carried on the person) and herbal recipes. She was also known as 'Clever of Tongue' for her assertiveness. In one spell she was called 'more clever than a million gods'. She was believed to have taught the ancient Egyptians how to make bread, spin flax into linen thread, weave clothing, and also the skills of reading and medicines.

Her worship eventually spread to Rome, where it was called 'superstition', as were Judaism and Christianity, and promptly forbidden in favor of the cult of the deified Roman emperors. However, the religion of Isis was the most attractive of all the Oriental religions being imported from the eastern Roman Empire; and Emperor Caligula eventually sanctioned an official temple to be built in Isis' honor.

Some of her many titles were: Queen of the Earth, Queen of the Stars, Magna Mater (of the Romans), Isis the Great, She Comes Who

Is Great, Mistress of the Land of Women, (perhaps referring to an early matriarchy). Her popularity outside of Egypt was phenomenal. Christianity had a difficult time destroying her worship; and may have incorporated some of her imagery and attributes into the worship of Mary, the Mother of God. *
(8)

Goddess Ma'at

Mother Goddess Ma'at of Egypt is one of the earliest ancestral Mother Goddesses. Her very name contains the mother syllable 'ma'. She stood for the Mother's laws upon which Egyptian civilization was founded: Truth, Order, Justice, and Morality. She was usually depicted wearing a large feather in her regal headdress. After death, Ma'at symbolically weighed the deceased's heart, with her feather on the other side of the scales of Justice. If the heart was pure and 'light as a feather', the deceased was allowed to enter the Field of Reeds, or everlasting life.

Pharaohs claimed to rule by the authority of Ma'at, and stressed in their Pyramid Texts how they had upheld the laws of the universe, which she personified. Her origins, however, go far back into antiquity before the Old Kingdom and the Pyramid Texts of 2500BC. She is Ultimate Wisdom, personified as female.

In her animal manifestation (before she was anthropomorphic, or made human) she was the Holy Cow who gave birth to the Sacred Bull of Memphis. Her feather may also have been symbolic of her other 'son', Horus the Falcon God. She was so recognizable in Ancient Egypt that her feather alone could represent her. In antiquity, the feather always symbolized a divinity that could transcend earthly existence and move freely between worlds, just as birds seem to do.

Because she also represented the primordial consciousness or conscience, she was also symbolized as an eye, ever-watching over her children. This is typical of mothers who have 'eyes in the back of their

---

* Marine archaeologists under Alexandria Bay, Oct. 1995, found remains of the legendary lighthouse of Alexandria, a 3,800-year-old Sphinx, and a 40-foot statue of a Goddess-Queen. The statue, weighing 12 tons, was robed as Isis. It is believed to have been submerged since AD 495, which would date her worship to even later into the historic era than previously thought.

Time Magazine, April 1996

heads'. As the ancient classless society of Ancient Egypt evolved into a political and militaristic theocracy (c. 2500 BC) with the Pharaoh at the top of the hierarchy of power, he co-opted the symbol of the ancestral Mother Goddess, Ma'at. Her ancient all-seeing mother's eye (internalized as moral conscience) became the Eye of RA, the sun God of the Pharaoh.
(9)

Goddess Manavegr

Manavegr, a Teutonic Moon Goddess whose name is prefixed by 'mana', was the Old European name of their ancestral Mother. She is the Goddess of 'man', which meant 'human person' originally. Patriarchal medieval scribes later omitted women from its meaning, until today 'man' means only male persons.
(10)

Mary

The Mother of God in the Roman Catholic religion, Mary, is the only female of divine status in the patriarchal biblically based religions: Judaism, Christianity, and Islam. Mary, as a composite of ancestral Mother Goddesses of antiquity, was probably named after Mari, the 3000 BC Syrian Goddess venerated for centuries in the Middle East, the same area of the world in which Mary herself originated. Other researchers compare her to Demeter; the stately, regal Mother Goddess of Greece who is depicted wearing the same draped garments and veils as Mary. In fact, it would be impossible to tell them apart from the way they were represented in statuary.

There is also an uncanny resemblance of Mary and the infant Jesus to the images of Ancient Egypt's Mother Goddess, Isis, and her infant, Horus. Both are portrayed with great tenderness holding their babies on their laps. The only difference is that Isis is usually bare breasted and Mary is fully draped, as is consistent with her de-sexualization under the auspices of ecclesiastic authorities. However, several rare representations of Mary nursing Jesus at her breast can be found in museums; but never in churches or on holy cards.

There are researchers who see Mary as a successor of the much loved Isis. The popularity of the ancient Egyptian Goddess was phenomenal outside of Egypt. She was known and revered even in Scandinavia, where she was the patroness of sailing and sometimes carved on the prows of ships. 'Isis Navigatum' was her title as patroness of sailors in the Roman Empire. Christianity had a difficult time destroying her worship and may have allowed the pagans it sought to convert, to have Mary as a replacement. The church further kept a close eye on Marian worship, even trying to suppress it by insisting Mary was not a divinity in her own right. However, it is a losing battle and Marian worship is as strong today as ever. There are new 'sightings' of her every year in many countries; and devotees flock to the sites where her 'vision' has appeared.

Many of Mary's most sacred shrines are in caves, which are reminiscent of the original Stone Age Mother Goddess and her followers who lived in limestone caves 30,000 years ago. Lourdes, France, is an example of the grotto cave site; her sacred spring runs through the cave with her healing waters in which pilgrims bathe and pray for cures.

I visited one such sacred site in Paris, where the Cathedral of Sacre Coeur rises above its foundation of underground caves and springs. Almost all of the cathedrals in France are dedicated to 'Notre Dame', 'Our Lady' Mary. Surely the cathedral of Notre Dame in Paris is one of the wonders of the world. The concrete spires appear to be made of concrete 'lace', a fitting tribute to 'Our Lady', Mary, who has been a symbol of all that is noble and pure for Christian men as well as women.

Unfortunately, her very 'purity' has sent a mixed message to Catholic females. It is biologically impossible to be both virgin and mother; so an unattainable role model is presented to women. Mary's sexuality has been totally obliterated, sending the subliminal message to Catholic women that they would do well to suppress their sensuality for the sake of virtue. This non-sexual Goddess is the direct opposite of every other Goddess in the ancient world, about 28,000 of who have been researched so far.

Non-Christian Goddesses were celebrated for their love, sensuality, fertility, and physical endowments. By casting human, and especially female, sexuality out of the realm of the sacred, the patriarchs placed it firmly in the realm of pornographers. By making sex sinful, impure and profane, in effect, the 'original sin', the church inhibited the self-esteem of the faithful at a very basic level of existence; and thus, set the stage for power, control, and manipulation of its members. Robbing Mary of her sexuality imposed an artificial standard of thought and behavior for women. This also did a terrible disservice to males who found it difficult to respect a woman who enjoyed her sexuality; and also set the stage for abusive relationships between the sexes.

But in spite of her de-sexualization, Mary has been an inspiration to me for my entire life. Her serenity, poise, dignity, compassion, maternity, and purity pulled me toward her when there were no other female images of divinity available to young women growing up in this country. Little did I know, as I recited her litany during the yearly May devotions at her grotto enshrined at St. Francis Church, that these same words were used thousands of years earlier by women devotees of Ishtar, Inanna, Aphrodite, Isis, Diana, Mari, and many, many other non-Christian female divinities who were the Goddesses of antiquity.

Her litany of names is still said with devotion by my seven year old grand-daughter, Casanndra:

> Holy Mary
> Holy Mother of God
> Mother of divine grace
> Mother most pure
> Mother most amiable
> Mother of our Creator
> Mother of good counsel
> Virgin most merciful
> Mirror of justice
> Seat of wisdom
> Cause of our joy
> Spiritual vessel
> Vessel of Honor
> Mystical rose
> Tower of David
> Tower of Ivory
> House of gold
> Ark of the covenant
> Gate of heaven
> Morning star

Health of the sick
Star of the sea
Comforter of the afflicted
Queen of Angels
Queen of Patriarchs
Queen of Prophets
Queen of Apostles
Queen of Martyrs
Queen of all Saints
Queen assumed into heaven
Queen of Peace
Pray for us!
(11)

Goddess Mami or Mawu

She is the ancestral Mother Goddess of the Dahomey of Benin, Africa. 'Mother of All', a rainbow colored serpent is her ally. The serpent was the ancient guardian of the women's fields and is depicted with Goddesses worldwide, linking the female to nature and the discovery of agriculture and medicine. Mami breathed her own breath (spirit) into all of her people. When they (her tribes) fight each other, they are fighting Mother because they all have her breath, her spirit. This is the mother principle, the beginning of justice.

Mawu is sometimes known as male in different regions of Africa, or an androgynous or dual deity, both female and male. This may be the result of some researchers assigning a gender to deities which were originally asexual.
(12)

Goddess Mbabe Mwana Waresa

To the Zulus of South Africa, she is the Great Rain Mother of All, the divine ancestress of the entire human race. The Zulus of Natal understood her as the personification of the waters of life, the birth waters. Other African tribal peoples, such as the Yemaya, worshipped her in the rivers, lakes, streams, and oceans.

Zulus are renowned for their beautiful and complex dances for all sacred festivals. When we bang pots and pans in the streets on New

Year's Eve, a Zulu observer would say we are invoking Mbabe Mwana Waresa in a rain dance to get her attention.
(13)

Goddess Maya

In Hindu mythology, the great mysterious energies of life and death are personified in their multitude of Goddesses and Gods. Maya, as an ancestral Mother Goddess, is thus the Creatress, the Creative Force at work in the universe. She is constantly bringing people and events in and out of existence, endlessly. She is usually shown with many arms and hands, each one making a different gesture, to show how busy she is.

In a wider philosophical sense, Maya also personifies the Illusion of Life. She teaches us that what we perceive through our senses can often deceive us; and things may often not be what they seem. In this sense, of the created, manifest world being illusory, she invites us to look deeper at people, places, events, ideas; to strip away preconceived notions (illusions) and get to the core of the matter. Thus she represents Intelligence also, pulling aside the veil of illusion; and Creativity, the art of making things manifest, making something new appear, that had not been apparent before.

She takes her place alongside Devi, Kali, and Shakti as the great female deities who partake of the dance of life with Brahma, Vishnu, and Shiva, the major Hindu male deities. Locked in an embrace, the female and male energies bring the world into being, sustain it, and release it to manifest itself again, differently.

Goddess Maya's name is a cognate of the Greek Goddess Maia, Ancient Egypt's Ma'at (pronounced Mayet), Ireland's Goddess Maga or Macha, Central America's Mayahuel, and Scandinavia's Maj. In her identification with education and knowledge, she is known as Mahavidya.
(14)

Goddess Memnet

Egyptian Goddess Memnet's name means 'memory'. The Greeks later borrowed her name for the science of 'memnonics', or memory-aides. The word 'memory' itself contains the mother-syllable, 'me', pointing to the reverence in Antiquity for those whose memories were trained to remember the entire history of the clan, before writing, when all knowledge was transmitted orally. Queen Hatshepsut, c. 1479 BC, built a colossal statue to Goddess Memnet at Memphis, Egypt.

Goddess Mu Lan

She was a legendary woman warrior of ancient China who was led into the mountains to be magically trained in the arts of war. She then returned to her village to right the wrongs done to the villagers by the warlords who ruled. She had the villager's grievances carved into her back with knives so she would not forget them. Mu Lan may actually have been a real woman who had villagers' names tattooed on her back. She then led avenging troops against the Emperor. The mother syllable 'Mu' prefixing her name suggests that she may have been an ancestral, fierce Mother Goddess of prehistoric China. Ancient Mother Goddesses, such as Ma'at of Egypt, were often credited with doling out justice, or the Mother's Law.

Nerthus

The ancestral Mother Goddess of all northern or Nordic Europeans was Nerthus, 'Mother of the Northern Earth', who gave her name to the direction of the 'North'. She was perceived as all-giving, bountiful, and nurturing humans through the bounty of her body, the earth, and its produce. The close association of female Goddesses with the plant world symbolically points to the female origins of agriculture. In Iron Age Scandinavia, her statue was pulled across the fields in a wagon, chariot, or sled, in spring, asking her to bless the fields and make them fertile. She may have been an early prototype of the originally female Santa Claus with her gift-laden sleigh.

She was pictured wearing long blonde braids, and a woven headpiece similar to the kore crowns of Greek Goddesses. These headdresses are sill worn today by Lithuanian, Polish, and Ukrainian, Swedish, and Hungarian ethnic dancers.

By the Iron Age, c. 700 BC, the warrior-centered tribes of Scandinavia changed Nerthus' gender and she became the god Njord or Niord. This suited the raiding Norsemen who venerated Njord as the god of seafarers and wealth.

There is scholarly disagreement about the connection of Nerthus to Njord. Some sagas portray them as consorts, which was a customary way of dethroning a Goddess or limiting her power by making her share power with a male deity; son, husband, brother, father, consort.

Caucasian invaders, beginning about 4,000 BC, profoundly altered the mythology of all indigenous peoples. They would be called Vikings much later, c. AD 100.

Caucasians imposed a patriarchal worldview on the formerly peaceful matrifocal agrarian societies. This was accomplished in part by dethroning the ancestral Mother Goddess, a unifying symbol among indigenous tribal cultures. Once their spirituality was forcibly removed (destruction of statues, 'idols', temples, slaying of priestesses and kings and queens) they were more amenable to control by outsiders. The sky gods of thunder and war replaced the earth mothers; or sometimes the local deities were miniaturized and pushed underground.

These are called trolls, elves, wood spirits, sprites, fairies, leprechauns, goblins and gnomes; and are sometimes allowed to retain their magical qualities.

The destruction of the old order and the imposition of the new deities of the conquerors are often preserved in sacred texts, epic poems, and Holy Scriptures. In Norway and Iceland these sagas are known as the 'Edda's'.
(15)

Nu-Kua

The 'Woman Kua' was an ancestral Mother Goddess of ancient China, 2800 BC and earlier. She was sometimes depicted as an Empress with magical powers. Although she is mentioned in the earliest texts, she is better known from writings of the much later Han Dynasty, c. AD 100. In these later texts, she was demoted to the sister or consort of the better-known Fu-hei, a sage.

Nu-Kua, as an early ancestral Goddess, is only mentioned twice in the 'Shin-hai Ching', the sacred scriptures of China, full of gory details and myths, similar to the Hebrew Old Testament and the scriptures or sacred writings of many cultures worldwide.

Nu-Kua was credited with being the first human on earth, who made herself a companion out of clay so she would not be lonely. She

was the divinity who imparted knowledge, agriculture, marriage and family, created the directions, the heavens, and tamed wild animals, all in a day's work for most women.
(16)

ROMAN	GREEK	EGYPTIAN	ROLE
Venus	Aphrodite	Isis	Goddess of love and beauty
Mars	Ares	Seth	God of war
Diana	Artemis	Sekhmet	Goddess of hunting and protector of wild animals
Minerva	Athena	Ra-ta-uit	Goddess of wisdom, warfare & crafts
Ceres	Demeter	Mut	Goddess of grain, farming and soil
Pluto	Hades	Osiris	God and king of the underworld
Vulcan	Hephaestus	Hephaestus	God of fire, volcanoes, and industry; blacksmith to the gods
Juno	Hera	Isis and Ma'at	Queen of the gods; goddess of marriage and childbirth
Mercury	Hermes	Aphrodite	Messenger of the gods, patron of travelers, merchants, and thieves
Vesta	Hestia	Hathor	Goddess of the hearth and home
Saturn	Kronos	Nut	Divinities of Time Keeping or Passage of Time
Proserpina	Persephone	Nepthys	Goddess queen of the underworld; goddess of spring
Neptune	Poseidon		God of the sea and earthquakes
Jupiter	Zeus	RA	King of the gods; protector of justice and social order
Apollo	Apollo	RA	God of the sun, arts/music, archery, prophecy, and medicine
Bacchus	Dionysus	Min	God of wine and revelry
Isis	Au Set	Isis	Great Mother Goddess, Queen of earth and stars

Table of Goddesses and Gods

Romans copied the deities of Greece because it (Greece) was a much more advanced civilization by the time the Romans conquered it, probably around 200 BC. The Greeks borrowed much from the high civilization of ancient Egypt, especially in medicine, religious concepts, etc. which the first Christians (who were Roman Catholics) then copied from the Greeks.

The Catholic male hierarchy copied the Roman Empire's political organization: Pontiff, Priest, Nuns (vestal virgins), Diocese, and Cardinal. Some deities do not have Egyptian counterparts because ancient Egypt had a different value system and did not have a War God, like the Roman's Mars.

Goddess Isis (AuSet, the Spirit/Creatress) encompassed most female inventions or attributes.

Goddess Bibliography

1. *The Woman's Encyclopedia of Myths and Secrets*, Barbara G. Walker, CA, Harper & Row, 1983
2. *The Greeks and Their Gods*, W.K.C.Guthrie, Boston, Beacon Press, 1966
3. Ibid
4. *When God Was a Woman*, Merlin Stone, NY 1976
5. *Goddesses in World Mythology*, Ann & Imel, NY, Oxford Univ Press, 1983
6. *The Woman's Encyclopedia of Myths and Secrets*, Barbara G. Walker, CA, Harper & Row, 1983
7. Ibid
8. *Goddesses in World Mythology*, Ann & Imel, NY, Oxford Univ Press, 1983
9. Ibid
10. *Dictionary of Word Origins*, John Ayto, NY, Little, Brown Co. 1990
11. *Goddesses in World Mythology*, Ann & Imel, NY, Oxford Univ Press, 1983
12. Ibid
13. Ibid
14. Ibid
15. Ibid
16. Ibid

CHAPTER IX:
The Mother Syllable or Mother Tongue

She-Speaks-Who-Is-Great

Because the female has not been highly valued for the past 4000 years, due mostly to a one-sided system of social and political organization called 'patriarchy', it is difficult for researchers to compile a complete, authentic, unbiased history of women, including the vast expanse of time (roughly 300,000 years) which we call 'prehistory'.

With my intense curiosity in this subject, I devised a way to trace female origins through language fossils, or words. The roots of many of our words reach far, far back into the dawn of humanity. One of these fossils is 'ma', which I believe was possibly one of humanity's earliest vocal sounds.

My reasoning is as follows:

After prototypical humans began walking upright, (a major evolutionary step in human development), their skulls elongated, and there was more room within the cranial cavity for the growth of more brain cells. The configuration of the tongue, palate, teeth, glottis, and lower jaw, likewise changed; allowing for a wider range of vocalization than was present in other animal species.

Little by little, with the combination of increased mental activity and mouth and throat coordination, the new hominids (our ancestors) were able to communicate by more than guttural sounds, sign language, facial expressions, and body language. They now had a way to express their needs in an attempt to have those needs met by others in the group; that is, language.

We know that one of our primal needs, in order for life to sustain itself, is food. The infant, because of total dependence on the mother, would have had the strongest motivation to ask to be fed. Most adults and children over the age of two-years could probably have found something edible in their environment on their own, except under the most adverse of circumstances. Because of a moving together or 'smacking' as a universal expression of a desire for food, it is not too far fetched to assume that a baby's first words would be motivated by its hunger pangs, or a desire to eat (maybe just for the sheer pleasure of it). The mother's breast may have been the only available source of food for a hungry infant in antiquity.

Aside from crying, which may not have worked all the time, the infant, out of intense need, would have been highly motivated to find alternate ways to attract the attention of its mother and let her know it was mealtime. The sound most likely to have been the first 'word' any infant spoke, no matter where the infant lived, would therefore have been a bringing of the lips together, in an opening and closing motion, sounding like 'mum-mum' or 'num-num'. Eventually, the primal sound of a suckling infant at the mother's breast became 'ma-ma', the prehistoric Indo-European root meaning 'breasts', and 'mother'.

The mammary gland is an obvious derivative, as is also the root of the word 'mammal', an animal that suckles its young. There are obvious cognates in many other languages: Latin, mammals and mater; Greek, mamme; French, mamman; Italian, mamma; English, mamma, mom, mother; Welsh, mam; Russian, mama; Lithuanian, motere; German, mutter, and so on throughout the entire range of global languages.

Unfortunately the word 'father' does not have an ancient lineage because the concept of paternity and the male's role in reproduction was not clearly understood in antiquity. And even when animal herders in the Caucasus may have discovered the secret of the inseminating role of the male's semen, c. 5000 BC, the reproductive process was misunderstood for many millennia. It was widely believed that the entire embryonic infant, the blastocyst, was contained within the male's sperm; and that the female body provided more or less just an incubator/womb for the fetus to develop to term.

With this erroneous mindset, it is easy to see why male sperm was deified for thousands of years; and why the male was elevated to the status of God, the Father; displacing the Mother Goddess who had held her primacy for all the millennia of previous human existence. It was not until the mid-1800's AD that the female ovum was discovered, after the invention of the microscope. However, ingrained concepts die hard; and the world's major religions still institutionalize the falsehood of male supremacy (patriarchy), even though we now know that 50% of the genetic information (DNA) is encoded in the mother's contribution.

Perhaps the ancient Stone Age matrifocal societies were more intuitively aware of the mother's enormous contribution to the gestating infant than we are today with all of our technology.

Thus, the mother syllable, 'ma', because of its roots in the very infancy of humanity, became my symbolic thread from my foremothers' tattered string skirts. I followed this 'string' figuratively backward in time and was able to trace the ancient female origins of many words.

Since there was no standardized language or spelling in our earliest existence as the human race, other syllables beginning with 'm', the primal sound of a suckling baby at the breast, can also be used to track our earliest maternal beginnings. Me, mi, mo, mu, and my, can also be used as cognates for ma, the mother syllable.

This chapter will be devoted entirely to mother syllable words, including Goddess names. My list will in no way be conclusive but only representative. The readers are invited to begin their own journey backward in space and time by using the mother syllable as a tracking tool.

These words that I call Mother-words are found in many languages. Greek, Arabic, Farsi, Turkish, Hindi, Lithuanian, Latin, Italian, French, Spanish, German, and English carry words that point to female origins of the arts of civilization in our ancient past.

Female origins in words:

Ma

Ma is the Indo-European root word for 'mother', suggested by the burbling of a suckling baby, which can be traced back into prehistory. The English, Russian, Italian, and French 'mama' are derived from it as are Latin 'mater', Lithuanian 'mamyte', Welsh 'mam', Greek 'mamme', Ancient Egyptian, 'mut'. (Goddess Mut's name meant both mother and life.) East Indian honorific title is 'ma', for a female spiritual teacher in the Tantra faith, 'maha', for a male. Mahatma Ghandi, for instance, was called the 'Great Revered Mother', even though he was a man.

Gloria Bertonis, with Carol Miranda

Ma'at

Egyptian word for both mother and matter. It is also primordial mud of the Nile from which all life came forth. Goddess Ma'at was the ancestral Mother Goddess of ancient Egypt. She symbolized justice, the intrinsic order of the universe, truth, and all that was righteous and good.

Ancient Egyptians honored their Great Goddesses as representational women, who were known to have played crucial roles in the creation of the world, such as agriculturists, domesticators of animals, potters, artists, writers, weavers, priestesses, musicians, doctors, mathematicians, educators, and time-keepers. Goddess Ma'at's origins go far back into antiquity, before the Old Kingdom and the Pyramid Texts of ancient Egypt. Pharaohs attributed Goddess Ma'at with their authority to govern; and stressed how they upheld the laws of the universe she embodied; truth, justice, and moral integrity. She was so well known in ancient Egyptian civilization that her feather alone could represent her. She was usually depicted with a feather behind one ear, symbolizing her heart so pure that it was 'as light as a feather'.

She is still honored by young black incarcerated males reclaiming their African heritage in the Federal Prison at Frackville, Pennsylvania. Their cultural association is called "Ma'at Association for the Advancement of Truth". I attended a lecture by a discharged prisoner who spoke of how much the Goddess Ma'at Association had helped him and many others regain their self-respect and a code of ethical behavior.

Machete

A sharp, large, curved knife used in agriculture. Machete is the mothers' knife with which women cleared underbrush and later appropriated by men for use in protection of the clan in warfare.

Magneh

Headscarf worn by Muslim women in Iran. The headscarf is sewn up the front, rather than tied, to make sure it does not loosen lest a wisp of hair escape. It is forbidden for a devout Muslim girl or woman to show any hair in public. At puberty, girls are taken to special stores to be fitted for their magneh in some Muslim countries. An ill-fitted scarf can interfere with hearing.

Madrasa

A religious school. Mothers have always been their children's first teachers, since the beginning of humankind, so it is fitting that a school be called 'the mother's place'. Most children were home-schooled before the 1800's when public education was instituted in many Western countries.

Maenad

In archaic Greece, a female follower of the wine-god Dionysos, son of Goddess Diana. When inspired by his spirit contained in the wine, she became a free woodland spirit, a 'maenad'.

Magan

A wealthy 'mother' city of the Bronze Age in southern Arabia, on the Persian Gulf. In 2500 to 2000 BC it flourished. Today it is called the United Arab Emirates.

Magazine

The original meaning of magazine was 'the house where the mothers stored their excess foods', seeds, roots, and tubers to be used for the next food crop. The magazine may originally have been a pit dug in a Stone Age cave floor. Magazine has an ancient lineage in several languages: magasin (French), magazzine (Italian), makhazin (Arabic). Under patriarchy, the magazine became the storehouse for weapons. Today's magazines are storehouses of information; which makes our foremothers very proud.

Magma

Hot molten rock from deep under the ground. Magma can move towards the surface of the soil in an earthquake and release carbon dioxide. Once it reaches the earth's surface, we call it 'lava'. Since earliest times when women learned to grow food from seeds, earth was viewed as a metaphysical food-providing mother. So it is only fitting that Mother Earth's 'insides' be named magma, or 'inside the mother'.

Maguey

A cactus plant, whose milky juice was fermented, possibly by women, into an intoxicating milky juice used to relieve the pains of childbirth. It was mentioned in Aztec writings of the deity Quetzalcoatl who drank the sap of the maguey. The Aztec priests may have used it as a consciousness-altering potion for religious rituals, much like priests use wine today.

Mahmood
Praise. Nearly all men praise their mothers, in every culture and every time period. 'Mahmood' may literally mean 'praise to mother'. It also means 'praised by Allah' when used as a man's name in Iran.

Mahtob
Moonlight. The moon was perceived as a female divinity in ancient Persia (present-day Iran.) Today Mahtob is a female name in Iran.

Mahzigen
People of the motherland. This is the name of the Berbers of the Atlas Mts. of Morocco-the name they call themselves. Ta'mazight is the mother-tongue of the Berbers totally distinct from Arabic, the official language of Morocco.

Maia (Greek)
Means 'she who makes the flowers and grass grow again every spring.' This is one of the earliest names of Mother Earth in antiquity. Her name survives in the name of the month of May, named after her. Goddess Maia's feast day, the first of May, or May Day is still celebrated in certain parts of the world where the boys and girls dance around a Maypole in a symbolic mating game. It was cruel irony that the soviets used the Mother's Day to celebrate militarism.

Maia was an early name of the 'Mother of All' in the Greco-Roman world. Magna, great and large, derives from this.

Mailicheia
Ancient Greek title of a female divinity who was 'easy to be entreated, the gentle gracious one'. She was the divinity of purification after kindred blood was spilled in inter-tribal warfare. It was an adjective used in honoring Goddess Demeter in archaic Greece.

Maimaktes

In archaic Greece, a title of a deity meaning, 'one who gets enraged when one's kin's blood is shed; and who pants and thirsts for justice'. Kinship was reckoned through the mother in almost all ancient societies, before knowledge of the male's contribution to reproduction.

Maiua

This is the Latin root of 'majesty'. Both of these words point to early maternal origins of ruler-ship. Mothers were the first majesties (queens) in Africa and the rest of the world. The right to rule was often passed on through the females of the family. This is the reason Egyptian Pharaohs had to marry their sisters. The sisters were the ones who had the power to rule and confer divine kingship on the males of the ruling dynasties. In Arabic tradition, 'sister' does not always denote a biological sister. Because there was no word for 'sweetheart' in ancient Egypt, 'sister' came to mean a man's beloved, as well as meaning a sibling.

Mahdi

A Messiah. The twelfth imam (teacher) that disappeared centuries ago and will reappear with Jesus on the Last Judgment Day of the Muslims. This word has the same root as the Hebrew 'Messiah' and both Semitic groups worshipped female divinities before their patriarchal shift to all-male religions. The Muslim Mahdi is prayed to on his birthday, May sixth, to grant special favors to the devout.

Majlia

A monthly salon held in Saudi Arabia homes or other buildings where the group hears lectures or discusses interesting topics. Originally women may have gathered in each other's homes for religious and educational discussions.

Makuna

The spirit or soul of Australian aborigines: the Makuna tribe; also the name of the Makuna tribe itself.

Malic

An Oracle, able to foretell the future. Today we would say 'psychic' to describe a person who has this ability. In the earliest days of human societies, this skill may have been associated mostly with mothers who may have been perceived as having much more knowledge of the past, as well as the future, out of sheer necessity.

Mallet
Early female tool used in crushing grain to feed to their infants and toddlers.

Mamlaka
(cognate of mother's milk, lactate) The ideal Muslim nation envisioned by some devout Muslims.

Mammetam
Babylonian Creatress of Destiny who allotted life and death but did not reveal the day of death. Mammetam was an important Goddess in the earliest written literature, the Sumerian 'Epic of Gilgamesh'.

Man
Man is 'he' who came from a woman. The word 'man' originally meant 'moon' in Scandinavia, Rome, and throughout Europe. 'Man' meaning 'moon' has origins in Sanskrit as well. Because the moon was believed to fertilize women before paternity was understood, the moon eventually took on male connotations; hence, 'man in the moon'.

In old English, 'man' meant 'human being' or 'person'; but with the progressive devaluing of the female that reached its height in the women's holocaust of the Medieval Catholic Church, 'man' came to mean only male persons.

Another possible etymology for 'man' is the Latin 'manus' meaning hand. 'Manus' is also a mother-syllable word. It must be remembered that mothers were most likely the first manufacturers of food, clothing, baskets, pottery, textiles, and medicines as well as child bearers.

Mana
A supernatural mother-power believed by indigenous Melanesians and Polynesians to be present in certain people, objects, and nature.

Anthropologists used the term for supernatural power and applied it to other cultures. It is also the biblical term for the food that helped Hebrews survive in the desert.

Manes
The 'shades' or spirits of the dead in ancient Greece who became Goddesses of the Underworld and prophesied in the form of ghosts or invisible energy essences.

Manger
Derived from the Latin, 'to eat'. The mothers of the earliest humans provided almost all food, first from the breast milk, then from forays into the bush to collect all edibles. Manger, the place where animals ate, and Jesus was born, is appropriately a mother-word.

Manifesto
Originally meant something that could be grasped by the hand (Latin-manus), like an infant coming out of its mother's body. Maternity was palpable, obvious, while fatherhood was not. Women also created the earliest rules of morality, the mothers' manifesto or 'mutterecht' in German, Mother-Right. Today we know this early maternal manifesto as the 'Common Law' or Humanism.

Männerbund
A prehistoric band from which Nazi's claimed fictitious descent. A super-human race.

Manteau
A heavy dark coat worn by women when they go outside the home in the Islamic Republic of Iran. This is supposed to make women 'invisible' so they will not tempt men to look at them. This Islamic custom may have originated as a means to protect women from male harassment, but has come to symbolize male dominance and female compliance in some instances.

Mantle
A covering worn over the shoulders, and possibly one of the earliest articles of clothing created by women weavers. Used as a head and

shoulder covering in Middle East, the Virgin Mary was always depicted wearing a mantle. It could easily be removed by the women and used to blanket her infant, or be tied into a carrying sling. The mantle, a lovely fabric woven by women, came to be associated with royalty. Since kings were originally one's kin, his mother may have been the one who wove his mantle and placed it over his shoulders as a sign of rulership which resided in the female in early matrifocal societies. The mother/matron/monarch thus vested her son, grandson, brother, etc. with her divine right to rule their tribe.

Mar
The Latin word for sea, which produced the Old English, 'mer', from which 'mermaid' is derived. Life itself is believed today (as in the past) to have begun in water; just as human life develops in the amniotic sac of fluid in the mother's womb. 'Mar', then, is the 'mother's waters' which gave birth to all things on land and in the water. 'Marine' and 'maritime' are obvious derivatives, as are the feminine names Marie, Mary, Marian, Marianne, Miriam, Marcella, Martha, Margaret, Margit, Marilyn.

Marabout
The beehive-shaped tomb of a local hero, heroine, or saint at which social and devotional activities are held in Muslim countries. These burial sites may have originally been the final resting places of ancient Clan Mothers. Now they honor mostly deceased men.

Mare
A mare is a female horse, or equine mother. The mare's sexuality as well as her maternity was highly valued in prehistory. It is said that in ancient Ireland, the High King was required to mate publicly with a mare in order to demonstrate his superior virility, thereby winning the approval of the Mother Goddess (personified as a mare) to rule. This custom was later changed to bathing in mare's milk, the previous custom perhaps being too demanding.

Margaritaria
Roman word in antiquity for a dealer in pearls, often a woman.

Mari

An ancient Goddess of Syria, usually depicted with wide, all-seeing eyes. Her name is the Indo-European 'mari' meaning 'primal mother's waters', amniotic fluid of the womb, sea, ocean, river, and water. Her name evolved into 'Mary', the generic name of the Mother Goddess of Christianity, who encompassed some of the attributes of the pagan Mother Goddesses, such as Star of the Sea, Queen of Heaven, Our Lady of Grace, Virgin Most Pure, etc. The usual blue of her dress evokes her watery origins.

Markab

A boat. Mothers may have used hallowed-out tree trunks as a boat or reed rafts to calm their infants on water (streams) long before sailing took place.

Mars

Mars was originally an outdoor, woodland deity of an ambiguous, non-sexual nature. Because the Romans named the red planet, Mars, it is probable that Mars may originally have been female, and associated with the moon that was believed to cause menstrual blood to flow from women. It is this association with red blood that may have led to Mars' designation as the god of war. The month of March may have been named after the Roman god of war because the Roman Empire began its preparations for war in spring, designating the 15th (of March, May, July or October or the 13th day of any other month in the ancient Roman calendar) as the 'Ides of March', with the ominous suggestion of future disaster to those who threatened the Roman Empire's expansion.

In the genealogy of Mars, one can see the progression of the divinity from a non-sexual woodland spirit, to life-giving female moon deity, to death-bringing military god. This ideological progression began c. 4000 BC and has continued to the present day until virtually every world culture has altered the gender of its' original Mother Goddess.

Marylya

A magic invisible fence of Siberian tribal peoples, signifying a defended territory protected by the friendly spirits of the clan mothers and local heroes or brave hunters. Building this protective spiritual wall was originally the work of the female shamankas who led the community where everyone was an equal participant in the ritual of protecting the village from evil. Later, the helpful spirits were seen as exclusively the spirit helpers of the male shamans; and their rituals became individual performances rather than communal group activities.

Mash

The grain that was crushed and prepared with water and enzymes, sweeteners, and flavorings in the preparation of beer. Mash was also an early baby food; grain chewed up by mothers and placed in the baby's mouth on her fingers. (Feeding was most likely done from mouth to mouth perhaps the origin of kissing.) If she added some water and honey to it, she would have invented the earliest fermented beverage we call 'beer'.

Mashrabiyyeh

Latticed windows used in women's quarters of the home and the harem. They were intricately carved so no one could see the woman peeking thru the tiny openings into the courtyard below where she was not permitted.

Masjed

Place of worship in Farsi. Mother Goddesses were the earliest divinities of Persia, as in every country worldwide. The place of worship would have been called 'the mother's house'.

Mass

May derive from Hebrew 'matzah', Greek 'maza' and Latin 'massa', meaning the mothers' barley cakes and later bread or nourishment provided by the womenfolk. The early Christian's 'mass' was a food sharing or communal dinner called 'agape' (love feast in Greek). The men and women present shared memories of Jesus and vowed to live according to his example. In its early years, Christianity believed women had equal status in the religion which Jesus taught; unlike the Hebrews who assigned women inferior status in the religion of his ancestors. Later Christian hierarchies of power reversed Jesus' teachings and examples and disallowed women from taking Holy Orders; even though Jesus' chief disciples had been the three Marys: 'Mary', mother of Jesus, 'Mary' Magdalene, and 'Mary', sister of Martha the homemaker, and not the 12 (all men) apostles.

Massebah

Standing stone of ancient Canaan (Syria and Palestine). It represented Mother Earth, older than time. Sometimes a rudimentary face was carved on it. Massebahs correspond to the menhirs, standing stones of Western Europe, British Isles, and Ireland. Some of the stones are slightly stooped, symbolizing an old woman, ancient Mother of the Earth.

Mast

In the Indo-Iranian Urdu language, it means 'drunk'. Mothers have always needed powerful pain relievers from the beginning of time for the labor pains of childbirth. Women foragers learned very early which plants had narcotic properties (narcosia means sleep) and may have appeared drunk, when under the influence of a midwife's pain-relieving intoxicants while in labor.

Matador

In ancient Crete, both females and males engaged in bull sports. In current usage, the matador is one who kills the bull in Spain's bullfights. It derives from 'mata' to kill, and 'dor'- God. Bullfighting has attained semi-religious status in Spain where the bull is treated like a national deity after it dies bravely in the arena.

Matins

Early morning. In the ancient world, and even today, morning may have been the time when only the mothers were awake: Morn or mother's hours. Mothers were awake to feed their infants, adjust the wick of the oil lamp, prepare the food for the rest of the family's breakfast, tend to animals, and the hearth fire, and make the daily bread.

Matorin

In the Cheyenne language, 'House of the Bear Mother', located on a hill near the mouth of the Cheyenne River in South Dakota. There,

Cheyenne women prayed at a boulder where Mother Bear's spirit was believed to be in residence. They prayed for female strength and healing power. No male was permitted to touch the stone under threat of a withered arm. Sacred stones were widespread in the ancient world, as well as today's world where the Ka'aba, said to be a black meteorite, is the focal point of millions of pilgrims who circumambulate the stone at Mecca, Saudi Arabia, during pilgrimages.

Matriarchy

Matriarchy is a form of socio-political organization in which the females control the power to make the rules and govern the society. We do not know if a matriarchy in the strictest political sense ever existed. However, we do know that matriarchies exist in the animal world; elephants and horses are but two examples of many others. We also know that early mythology was dominated by female divinities. The suggestion that matriarchies existed before a takeover by men was first put forth in the mid-1800's AD by Johannes Bachofen, a German classical scholar.

Mattock

One of the earliest female tools used in agriculture. This ancient mother-word connects females to one of the first agricultural tools used in soil cultivation.

Matzah

The bread baked by indigenous Semitic mothers, nomads, with no time to wait for the dough to rise, a flat, crisp, cracker.

Bread and cereal may be the most important invention in the history of humanity, as they have made life possible when there was no fresh food in winter.

In Judaism, the sacred mother-bread is 'matzoh'. Even though patriarchal religious traditions altered the meaning of the 'holy' bread (communion wafer), they could not alter the female association with grains, grinding them into flour, and baking them into breads, crackers, wafers, and cakes. This invention greatly improved the quality of life for early peoples and made survival possible at the end of the last Ice Age.

This is truly sacred, and a most miraculous gift of women to civilizations. It is a sad reflection of Father God religions that they do not choose to fully honor bread as the marvelous invention that it is and that women created it.

Mau
Means cat in the Egyptian language. The Egyptians treasured cats because they saved their grain supply by eating the rodents. Egyptian and Ethiopian cats were the first ones domesticated.

Mawadi
Water dwelling anaconda snake of the indigenous tribes of southern Venezuela, South America, called the 'rainbow serpent' because it is said to rise up in droves from the river, kill all the men and capture all the mothers and take them to their underwater home.

May
The month named after Mother Earth Goddess, 'Maia', of the Greco-Roman world. The first of May was traditionally the beginning of the mating season; and celebrated by dances around a maypole, probably a pagan phallic symbol. In France and England, a maid could leave a 'May basket' filled with goodies on the door handle of a boy she wanted as her mate.

Mazone
Mazone is 'Mother' in a prehistoric African language of Libya. Amazons were the pugnacious females who refused to allow men into their matriarchal society, according to legends. The Hebrew word for bread, Matzoh, may derive from the North African word for mother, 'mazone'.

Me
The declaration of a child coming to the awareness that she or he is a separate being from the mother, usually around the age of one and a half years. In psychology, this process is known as 'Individuation'.

Meal
Edible grain that was ground between stones by the mothers. Women also cleared the land, grew the grain from seeds they saved, and harvested

the sheaves. Mothers had to crush the hard grains so that their infants, toddlers, sick and elderly could eat the grains: wheat, emmer, barley, rye, rice, etc. Eventually, a meal came to mean all the foods served by the women who grew, harvested, preserved, stored, cooked, and served them.

Mecca
The sacred city of Muslim religion located in Saudi Arabia.

Medinah
Medinah is 'the Mother place', most sacred city of Islam. Birthplace of Mohammed in Saudi Arabia, AD 570. The medinah of a city was its central market place where mothers sold the textiles and rugs they wove, perfumes, pottery, produce, etc. that they made and grew, in order to help support their families.

Medusa
A magical female head that frightened men and exacted maternal justice. She was shown with a frightful face and wriggling snakes as hair. In Greek mythology, one glance from her was reputed to turn a man to stone (metaphor for death); as all that would remain of him would be his tombstone.

Meed
The mother's basic food; a meal. In archaic Greece, 'meed', the earliest recipe, consisted of barley flour and water. Today, we would call this 'gravy'. Meed was often used as a sacrificial offering or libation to the first clan mothers, who eventually became the Goddesses of Greek mythology.

Megara
The trench of an archaic Goddess heroine, or local hero in ancient Greece into which libations were poured. At first a megara was a natural cleft in rocks as hillsides or chasms into which offerings for Mother Earth were placed. The word derives from the Phoenician and Hebrew words for cave 'meghar' and 'meghara'. Both are Semitic words. A megaron was a cave in which early Greek mothers lived with their young; and

in which later religious offerings of food – honey, barley, wine, olive oil, were left for the original clan mothers who were revered by later generations. Certain clan mothers evolved into Goddesses, and megaras' caves came to be included in Greek temples, palaces, tombs, and Olympian sanctuaries.

Memsahib
This was a respectful title of English women in India during the Victorian era of British rule.

Meriah
The sacrifice offered by Kondh tribes of the mountains of India. In many ancient societies, a human was sacrificed as a last resort in an attempt to please a deity.

Merquita
Medieval name for a Turkish mosque.

Mescaline
A product of the peyote cactus, used as a sacrament in some Native Americans religions. Its use corresponds to the use of wine in Judaic-Christian religious rituals.

Mesquita
The name given by the medieval Spanish conquerors to Turkish temples. Almost all deities worshipped worldwide were originally female, therefore the home of the Goddess originally had a female root, as does mosque.

Metal
Metal derives from Greek 'metallon' which has a wide range of meanings, including a mine, in its original sense of belonging to Mother Earth. Metal also contains the root of Goddess Metis' name, the Goddess of Wisdom and Medicine. Metals have a long association with women, being first used as paint or make-up (red and yellow ochre, malachite). Women may have come across veins of metal while digging for roots and tubers in their daily gathering tasks. They may have worked with the

shiny metals and made jewelry or other adornments, amulets, charms, etc.

Metisponda

In archaic Greek religions, a form of devotion in which the devotee 'gave up' wine, bad habits like anger, and favorite foods in order to purify herself and be worthy of the Goddesses' blessings. The most ancient Mother Goddesses of Greece were the 'Semnae' the seminal ones, the foundresses of the tribes and clans. 'Metis' was the mother who meted out punishment for wrongdoing. 'Ponda' meant to weigh heavily, to reflect on one's shortcomings, to ponder. 'Metisponda' then, was the making of amends for wrong doing, similar to the Catholic confession and Lenten sacrifices.

Mezethakia

Greek, meaning little foods or appetizers. Greek mothers taught their children a profound reverence for food, as it was often very scarce and extremely difficult to grow in Greece's rocky soil. This reverence survived in the 'prayer before meals' of Christian families.

Mielikki

The Forest Mistress of a Scandinavian hero/heroine story. Mielikki sometimes spelled 'Malaike' means 'angel' in Swedish. Scandinavian hero stories were often prehistoric bear retellings with emphasis on men's heroic valor, as they gradually appeared to overpower the animal's superior strength. However, in the earliest myths, females often outwitted the animals by cunning.

Mihrab

Niche in mosque which points to Mecca, the site that must be faced when men pray 5 times per day.

Milk

Milk is the nurturing life sustenance in liquid form that comes from the breasts of female human mothers as well as mammal mothers. The availability of mothers' milk meant life or death to newborns throughout most of human history before formula replacements. Because of its life-sustaining nutrients milk has figured prominently in ancient mythologies worldwide, along with its source in the female breast. Early vessels, bowls, cups, chalices were all breast-shaped. The health giving properties of mother's milk were considered magical and this association lent itself to the breast and chalice as well. Morrigan, one of the triple ancestral Mother Goddesses of Ireland, was said to heal with her milk. Many Goddesses of antiquity, including Inanna of Mesopotamia, are depicted offering their breasts to humanity in a nurturing, nonsexual way. In much the same way, the bared breast in classical art represented 'charity' or 'giving of oneself' to nourish or to heal another with the life giving offering of milk.

Egyptian princes were nourished exclusively on cow's milk to bond them to the Divine Matriarchal principle of Ma'at, the ancestral Mother Goddess; and also to identify them in their subjects' minds with the cow-goddesses, Isis and Hat-Hor. The sacred cow, Hat-Hor is easily identifiable on wall and tomb paintings because she was always shown with large 'cow' ears. The cow is a sacred animal in India as well because of her maternity and nurturance. The term 'sacred cow' refers to the high regard with which the Hindus hold this milk-producing animal.

Milk has many uses and meanings in Goddess-honoring cultures. Mythical kings of ancient Ireland had to bathe in a broth of mare's blood and milk during their inaugural rituals.

The symbol for flowing water (broken downward lines) was derived from the mother's milk flowing from her breasts. In the Christianization of Ireland, flowing water replaced the mare's blood and milk in royal ceremonies.

In Africa, the basic Masai diet is milk mixed with an animal's blood. In my jewelry collection, I have a lovely gold pendant showing a Masai woman on her way to market holding two large casks filled with milk and blood, believed to greatly enhance physical strength. A galaxy, the Milky Way, represents the milk falling from the Queen of Heaven's breasts.

Mimetic

Imitating or learning. Later mimetic, or magical imitative ceremonies became religious. Anthropologists call imitating the process of nature and movements of animals to influence their behavior as 'sympathetic magic'. Most early Mother religions that honored a revered clan mother used drama as part of their magic rituals. It may have included a reenactment of the act of giving birth, the breaking of the waters, the crown of the baby's head coming forth. This is memorialized as the rite of baptism in Father God religions.

Minaret
This is the tower atop a mosque from which the muezzin summons the faithful to daily prayers in Muslim countries. He chants a verse from the Koran and can be heard over wide distances. Today it is usually a recording that is played five times a day.

Mitochondria
The DNA that is inherited only from the mother. It is called the 'power house of the cell'. Nuclear DNA is inherited from both the mother and father.

'Mitochondrial Eve' is the name given by some biologists to the black African female who may be the source of most mitochondrial DNA in the present human world population.

Mizmer
Droning woodwind instrument similar to the oboe. It is used in the music of Egypt and may have been originally used in birth rituals to ease the birthing mother's labor pains and re-energize her for the difficult task of bringing forth a new life.

Moggadem
In Berber Arabic, the title of the village chief in Morocco. It is related to many words of political power that may have been passed down through the tribal mothers in prehistoric times: mayor, magistrate, master, mistress, manager, minister, mahatma, mustafa, major, majesty.

Moguls
Muslim Mongols that invaded India, and also Persia (Iran)

Mohammad
An Arab trader and mystic who founded a new religion in Saudi Arabia,

c. AD 600. Islam is a religion that incorporated elements of Judaism and Christianity.

Moharram

Month of mourning. Month is a mother-word derived from moon and menses, the two devices by which Paleolithic females calculated the passage of time. Moharram is a logical extension of moon (moh) and sorrow (harram), which also means harm.

Mohmorid

Praised in Arabic. Mohammad is a cognate, meaning 'highly praised'.

Mola salsa

This was a Roman condiment, or a salted meal. It was the food of the ancestral clan mothers. It was sprinkled on an altar stone as a sacrifice at the tomb of a deceased foremother or local heroine or hero. 'Mola' refers to 'mother food', or cereal grains; salsa means 'salt'.

Moloch

Androgynous Phoenician deity sometimes depicted as a coiled snake. A snake was often used in ancient art to symbolize a divinity that was neither male nor female. One cannot tell the gender of a snake unless the she-snake is wrapped around her eggs.

Monolith

A large unusually shaped stone that was used as the precursor of a statue in the late Stone Age and early Neolithic era. It was thought to represent the first maternal ancestress or 'spirit-of-the-place'. Later these huge stones were carved to represent full-figured pregnant clan Mothers. At Malta, c. 5000 BC, the monoliths were thought to be the resting places of the Goddess Mother. A monolith at Mecca, Saudi Arabia, (possibly a meteorite encased in a structure) is believed by many to be sacred to their faith.

Monster

Because it is a 'mother word', in my opinion a monster was originally a very angry mother; furious and fearsome in her wrath, who scared men into behaving right towards women, children, and other men. Many early Greek monsters were female. Gorgons had hideous faces and outstretched tongues, Medusas had slithering serpents in their hair, etc.

Moon and Moonlight

The moon is the astral body that had many symbolic female connotations in antiquity. It was believed to cause the menstrual cycles as well as impregnation, before the role of the male was understood. We now know that our ancestors were correct in their assessment of the moon's gravitational effect on all earthly fluids, including menstrual blood. Because menstruating women were believed to have something dying within their bodies that caused them to bleed, such as a miscarriage, abortion, disease, the moon came to have sinister connotations as well as positive; thus the idea of 'lunacy' or moon madness and mania.

It is important to remember that the sun, moon, and stars, were early deities in the evolution of humanity's religious awareness. Because the moon changed the shape of her 'body' as she went through her three monthly cycles, by waxing, becoming full, then waning, Goddesses were often thought of as trinities also.

The Greek triad of Moon Goddesses consisted of Artemis, Selene, and Hecate. This close association of women with the Goddesses in the moon no doubt lent a considerable aura of power, divinity, and magic to *Women in Prehistory*.

An entire symbol system developed in the Stone Age based upon the mysteries and female cycles of the moon and menstruation. The symbols and the myths they embodied spread from Spain to Central Asia, and by the Neolithic period (New Stone Age) had reached Africa, Europe, and Asia. According to the agricultural lunar calendar, holy days began by the light of the moon deity. We know these sacred celebrations as Halloween, Christmas Eve, (Winter Solstice), New Year's Eve, Ramadan, Easter, and others.

Religious rites involving the moon eventually incorporated techniques of altered states of consciousness (sometimes brought on by ingesting plant derivatives with narcotic effects). These techniques of illumination are known as Shamanism, European Paganism, Hebrew Kaballah, Druidism, Kundalini, Tantric Yoga, and Sufism. Ecstatic dances may have prompted descriptions of 'lunacy' by the uninitiated who observed them.

Pre-Islamic Arabic people may have worshipped the moon. Various constellations were called 'Houses of the Moon', and the zodiac was known as 'The Girdle of the Goddess Ishtar'. The crescent of the waxing moon is the symbol of Islam today, a fitting reminder of matriarchal origins.

Morgh

Prayer stone. This lump of clay is placed on the floor so that the head will not touch anything made by a human while doing the daily prostrations. Clay has ancient female (mother) associations, since the times when women fashioned vessels of clay to cook, serve, and store the food they served to their families. It is called 'earthen ware' and still retains an irresistible charm.

Mosaic

A piece of ceramic tile. Women of the Ukraine, circa 25,000 BC, may have invented ceramics. Women learned the controlled use of very hot fire to use in hardening the clay female figurines and vessels they sculptured. Ceramics and mosaics are very early art forms.

Moslem

A follower of the religion of Islam.

Mosque

Temple of worship

Mother

The English word that derived from the ancestral Indo-European word for mother, 'mater'. It was probably derived from the primal syllable 'ma' suggested by the sounds of a suckling infant, which also lies behind 'mammal', the animal species that suckle their young at the female's breasts.

The mother is the creatress of new life who forms the growing embryonic child from her own body after her ovum is fertilized by a male's sperm. All nutrients are leached from the mother's own body as the fetus enlarges and becomes a human female or male infant. The calcium from the mother's teeth and bones form the growing infant's skeletal frame. Iron from the mother's hemoglobin forms the baby's blood, and so on.

Christianity minimized the female's contribution to the creation of new life by teaching in the Baltimore Catechism: "Who made you?" Answer: "God made me". In reality, the mother made the child of her own flesh and blood with a genetic contribution from the child's father. Ancients recognized the enormous contribution of mothers and elevated them to the status of deities called 'Goddesses'.

The word itself derives from the 'ma syllable', the sound suggested by a baby suckled at the mother's breast. Our word, 'mother', comes from the Latin 'mater' which has cognates in all Indo-European languages as well as some African and Asian dialects. The Greek is 'meter', German 'mutter', Dutch 'moeder', Scandinavian 'moder', Lithuanian 'motere', French 'mere', Spanish, 'madre', Italian, 'mama', Armenian,'mamuti', Chinese,'mucin', African,' mazone', 'mami', Arabic, 'umma'.

After hominids became bipedal (learned to walk on their two legs instead of four), after their cranial cavities elongated and made room for more brain cells to multiply, after they began using rudimentary tools of bone and flint and stone and sticks, antler and wood, the next major evolutionary step forward was the use of language. And the first word very likely spoken as infants was 'ma'- the mammary gland, the milk, life itself, the Mother.

Motika

The mother's tool, a heavy hoe, which every rural Bulgarian carries to the field, to plant a personal plot of land. The mother-word, motika, points to the female roots of farming in Bulgaria, c. 6000 BC when it was known as Thrace. It was a very progressive matrifocal civilization, with women wearing copper and gold jewelry, making lovely polished household pottery and revering a Goddess of Pregnancy-Fertility-Life-Death. Many words like 'motika' in every culture of the world contain pieces of the suppressed history of women coded permanently in the language itself.

Moussem

A Berber tribal fair in Morocco. Originally, women brought the textiles they manufactured in their huts or tents to sell or barter for pots, food, animals, and other things needed by their families. Berber tribal women wove saddles, blankets, rugs, robes, trousers, shirts, turbans, for their men folk and families. They brought their surplus woven textiles to regional trade fairs where bachelors could find a bride, become engaged instantly, court her publicly, and marry her on the spot.

Muchin

Chinese word for 'mother'.

Muezzin

A man who calls to prayer all males. A cognate of 'music'. The word music is derived from the Greek female 'muses'- Goddesses who invented all the arts.

Mujawand

Most melodic and popular style of recitation of Koran; used at weddings and celebrations

Mulher

A Portuguese word for Mother.

Mullah

A cleric who also acts as a judge in legal cases. Muslim religion originated in the Arab world of AD 630, where women formerly had as many freedoms, wealth and choices as men.

Mummification

The process of restoring the dead to lifelike appearance or 'eternal life' by using fragrant salts, herbs, and resins. Goddess Isis was credited with inventing the process in ancient Egypt.

Mundus

The world, Latin. Every child's first world is the maternal body; first her breasts, then her arms, face, voice, and body. The child's world before birth is inside its mother's body. Therefore, it is appropriate that 'world' be a mother-word: mundus, 'where my mother is'. The English word, mundane, is derived from Latin and means 'the everyday, the ordinary', the domestic, the world of the mother.

Murder
Originally the one who killed a mother. In early matriarchies, kinship was reckoned through the mothers, and the relationship to the mother has always been the holiest of human relationships. Therefore, a particularly horrible fate awaited one who slew their mother. Today, although it's meaning has become more generalized, murder is still the most heinous and unthinkable crime.

Musa
House of the mother in the Armenian language.

O'mama
This is the traditional headdress of men in Saudi Arabia. Twisted into a turban, the length of silk or other fabric was most likely woven by mothers, wives, or sisters of the wearer.

Words for Mother in several languages:

Ma'at	Ancient Egyptian
Macha	Gaelic Irish
Madre	Spanish
Mahat	Ukrainian
Mai	Thailand
Mama	Italian
Mamati	Armenian
Mamakuna	Hawaiian
Mammetan	Sumerian
Mami	African and Czech
Mamu	Alaskan
Mater	Latin
Matrika	Russian
Mammyje	Hindi
Mater	Latin

Mazone	Ancient Libyan (African)
Mbote	Swahili (African)
Mére	French
Met	Ancient Egyptian
Meter	Greek
Mithra	Ancient Persian (Iran)
Motere	Lithuanian
Mother	English
Msadi	Botswana (African)
Mouima	Moroccan
Muchin	Chinese
Mudui	Ndemba (African)
Mulher	Portugese
Mut	Ancient Egyptian
Mutter	German
Mzee	Swahili (African)
Umma	Arabic

Measurement Words Derived From the Mother-Syllable:

Many	Mile
Mass	Milestone
Math	Milligram
Measure	Millimeter
Measurement	Million
Mega	Moderate
Megameter	Money
Mensurate	Month
Meridian	More
Meter	Multi
Metric	

References:

1. *The Sacred Paw*, Sanders & Shepard, NY, Viking, 1985
2. *The Wisdom of the Serpent*, Hutchinson & Oates, NY, 1989
3. Saudi Aramco World, Aramco Services Co., Houston TX, Sept-Oct 2001, Vol. 52 #5
4. *Dictionary of Word Origins*, John Ayto, NY, Little Brown & Co., 1990
5. *The White Goddess*, Robert Graves, NY Vintage Books, 1958
6. *God has Ninety-Nine Names*, Judith Miller, NY, Simon & Schuster, 1996

Chapter X:
In Conclusion

She-Comes-In-Her-Goddess-Power

In 1970, a social evolution began, that promised to empower woman by opening up opportunities for women that had long been denied to generations before them. I was 38 and had just given birth to my sixth child. I hoped that one day in the future I would be a part of this exciting new world opening up for women.

I had been a teenager, when I became pregnant with my first child and had to drop out of college to raise my baby after I married, as there were no daycare centers in 1951.

Twenty years later, I had six children, but still had no skills or training with which to get into the marketplace and earn a paycheck which all my friends were doing and enjoying. I did not even have an identity by this time, as I had been Mommy or 'Mrs.....' for so long that I very rarely heard my own name, 'Gloria'.

Little did I know that in three more years I would regain my own identity, empowering me with knowledge and self esteem while still maintaining my long cherished roles as wife and mother.

In my need for mental stimulation, I enrolled at the local Community College for one Saturday morning class in Psychology, as I still had an enormous workload at home. Almost instantly my brain welcomed the intellectual challenge provided by the college environment. My self-respect, self-esteem, and self-confidence, were restored, as my friends, husband, and children began to regard me in a new way.

While I realized that giving birth to six healthy children, raising them to be productive adults and building a peaceful, beautiful, nurturing home for my husband and children, is the most essential, worthwhile, and honorable vocation; it is still today undervalued, unappreciated and under paid. A woman is the most beneficial member of the Community.

Where there is a woman in the home, there is usually a life creator, nurturer, care taker of the children, the handicapped, the sick, the elderly, the disabled, those in recovery, and the dying.

Women can no longer deride our own knowledge and self worth. We must bond together in friendships and in sisterhoods to help each other survive in an increasingly complex world that does not always value women. We will find that women played a far greater role in society than has been credited to them.

We need to pay closer attention to the bath and beauty products seductively marketed to beautify us, to the tanning and nail salons, cosmetics, hair products, and home fragrances, so beautifully marketed. Women and young girls buy these products which can be harmful to their health. We need to warn each other of these hazards and remind each other to clean out our bathrooms and kitchens that may also contain cleaning solutions and unhealthy processed foods. We need to be smarter, and to stand up to the multi-billion dollar industries that have targeted us as 'easy prey'.

I speak from personal experience for I have developed a painful syndrome, fibromyalgia, which I believe was caused by lifetime exposure to hidden toxins in the cosmetics and cleaning solutions I used with the best of intentions.

In the past thirty years since I have raised all six of my children, helped with my seven grandchildren, and eight great-grandchildren. I have read over 1000 books in nearly all fields of knowledge. While earning a Masters Degree in Psychology, I also studied anthropology, archaeology, biology, word origins, history, genetics, theology, metaphysics, mythology, nutrition, philosophy, and many of the world's cultures and religions.

This book is a culmination of my research, travels, studies, and insights; and my sister's skill of putting it all together into a readable text. We did this so all the women in our lives will know that females were long considered not only super-human, mysterious, magical beings; but also divinities, Goddesses. The mother creatresses from whom all indigenous people trace their origins, became Goddesses eventually, after thousands of centuries of being passed on as oral history.

For we are all 'god/makers in the process'. Today, we recognize the deifying of Marilyn Monroe as a goddess of beauty, Princess Diana as a great humanitarian, Elvis Presley as a tragic singer and matinee idol, as well as many others. Some are legends in their own time as: Oprah, Elizabeth Taylor, and the stars of stage and screen. So too, the Goddesses, whose identities were thought to be long lost in the mists of prehistory, have survived in myths, religions, and legends.

A mother goddess could have been a composite of actual women, usually clan mothers, who have lived in the farthest reaches of history (her story).

But their lovely names have survived:

Athena: who taught her children to grow olive trees, in ancient Greece and make life-giving olive oil.

Ishtar: guiding star of Sumerian Iraq's highest civilization.

Mulan: legendary Chinese warrior who had the names of wronged villagers tattooed onto her back so she would not forget to avenge injustices.

Mahavidya: Hindu mother goddess of knowledge and education.

Mami: The ancestral mother of the African Dahomey people, who taught maternal values as the origins of all justice.

Isis: ancient Egyptian mother who taught people to make bread, spin flax, and weave linen.

Hecate: of old Europe, known as a midwife, herbalist, and doctor.

Guadalupe: unifying spiritual Mother of Meso-Americans.

Diana: skilled Roman huntress who was herself hunted.

Demeter: devoted mother who searched to the ends of the earth and the underworld for her kidnapped daughter seized by a predator.

Aphrodite: the most beautiful of her day, the symbol of sexual desire.

Ceres: who may have invented cereal perhaps the greatest of all inventions which enabled humans to stay alive for millennia before refrigeration.

I want every girl in every corner of the world to grow up learning the lovely names of these and other Goddesses and what they represent. Their legends contain hints of origins of all the arts of civilized living of the world today. Agriculture, food preparation and preservation, weaving, the wheel, writing, pottery sculpture, music, medicine, manufacturing, astronomy, hygiene, time keeping, mathematics, chemistry, and more. Every girl needs the knowledge of our godmothers who were part of a long line of inventors, geniuses, creators, technologists, and civilizers.

A return to maternal values will shine a spotlight on the basic issues for a humane society. With more women in positions of political power, we may well be embarking on the century of the woman.

If our ancestors had not been incredibly intelligent and resourceful, none of us would be here today. We can now connect in a very real way with the Stone Age Divas, whose intelligence and resourcefulness guaranteed our own existence.

We can now trace our DNA hundreds of centuries backwards in time. I recently had my (maternal) DNA traced back to 28,000 BC in an unbroken chain back to Mesopotamia.

I call our ancient foremothers, 'Stone Age Divas', because it is quite possible that they were very glamorous in their day, not at all like the dismal way that they were portrayed in the past. From images they sculpted themselves from clay and ivory, they are shown with elaborate hairdressings, and jewelry, seductive string skirts, and quite possibly tattoos which were a very early art form.

DNA may very well be the biological equivalent of soul, that elusive concept that religions speak of. They tell us there is a part of us that never dies; an energy essence that cannot be killed. This is our DNA, the essence of who we are, which every female passes into the future when she gives birth. In this regard, she is indeed a Goddess...for she confers immortality on a man when she passes his genes into the future, insuring he will live forever as long as his genes are constantly reproduced into future generations.

Girls need to be aware of this awesome Goddess/power they possess when they birth future generations, by being more selective in their partners. Mothers must teach their sons and daughters that the female body is sacred, not to be violated or used by sexual predators, unnecessary plastic surgery, starvation or sexually transmitted diseases.

It is hard to maintain self-respect when girls are targeted and exploited by the advertising media. The female body is often a vehicle to sell these products that are often harmful to their health. Girls begin absorbing messages of self-hate at a very early age when they are constantly being told there is something wrong with every body part: complexion, eyes, neck, breasts, upper arms, teeth, waistline, armpits, legs, nails, hair, eyebrows, tummy, hips, buttocks, legs, finger nails and toe nails, even pubic hair and labia.

Girls should learn that true beauty comes from what we put inside our bodies, fruits and vegetables, which gives the face a glow of health from within; as well as our thoughts and a deep understanding of who and what we are, and an education that will give us a sense of our true being.

And with that power and knowledge and wisdom of our wonderful heritage as females, know, with absolute certainty and conviction, that we are Goddesses in every sense of the word. I am a Goddess, and so are YOU!

Gloria Bertonis, with Carol Miranda

In the immortal words of Shakespeare, "Thanks, thanks and evermore thanks to all of our amazing Goddess Mothers."

And more thanks... to:

My daughter, Patrice Wynne, owner of 'San Miguel Designs' and author of "The Womanspirit Sourcebook", N.Y., Harper & Row, 1988, and owner of the former 'GAIA Bookstore and Cultural Center in Berkeley, CA' has also been a dedicated midwife to the birth of this book. The Berkeley City Council named Patrice 'Woman of the Year' and she is also my personal treasure as a daughter, teacher and friend. She has led me on a stunning odyssey, discovering all that is fine, true, and most beautiful, adventurous and enlightening. My love and thanks!

And to my soul companion, Ed Weiser, who has been my loving life partner for over thirty years. He has been a patient sounding board for my unusual conclusions and has strengthened my resolve when these ideas were criticized. He helped me to stay focused while I lectured to community groups, and listened night after night as I read pages of handwritten manuscript. For carrying heavy-laden bags of visual aids to my lectures and classes, and for all his encouragement, I owe my heartfelt thanks.

My daughter Holley Ward Betz was always beside me providing financial, spiritual, and emotional support, as were my sons, Kerry, Jeffrey, Christopher, and Jason. To their never failing fonts of love, I give my love and my many thanks.

Thanks and appreciation to the creative talents of Pres Miranda, who did all the illustrations for us. You are a treasure, whose many abilities and talents amaze us all.

To my friends Maryly Hossain, artist and poet; Myrtle Kohr Johns, artist and lecturer; and Rosemary Suhre; who have enriched me with a constant flow of books, references, poems, luncheons, precious oils, and teas that have nourished my spirit in every way possible, my thanks for your support. To Rev. Rosemarie Carnarius, Irene Maziarz, Nancy Lesh, Bill Stroup, Charlotte Melville, and scores of others who encouraged both of us to continue going forward, I am grateful.

Gloria Bertonis, M.Ed.
Bucks County, PA
August 2010

Index

A

Abortifacients 135, 136
Aegean 16, 24, 77, 78, 183
Afghanistan 50
Africa 4, 5, 8, 14, 31, 37, 50, 53, 57, 60, 85, 91, 103, 123, 125, 147, 151, 182, 189, 195, 209, 221, 224
Agriculture 11, 28, 39, 44, 51, 64, 66, 146, 180, 183, 188, 195, 197, 199, 206, 216, 234
Ainus 139
Alaska 20, 139
Albanians 106
Al'Lat 19, 179, 180
Amaterasu 18, 179
Amazon 147, 161
Americas xii, 20
Anapurna 145
Anatolia 20, 24, 35, 36, 49, 50, 86, 103, 104, 108, 185, 188
Andes 114, 123
Animals xii, 3, 4, 5, 6, 8, 9, 10, 13, 14, 15, 17, 22, 28, 30, 31, 32, 33, 37, 39, 40, 41, 42, 43, 44, 45, 47, 51, 52, 53, 65, 67, 73, 74, 75, 76, 86, 88, 101, 107, 109, 113, 114, 122, 123, 128, 130, 133, 134, 137, 141, 147, 153, 154, 174, 180, 184, 185, 187, 199, 206, 211, 215, 220, 221, 227
Anise 159
Anna 144, 145
Anorexic 68
Aphrodite 106, 179, 181, 182, 194, 199, 233

Arabia 19, 37, 50, 207, 209, 216, 218, 222, 223, 228
Arinna 20
Armenia 49
Artemis 33, 159, 199, 224
Arunte Tribe 2
Aryans 36, 48, 50
Asia 14, 19, 48, 52, 56, 111, 116, 185, 224
Assyria 24, 49, 86
Astarte 1, 179, 187
Athena 93, 173, 179, 182, 183, 199, 233
Auel, Jean 39, 100, 119
Ausros Vartai 21

B

Balkans 35, 77, 80, 92, 103, 110, 183, 188
Barbarians 51
Barber, Elizabeth 100, 102, 108, 109, 119, 120
Barber surgeons 143, 144
Baskets 103, 187, 210
Bath, England 112, 153
Bear Goddess 76, 125
Bedouin 108
Bee Goddess 32, 110
Belladonna 140, 160
Berbers 116, 208
Bernatonis i, vi, 21, 109, 120
Bible 37, 57, 64
Bipedalism 3, 4, 8, 9
Birds 5, 9, 17, 27, 73, 101, 107, 109, 183, 191
Birth vii, xii, 7, 30, 39, 41, 56, 58, 74, 76, 83, 128, 129, 137, 143, 146, 149,

151, 171, 184, 188, 189, 191, 195, 212, 222, 228, 231, 234, 235, 236
Blood xi, 1, 16, 28, 44, 67, 74, 93, 95, 134, 137, 138, 162, 164, 165, 172, 208, 209, 213, 221, 224, 226
Bog burials 110
Bona Dea 145, 179
Bonding 39, 40, 41, 76, 180
Boršcht 160
Bride price 47
Brigid 151
Bronė 109
Bronze Age xvii, 7, 16, 26, 30, 37, 44, 47, 48, 49, 51, 53, 54, 57, 61, 62, 64, 65, 66, 80, 100, 105, 106, 132, 180, 207
Bulgaria 76, 77, 84, 188, 226

C

Caduceus 63, 69, 145, 147
Camphor oil 141
Carpets 107, 116
Catal Huyuk 35, 108
Catholicism 21, 89, 189
Caucasus 35, 36, 49, 204
Caves 5, 14, 15, 40, 41, 74, 78, 86, 88, 102, 193, 219
Celts 48, 49, 79, 80, 148, 150, 151
Chaldeans 37, 50
Chamomile 117, 161, 162
Chariots 26, 49, 50, 82
Chavins 38
Chieftain 66, 82, 150
Chimpanzees 3, 5, 8, 14, 31
China 14, 48, 90, 111, 122, 123, 136, 150, 155, 157, 165, 166, 197, 198
Christians 20, 29, 32, 200
Clan Mother 126, 178, 222
Cleopatra 60
Cloth 59, 70, 107, 109, 111, 112, 114, 149
Clothing xi, 13, 15, 16, 34, 37, 42, 52, 59, 61, 68, 78, 97, 98, 100, 103, 104, 107, 110, 112, 151, 190, 210, 211, 247

Cloves 141
Coatlique 184, 185
Containers 103, 113, 138
Contraception 70, 135
Convents 138, 142, 143
Corn 30, 130, 145, 146, 180
Corn Mother 145, 146
Crete 26, 33, 63, 71, 78, 81, 82, 84, 215
Crocheting 97, 110
Cro-Magnons xi, 8
Cucuteni culture 84
Curanderas xviii, 9, 69, 154, 157
Cybele 185, 186

D

Daino 21
Datura 152
Demeter 1, 7, 33, 69, 146, 179, 192, 199, 208, 233
Denmark 99, 100, 104, 105, 110
Diana 179, 194, 199, 207, 232, 233
Diarrhea 131, 141, 162
Digitalis 139, 157, 164
Doctors xv, 9, 10, 63, 121, 122, 125, 126, 128, 131, 142, 144, 149, 153, 157, 165, 188, 206
Dogs 39, 44, 52
Dress 125, 213
Druids 80, 147, 168
Dyes 110, 116, 117

E

Ea 186
Earth xi, 1, 9, 17, 20, 29, 37, 40, 52, 54, 55, 56, 65, 74, 75, 76, 77, 86, 88, 100, 102, 110, 145, 151, 152, 153, 165, 171, 180, 181, 184, 185, 186, 187, 188, 190, 197, 198, 199, 207, 208, 215, 217, 218, 219, 233
Easter 147, 186, 187, 224
Egypt 7, 18, 20, 24, 32, 36, 43, 48, 49, 50, 52, 54, 57, 58, 59, 60, 61, 63, 65, 67, 71, 75, 84, 86, 87, 88, 90, 91, 92, 93, 106, 108, 126, 128,

129, 130, 135, 136, 148, 149, 152, 153, 158, 159, 184, 188, 189, 190, 191, 192, 193, 196, 197, 200, 206, 209, 222, 227
Ehrenberg, Margaret 90
Eisler, Riane 35, 252
Eleusinian Mysteries 16
England 17, 65, 112, 121, 123, 137, 139, 142, 143, 153, 162, 172, 178, 217
Enheduanna 54, 55
Eostre 147, 186
Erzuli 147
Esther 147, 186, 187
Estonia 49
Estrogen 8, 147, 186, 187
Eurasians 50
Euronyme 187
Europe xi, 5, 10, 14, 21, 22, 23, 24, 25, 26, 32, 37, 42, 47, 48, 49, 52, 57, 61, 62, 68, 73, 74, 75, 76, 77, 79, 80, 83, 84, 85, 86, 90, 103, 105, 108, 109, 110, 111, 112, 128, 130, 133, 134, 135, 136, 137, 142, 143, 147, 159, 160, 162, 171, 173, 188, 210, 215, 224, 233
Eve 58, 64, 196, 222, 224, 247
Evil Eye 58, 59, 60, 130
Eye 28, 30, 58, 59, 60, 103, 117, 126, 130, 153, 154, 189, 191, 192, 193
Eye Goddess 154

F

Farming vii, xvii, 11, 28, 53, 64, 108, 132, 199, 226
Fatherhood 2, 6, 28, 39, 121, 181, 211
Feminist xv, 4, 11, 30, 67, 69
Finland 108
Fire xv, 14, 39, 72, 82, 98, 161, 173, 199, 215, 225
Flax 59, 109, 110, 112, 183, 190, 233
Food gatherers 3, 11, 114
Foragers 4, 5, 73, 122, 124, 125, 215
Foxglove 139, 157, 164

France 7, 12, 31, 32, 33, 34, 98, 100, 101, 102, 123, 133, 142, 143, 167, 178, 193, 217

G

Gaia 1, 179
Germany 76, 111, 122, 137, 143, 148, 157, 186, 188
Gimbutas, Marija 21, 22, 23, 24, 25, 34, 35, 36, 75, 78, 95, 100, 105, 110, 119
Glyphs 58, 79, 83, 85, 114, 117, 154
Gnostic Gospels 63
Goddesses v, vii, viii, ix, xi, xv, 1, 7, 12, 13, 16, 17, 18, 19, 20, 21, 22, 23, 24, 26, 28, 29, 30, 32, 33, 34, 35, 36, 37, 38, 45, 47, 49, 50, 51, 53, 54, 55, 57, 58, 60, 61, 62, 63, 64, 65, 66, 67, 68, 69, 71, 72, 73, 74, 75, 76, 77, 79, 83, 86, 87, 88, 92, 93, 94, 95, 98, 100, 101, 106, 107, 110, 111, 112, 115, 119, 122, 123, 125, 127, 128, 129, 130, 131, 139, 145, 146, 147, 148, 149, 150, 151, 152, 153, 154, 155, 156, 159, 160, 171, 173, 175, 176, 177, 178, 180, 181, 182, 183, 184, 185, 186, 187, 188, 189, 190, 191, 192, 193, 194, 195, 196, 197, 198, 199, 200, 201, 204, 205, 206, 207, 208, 210, 211, 212, 213, 214, 217, 218, 219, 220, 221, 223, 224, 225, 226, 227, 230, 231, 232, 233, 234, 235, 250, 251, 252
Gods viii, 13, 14, 18, 32, 33, 36, 38, 61, 73, 87, 127, 128, 130, 181, 182, 183, 185, 186, 188, 190, 196, 198, 199, 250
Grandmother 126, 148, 152, 160, 169, 247, 248, 249
Great Cosmic Mother 29, 30
Greco-Roman 136, 146, 158, 169, 170, 190, 208, 217
Greece 20, 33, 36, 48, 60, 61, 63, 76, 93, 106, 107, 119, 130, 135, 136, 159,

167, 173, 185, 188, 192, 199, 207, 208, 209, 211, 218, 220, 233
Guadalupe 130, 131, 154, 184, 185, 233
Guilds 135, 143, 144
Gynecology 129, 134, 144

H

Hallucinogens 122, 125
Hathor 128, 130, 149
healing hand 126
Hebrews 37, 50, 211, 214
Hecate 1, 122, 123, 129, 148, 179, 188, 189, 224, 233
Hera 179, 199
Herbs 9, 11, 40, 89, 101, 102, 115, 123, 133, 135, 137, 140, 145, 146, 147, 150, 152, 153, 154, 157, 158, 167, 169, 170, 173, 184, 227
Hexers 122, 134, 148, 157
Hildegarde of Bingen 137, 142, 143
Hindus 62, 148, 221
Hirohito, Emperor 18
Holistic healing 123, 128, 249, 250
Homer 106, 146
Hominids 3, 4, 5, 6, 7, 8, 203, 226
Horns viii, xi, 22, 30, 130
Horses 32, 35, 36, 37, 42, 45, 47, 48, 49, 50, 52, 56, 66, 82, 150, 216
Horus 7, 59, 61, 128, 149, 189, 191, 192
Hospitals 71, 142, 143
Housewives 128, 141, 144, 174
Hungary 48, 76, 109, 123
Huns of Hawaii 48
Hunters 74, 123, 124, 125, 213
Hygiene 148, 234

I

Ideogram 79, 117
Inanna 54, 55, 86, 93, 179, 194, 221
India 20, 36, 48, 49, 50, 52, 57, 62, 80, 85, 93, 101, 109, 112, 145, 148, 150, 152, 157, 170, 181, 184, 189, 219, 221, 222

Indo-European 25, 37, 48, 49, 50, 51, 57, 62, 107, 121, 204, 205, 213, 225, 226
Indra 36, 57, 62
Infanticide 43, 56, 136
Inquisition 10, 70, 135
Inuit 97, 98, 139, 172
Iran 24, 36, 48, 49, 50, 56, 111, 116, 126, 136, 206, 208, 211, 222, 229
Iraq 24, 36, 48, 49, 56, 62, 71, 84, 86, 87, 93, 103, 108, 111, 116, 126, 136, 186, 233
Ireland 20, 85, 131, 135, 136, 147, 150, 151, 157, 172, 189, 196, 212, 215, 221
Iron Age xii, xvii, 30, 36, 45, 48, 197
Ishtar 179, 186, 194, 225, 233
Isis 1, 7, 20, 58, 59, 60, 61, 81, 93, 128, 130, 149, 179, 189, 190, 191, 192, 193, 194, 199, 200, 221, 227, 233
Islam 19, 67, 192, 218, 223, 225
Isles of Aran 112
Ix-Chel 115, 149

J

Japan 18, 19, 123, 139, 150, 248
Jarmo 108
Jericho 77, 81
Jesus 7, 61, 112, 126, 178, 187, 192, 209, 211, 214, 215
Jewelry xi, 24, 42, 52, 53, 66, 74, 78, 91, 92, 102, 105, 106, 126, 129, 220, 221, 226, 234, 247

K

Kachina Mana 146
Kali 1, 93, 184, 189, 196
Kami 19
Kazakhstan 37
Kilim rugs 117
Knots 74, 91, 101, 129, 132
Korea 19
Kurds 116, 117
Kush Mountains 50

Kwan Yin 19, 150

L
Lascaux 31, 102
Laussel 12, 85
Lavender 141, 167
Leeches 138
Lenni Lenape 113
Lespuque 98, 100
Linen 34, 52, 59, 92, 109, 112, 129, 130, 135, 169, 190, 233
Litany 194
Lithuania 18, 20, 21, 34, 107, 108, 109, 110, 120, 159, 170
Lucy 3

M
Ma 93, 205
Ma'at 58, 60, 93, 191, 192, 196, 197, 199, 206, 221, 228
Macedonia 76, 78, 104
Macha 150, 151, 196, 228
Machete 206
Madonna and Child 76
Madrasa 207
Maenad 207
Magazine 42, 117, 155, 191, 207
Magic xii, 27, 60, 87, 95, 107, 119, 123, 126, 127, 128, 149, 152, 155, 156, 190, 213, 222, 224
Magma 207
Magna Mater 186, 190
Magneh 206
Maguey 207
Mahdi 209
Mahmood 208
Mahtob 208
Mahzigen 208
Maia 1, 196, 208, 217
Mailicheia 208
Maimaktes 209
Maiua 209
Majlia 209
Makuna 209

Malic 209
Mallet 210
Mami 195, 228, 233
Mamlaka 210
Mammetam 210
Man 3, 5, 16, 120, 131, 157, 166, 178, 192, 205, 208, 209, 210, 218, 227, 234, 249, 252
Mana 146, 192, 210
Manes 211
Manger 211
Manifesto 211
Männerbund 211
Mantle 211, 212
Mapuchi Indians 125
Mar 212
Marabout 212
Mare 39, 212, 221
Margaritaria 212
Mari 192, 194, 213
Marijuana 125
Markab 213
Mars 20, 36, 57, 199, 200, 213
Mary 7, 21, 30, 61, 112, 130, 131, 154, 185, 191, 192, 193, 194, 212, 213, 215
Marylya 213
Masai 151, 221
Mash 214
Mashrabiyyeh 214
Masjed 214
Massebah 215
Mast 215
Matador 215
Matins 215
Matorin 215
Matriarchy 65, 191, 216
Matrifocal 35, 36, 66, 67, 84, 88, 92, 184, 188, 198, 205, 212, 226
Mattock 216
Matzah 214, 216
Mau 217
Mawadi 217
May 120, 194, 208, 209, 213, 214, 217
Maya 114, 120, 196

Mayahuel 196
Mayans 115, 154
Mazone 217, 229
Mbabe Mwana 195, 196
Medicine vii, 9, 10, 16, 20, 63, 69, 70, 88, 89, 101, 121, 122, 123, 124, 125, 126, 127, 128, 129, 130, 131, 132, 133, 134, 135, 137, 138, 139, 141, 142, 143, 144, 145, 146, 147, 148, 149, 151, 152, 154, 155, 157, 159, 160, 161, 163, 165, 168, 173, 175, 176, 190, 195, 199, 200, 219, 234
Medinah 218
Mediterranean 24, 26, 42, 43, 49, 50, 61, 152
Meditrina 151, 152
Medusa 218
Meed 218
Megara 218
Memnet 196, 197
Memsahib 219
Menhirs 62, 215
Menses 17, 73, 74, 189, 223
Meriah 219
Mescaline 219
Mesopotamia xviii, 24, 36, 47, 49, 50, 56, 62, 71, 84, 86, 103, 108, 111, 126, 127, 136, 221, 234
Mesquita 219
Metal 35, 52, 53, 105, 132, 134, 219
Metis 219, 220
Metisponda 220
Mexico 85, 115, 130, 154, 157, 250
Mezethakia 220
Middle East 24, 32, 41, 48, 49, 50, 52, 57, 61, 65, 75, 77, 80, 87, 103, 126, 130, 136, 192, 212
Midwives 9, 53, 68, 132, 133, 134, 135, 136, 138, 142, 144, 149, 167, 168, 174, 188
Mielikki 220
Mihrab 220

Milk vii, 16, 28, 43, 44, 45, 51, 52, 86, 131, 169, 171, 180, 181, 189, 210, 211, 212, 220, 221, 226
Mimetic 221
Minaret 222
Minerva 17, 112, 153, 179, 199
Mitochondria 222
Mizmer 222
Moggadem 222
Mohammad 222
Moharram 223
Mohmorid 223
Mola salsa 223
Moloch 223
Momoy 152
Monasteries 142, 143
Money 10, 52, 71, 74, 89, 133, 229
Mongolia 37
Monolith 223
Monotheistic 29
Monster 223
Month 13, 16, 73, 134, 208, 213, 217, 223, 229
Moon viii, xvi, 13, 15, 17, 19, 20, 26, 29, 30, 44, 55, 73, 74, 75, 115, 146, 147, 151, 180, 181, 188, 189, 192, 208, 210, 213, 223, 224, 225
Moonlight viii, 208, 224
Morgh 225
Morrigan 150, 189, 221
Mosaic 225
Moslem 20, 225
Mosque 219, 220, 222, 225
Mother i, xi, 1, 2, 4, 6, 7, 8, 16, 18, 19, 20, 21, 22, 28, 29, 30, 33, 34, 35, 36, 37, 39, 40, 41, 43, 44, 45, 47, 49, 51, 53, 56, 57, 58, 60, 61, 62, 65, 67, 68, 70, 71, 74, 75, 76, 77, 79, 83, 92, 93, 110, 112, 121, 125, 126, 128, 129, 131, 140, 141, 143, 144, 145, 146, 148, 149, 150, 151, 152, 157, 158, 161, 168, 170, 171, 178, 179, 180, 181, 182, 184, 185, 186, 188, 189, 191, 192, 193, 194, 195, 196, 197, 198, 199, 203, 204,

205, 206, 207, 208, 209, 210, 211, 212, 213, 214, 215, 216, 217, 218, 219, 220, 221, 222, 223, 225, 226, 227, 228, 229, 231, 232, 233, 247, 248, 250
Mother Goddess xi, 16, 20, 22, 28, 29, 30, 33, 34, 35, 36, 37, 45, 47, 49, 53, 57, 58, 60, 67, 71, 74, 75, 76, 79, 83, 92, 146, 150, 178, 184, 185, 186, 188, 189, 191, 192, 193, 195, 196, 197, 198, 199, 204, 206, 212, 213, 221
Mother syllable 20, 121, 191, 197, 203, 205
Motika 226
Muezzin 222, 227
Mujawand 227
Mulher 227, 229
Mullah 227
Mummification 227
Mundus 227, 228
Murder 228
Musa 228
Muses 227
Muslim 206, 209, 210, 212, 218, 222, 227
Mustafa 222
Myrrh 135, 136
Myrtle 135, 136, 236
Mysteries 1, 16, 17, 120, 224
Mzee 229

N

Narcotic 125, 215, 224
Native Americans xvii, 13, 15, 16, 17, 28, 30, 38, 112, 113, 116, 125, 146, 163, 166, 172, 219
Naturopaths 69, 142, 188
Near East 47, 52, 57, 61, 62, 75, 80, 81, 90, 92, 108, 185
Needle 98
Neolithic xvii, 21, 22, 24, 26, 30, 32, 34, 36, 42, 44, 49, 51, 53, 61, 62, 65, 66, 67, 68, 76, 77, 78, 79, 82, 84, 85, 86, 88, 92, 103, 106, 108, 109, 110, 125, 132, 139, 161, 181, 183, 223, 224
Nepthys 199
Nerthus 197, 198
New Zealand 31
Nightshade 160, 169
Ninhursag 76
Noblewomen 142, 143
Norse 153
Nubia 106, 189
Nu-Kua 198
Nut 69, 184, 199

O

Ogham 11, 85
Okinawa 18, 19
Olmecs 38
O'mama 228
Oshun 145
Our Lady 130, 131, 184, 193, 213

P

Paleolithic xii, xvii, 5, 7, 12, 14, 15, 16, 24, 29, 30, 31, 40, 41, 61, 62, 65, 72, 74, 76, 77, 85, 98, 99, 100, 102, 103, 109, 122, 123, 181, 223
Palestine 24, 42, 50, 51, 215
Papyrus 59, 79, 84, 92, 126, 128, 130, 153, 190
Parsley 135, 169
Paternity 2, 6, 28, 54, 121, 124, 181, 204, 210
Patriarchy 2, 19, 47, 53, 54, 56, 57, 58, 63, 67, 68, 90, 181, 184, 203, 205, 207
Pazyryks of Siberia 111, 117
Pennsylvania Dutch 122, 188
Peppermint 170
Persia 20, 116, 208, 214, 222
Peyote 125, 219
Phallic symbol 217
Philippine Islands 31, 123
Philistines 50
Phoebe 20

Phoenicians 37, 50, 71, 84
Pictograms 75, 86, 93
Piggott, Stuart 116
Pinkham, Lydia 141
Pinworms 141, 171
Pope 57, 142, 188
Pottery 21, 22, 65, 77, 85, 86, 92, 93, 183, 210, 218, 226, 234
Pregnancy xi, 12, 15, 16, 17, 28, 37, 44, 51, 67, 74, 77, 83, 85, 88, 93, 100, 106, 131, 146, 151, 170, 226
Prescriptions 70, 136, 141, 151, 152, 157
Priestess 33, 54, 55, 87, 89, 125, 126, 146
Primates 3, 9
Prozac 172
Prussia 49
Pueblo 154
Pulque 125
Pyramid Texts 18, 54, 90, 191, 206

Q

Queen of Heaven 20, 180, 213, 221
Queens xv, 91, 92, 144, 198, 209

R

RA 18, 58, 60, 128, 130, 192, 199
Recipes 70, 128, 136, 141, 151, 152, 157, 190
Reincarnation 14, 67
Religion vii, xi, 1, 2, 11, 15, 19, 20, 29, 30, 47, 61, 64, 65, 68, 71, 79, 82, 87, 90, 92, 123, 125, 126, 128, 130, 142, 145, 148, 149, 180, 184, 185, 186, 187, 189, 190, 192, 214, 218, 222, 223, 225, 227, 247, 249, 251
Reproduction xv, 2, 9, 37, 48, 62, 64, 65, 93, 100, 131, 135, 151, 181, 204, 209
Rhodes 33
Rock painting 32
Rocks 9, 62, 67, 85, 137, 185, 218

Romania 23, 76, 78
Romans 20, 49, 80, 122, 130, 153, 167, 171, 182, 185, 186, 190, 199, 200, 213
Rosemary 135, 236
Rue 133, 136, 158, 170, 171
Rugs 52, 107, 109, 116, 117, 218, 227
Runes 79, 80, 89
Russia 37, 48, 49, 50, 100, 104, 106, 111

S

Salta birštai 160
Salus 152
Saule 18
Savior 61, 149
Scandinavia 20, 80, 94, 109, 135, 189, 190, 193, 196, 197, 210
Scotland 70, 111, 144, 250
Sekhmet 152, 153, 199
Semites 37, 50, 84
Serbs 106
Serpent 26, 63, 64, 145, 187, 195, 217
Sexuality 7, 51, 62, 63, 64, 149, 181, 182, 188, 193, 194, 212
Shakti 196
Shamankas xviii, 9, 69, 122, 125, 157, 214
Shamans 19, 89, 123, 125, 157, 169, 214
Shekinah 20
Siberia 37, 41, 111, 117, 125, 157
Sisters of Charity 142
Slavs 36, 49
Slovakia 49
Songs 1, 3, 21, 66, 91, 109, 110, 138
Sonja 18, 20, 154
Spain 32, 123, 143, 185, 215, 224
Sperm 6, 7, 17, 44, 45, 47, 55, 56, 57, 73, 76, 136, 204, 225
Spider Woman 154
Sprang weaving 106
St. John's Wort 140, 172
Stone Age v, vii, xi, xii, xvii, 1, 2, 5, 7, 12, 13, 14, 15, 24, 29, 30, 32, 40, 42, 43, 74, 85, 86, 98, 101, 104, 105,

106, 112, 123, 124, 125, 131, 135, 144, 180, 183, 187, 193, 205, 207, 223, 224, 234
String 74, 91, 98, 99, 100, 101, 102, 103, 104, 105, 106, 108, 111, 130, 132, 149, 205, 234
String skirt 98, 99, 100, 101, 104, 105, 106
Sulis 17, 18, 20, 112, 153, 171
Sumeria 84, 87, 93, 186
Sun 17, 18, 19, 20, 21, 26, 30, 58, 112, 146, 147, 153, 154, 180, 181, 184, 186, 187, 189, 190, 192, 199, 224
Sunna 153, 154
Surgeons 132, 142, 143, 144
Sweden 20
Switzerland 110, 139, 161
Symbols 15, 20, 21, 22, 23, 24, 30, 33, 34, 35, 58, 60, 62, 65, 69, 71, 72, 73, 74, 75, 78, 79, 80, 81, 83, 85, 86, 87, 88, 89, 95, 104, 112, 114, 117, 123, 129, 130, 132, 153, 180, 184, 185, 187, 224
Syria xviii, 24, 36, 106, 123, 213, 215

T

Ta'mazight 208
Tattoos 91, 98, 106, 234
Tea 140, 141, 158, 159, 160, 161, 162, 163, 164, 165, 166, 167, 169, 170, 171, 172, 173, 174, 175
Textiles 37, 47, 52, 65, 83, 97, 102, 103, 110, 111, 112, 114, 115, 117, 119, 132, 133, 154, 210, 218, 227
Theocracy 19, 192
Thrace 188, 226
Thunder God 35
Tlazolteotl 154
Tools v, xi, 3, 5, 6, 8, 9, 14, 53, 102, 104, 124, 126, 216, 226
Totem 30
Trinity 29, 150, 189
Triple Goddess 29
Tripolyte culture 111
Troy 116

Turkey 20, 24, 33, 35, 36, 49, 50, 56, 103, 104, 108, 116, 117, 130, 185, 188

U

Ukrainian 197, 228
Uzbeks 116

V

Valerian 140, 173
Valium 140, 173
Venus 12, 62, 85, 100, 178, 182, 199
Venus of Willendorf 62
Vervain 174
Vesta 20, 107, 199
Vestments 107
Veterinarians 123, 134, 142, 148, 189
Vikings 190, 198
Vinča 23, 24, 35, 77, 78, 79, 104
Vinča culture 23, 78, 79, 104
Violence 26, 36, 49, 51, 54, 56, 57, 72, 90
Virgin 21, 131, 154, 183, 185, 193, 194, 212, 213
Virgin Mary 21, 185, 212

W

Warfare 50, 52, 53, 56, 65, 67, 82, 90, 150, 199, 206, 208
Wealth 3, 11, 37, 42, 45, 47, 48, 51, 52, 53, 59, 64, 65, 67, 82, 106, 108, 126, 139, 197, 227
Weaving vii, 65, 83, 97, 98, 103, 104, 106, 108, 109, 113, 114, 115, 116, 117, 133, 149, 154, 183, 234
Wicca 11, 125, 144
Witches xviii, 9, 10, 11, 68, 70, 125, 133, 134, 135, 137, 144, 157, 159, 160, 164, 188
Wolf hair 174
Women v, vii, xi, xii, xv, xvii, xviii, 1, 2, 3, 4, 6, 9, 10, 11, 12, 13, 15, 16, 17, 18, 19, 20, 21, 22, 24, 28, 30, 33, 36, 37, 39, 40, 41, 42, 43, 44, 51,

52, 53, 54, 55, 56, 57, 59, 60, 61,
62, 63, 64, 65, 66, 67, 68, 69, 70,
71, 72, 73, 74, 75, 76, 77, 78, 79,
80, 82, 84, 86, 87, 88, 89, 90, 93,
94, 95, 97, 98, 99, 101, 102, 103,
104, 105, 106, 107, 108, 109, 110,
111, 112, 113, 114, 115, 116, 117,
119, 120, 121, 122, 123, 124, 125,
126, 128, 129, 131, 132, 133, 134,
135, 136, 137, 138, 139, 140, 141,
142, 143, 144, 145, 146, 148, 149,
150, 151, 152, 153, 154, 157, 158,
160, 161, 163, 166, 168, 170, 171,
172, 173, 174, 177, 178, 179, 180,
181, 182, 183, 184, 187, 188, 191,
192, 193, 194, 195, 199, 203, 206,
207, 209, 210, 211, 212, 213, 214,
215, 216, 217, 218, 219, 224, 225,
226, 227, 231, 232, 233, 234, 247,
248, 249, 251, 252
Wool 59, 109, 110, 111, 112, 113, 116,
117, 120

Y
Yarrow 174
Yoruba 145
Yugoslavia (former) 35, 76, 78, 79, 105,
183

Z
Zeus 36, 57, 181, 188, 199
Zostra net 107
Zulu 196
Zurstai 107

About the Author

Gloria Bertonis earned a Bachelor of Arts and Master of Education in Counseling and Psychology at Antioch University in Pennsylvania as well as an Associate of Arts degree in Early Childhood Education from Bucks County Community College. She has lectured at the Unitarian-Universalist Congregations, presented seminars to the community and civic groups for a number of years, appeared as a guest commentator on WWBD, Philadelphia, WBUX, and WPEN at the University of Pennsylvania.

Gloria has taught adult evening education classes on Psychology, Self-Esteem, Assertiveness, Stress-Management, and taught women's study groups under the auspices of the Unitarian-Universalist Organization. As the Director and Founder of the Whole Life Learning Center in Bucks County, PA, she provided courses in World Religions, World Cultures, World Philosophies and Psychology.

She was a contributor to the "The Womanspirit Source Book", Patrice Wynne, NY, Harper & Row, 1988 and has contributed to Women in Religion as part of the Unitarian-Universalist Organization with articles and lectures honoring women in all phases of life. She has served as a community member of the Courier-Times Editorial Board in 1999 and has written many guest opinion columns for the newspaper.

In 2001, Gloria Bertonis was the recipient of an award from the United States Federal Government for her continuing work 'to right the historical injustices against women'. Eve Ensler of the famed play "The Vagina Monologues" has publicly acknowledged Gloria's research from the stage in San Francisco on March 8, 2002 and included her research in the play's programs. Gloria has had color features in the local newspapers including The Philadelphia Inquirer and the Buck's County Courier Times and the Doylestown Intelligenser.

Gloria Bertonis is the mother of six adult children, grandmother of seven children, and great grandmother to eight children. She enjoys her world travels with her cherished companion, Ed Weiser. She also collects antiques, including dolls, jewelry, perfumes, and vintage clothing and accessories which she wears when lecturing on earlier generations of women who effected changes in history which are held at the Bolton Mansion in Bucks County.

Gloria Bertonis continues to be a driving force in her community, through her current Guest Opinion Column for the local newspaper, and her continued lectures and speaking engagements.

Co-author and Editor, Carol Miranda, sister to Gloria Bertonis, urged Gloria to put her ideas and conclusions into book form. Thus began the pursuit of information between sisters from coast to coast over ten years ago.

Carol Miranda is a mother of 4 daughters, and the grandmother to 7 grandchildren. She also has four stepchildren. She is a graduate of Beacom College, in Wilmington, DE, and the Ikenobo Institute of Ikebana, Kyoto, Japan. She lives in Silicon Valley and worked as an Executive Assistant for 25 years. She is a professional high-style floral designer of Carol's Silk Art and the co-author and editor of this book.

Carol is retired and lives in San Jose, CA with her husband. Besides the happiness of being surrounded by her loving family and working on creative projects and floral art, Carol is in love with her maltese, Samantha, and her wonderful grandchildren who keep her smiling at every opportunity.

GLORIA BERTONIS, M. Ed.

Presentations:

Oceans of Emotions
Deep Relaxation and Relaxation Response to Stress
Mind Dynamics for the 80's
Psychology of Religion
Holistic Health-Healing-Living
Deep Relaxation & Physical & Spiritual Attainment
Mystery of Consciousness
Spirituality of Sex
The Spectrum of Love: Expanding our Love Potential Living is Your Higher Consciousness
New Age Spirituality
Adventure in Consciousness
Healing Pathways in the New Age
Consciousness – the Hidden Factor in Health
The Esoteric Path to Growth and Change
Conscious Living/Conscious Loving
Learning to Love Again
Eastern Wisdom – Western Relationships
Stress and Tension Management
Meditation – Altered State of Consciousness
Reprogramming your Personal Bio-computer (Brain)
Adventures in Awareness
Looking In and Looking Out – Psychology of Awakening
Oceans of Emotions
Metaphysical Love
The Partnership Way – Women's Spirituality
In Search of God's Grandmother – Religions of the Ancient World to the Present
Personal Empowerment through Psychology
Psycho Kinetics – Writing a New Script for Your Life
Web of Womanspirit
Alexander the Great: Man Behind the Legend
Cosmic Consciousness: Hidden Factor in Life, Love & Happiness

Salvation and Self-Actualization
Expanding Your Love Potential
WICCA: Legacy of the Goddess Mothers
Enlightenment as a Life Style, 1985
Cosmic Consciousness: Implications for Individuals & Society
Meshica, Land of the Mothers in San Miguel de Allende, Mexico
Myths, Lies, and Exaggerations (re: beauty industry and toxins)
Cailleach Bheurra, The Bear Mother of Scotland
Realm of the God Mothers: When Mothers were Gods
Hats in History: How Fashion Reflects History

Group Discussions:

Building New Relationships
Lifelines of the 80's: Humanism, Hypnotism & Holism
Coping with Emotions
Male Sexual Identity in the 80's
Are We All Psychic
Art of Communication
Spirituality of Sex
Healing Pathways through the New Age
Building New Relationships from the Embers of the Old Ones
Changing Attitudes – Changing Lives
Keeping Stress out of the Holidays
Living Fully in the Present Moment
Psychology of Self-Esteem
Love Seminar: Are You Using an Inadequate Loving Style?
Self-Knowledge for Self-Improvement
Changing Rules – Changing Roles
Human Potential: Options and Possibilities
If Life is a Journey, Who's Got the Map?
Opening up to your Psychic Self
Replacing the Old Negative Tapes in your Head with New Ones

Published Articles:

Holistic Self-Healing
What are Emotions?

Changing Our Attitude
Women in Religion: My Personal Response
The Rise of Feminine Spirituality
Living Fully in the Present Moment

Articles – Non-Published

Participating in the Development of Others
God
Love: An Inquiry into its Effectiveness
Guilt: Our Useless Emotion?
Awaken the Goddess Within
Ways of Growth Important for Women Right Now
Womanspirit: the Rise of Feminine Spirituality
How to Remain Peaceful in a Violent World
Love: A Working Definition
Expanding our Love Potential
In Search of My Soul: From Physical to Meta-physical
Reflections of Love
Emotional Needs
Existential Humanism
Rational Emotive Therapy: The Power of Positive Thoughts

Workshops:

Mind Dynamics in the 80's
Mind Force in the 80's
Enlightenment as a Lifestyle

Classes Taught:

Creating a Holistic Lifestyle
Emotional Group Therapy
Personal Success
Developmental Psychology: Psychology of Love, Growth & Creativity
Loving Relationships
Psychology of Self-Esteem
Positive Thought Management

Assertiveness Training
Metaphysics for Stress Relief & Life Enrichment
Cosmic Consciousness
Psychology
Psychology of Self-Development
The Spectrum of Love
The Chalice and the Blade: Politics and Spirituality, by Riane Eisler
Women Who Run with the Wolves, by Dr. Jean Shinoda Bolen
Yoga
Psychology of Relationships
Psychology of Consciousness
Realm of the Clan Mothers

Audio Tapes:

Relaxation Response for Spiritual & Physical Attunement
Beginning Yoga
The Chalice and the Blade
Alexander the Great: The Man behind the Legend
WICCA: Legacy of the Goddess Mothers

Contact: stoneagedivas@yahoo.com

Lightning Source UK Ltd.
Milton Keynes UK
UKHW041311190220
358982UK00001B/419